The Secret Leprosy of Modern Days

The Secret Leprosy of Modern Days

Narcotic Addiction and Cultural Crisis
in the United States, 1870–1920

TIMOTHY A. HICKMAN

University of Massachusetts Press

Amherst

Copyright © 2007 by University of Massachusetts Press
All rights reserved
Printed in the United States of America

LC 2006100129
ISBN 978-1-55849-566-1 (paper); 978-1-55849-565-4 (library cloth ed.)

Designed by Steve Dyer
Set in Monotype Bell
Printed and bound by The Maple-Vail Book Manufacturing Group

Library of Congress Cataloging-in-Publication Data
Hickman, Timothy Alton.
The secret leprosy of modern days : narcotic addiction and cultural
crisis in the United States, 1870–1920 / Timothy A. Hickman.
p. cm.
Includes bibliographical references and index.
ISBN-13: 978-1-55849-566-1 (pbk. : alk. paper)
ISBN-10: 1-55849-566-5 (pbk. : alk. paper)
ISBN-13: 978-1-55849-565-4 (library cloth : alk. paper)
ISBN-10: 1-55849-565-7 (library cloth : alk. paper)
1. Drug addiction—United States—History.   2. Drug control—United
States—History.   3. Narcotic laws—United States—History.   I. Title.
HV5825.H46 2007
616.86'320097309034—dc22   2006100129

British Library Cataloguing in Publication data are available.

For

Henry Caldwell Hickman,

who arrived only a few months
before this book did.

And of course, for

Nicola,

who brought him here.

Right and wrong ... must be eternal verities, but our standards for measuring them vary with our latitude and our epoch. We make our customs lightly; once made, like our sins, they trap us in bands of steel; we become the creatures of our creations.

—CHARLES CHESNUTT,
The House behind the Cedars (1900)

Slowly, unceasingly, "without haste, without rest," the wreaths of flowers are replaced by silken bands, and the bands of silk by chains of steel. The consciousness of liberty remains long after the bondage has become as fixed and certain as the grasp of fate.

—DR. LESLIE E. KEELEY, *Opium: Its Use, Abuse and Cure; or, From Bondage to Freedom* (1897)

CONTENTS

ILLUSTRATIONS

ACKNOWLEDGMENTS

I AM VERY GRATEFUL to the individuals and institutions that gave their support during the preparation of this book. In its earliest phases, the research was supported by a series of dissertation fellowships from the University of California, Irvine. In 1998, I received a resident research fellowship from the Francis Clark Wood Institute for the History of Medicine at the College of Physicians of Philadelphia, which made possible the research presented in chapter 2. That research was further supported by a Faculty Development Award during a postdoctoral year at the School of Humanities at UC Irvine. I received teaching relief from my colleagues in the History Department at Lancaster University through the auspices of the Lancaster Pamphlet Fund in 2003–4 and also a teaching sabbatical for the 2004–5 academic year, which gave me the time to complete the manuscript.

It is not possible to thank all the individuals who have influenced the final outcome of this project. If I could have incorporated all their comments, the result would have been a much better book. In its earliest phases, Alice Fahs, Brook Thomas, and Jon Wiener guided the project. They offered invaluable professional and practical advice for moving from a raw hunch to a finished piece of work. Likewise, Josh Meyer and Eric Ruckh endured countless hours of discussion and offered many critical insights during the project's early years. Jonathan Judaken and Torbjörn Wandel have had a profound influence on my thinking from the very beginning. They continue to do so.

Various historians of drugs and alcohol have also supported my work. The expertise of the anonymous readers at the University of Massachusetts Press was clear in their lucid and helpful comments. David T. Courtwright, David F. Musto, and Robin Room have been models of the way that senior scholars can and should support new developments in research fields which they themselves have defined. Their support has been exemplary, even of approaches with which they do not always agree. Caroline J. Acker, Nancy D. Campbell, William H. Helfand, Sarah W. Tracy, Joseph F. Spillane, and William L. White have all offered comments and encouragement, reminding me that there is a lively and collegial group of scholars who share an interest in the material that I explore in this book. Clark Dougan at the University of Massachussetts Press has offered support and encouragement throughout, and likewise, Carol Betsch and Sally Nichols have worked very hard to coordinate the editing and production team that oversaw the book's journey from rough manuscript to finished product.

Finally, my colleagues at Lancaster University, especially Paolo Palladino, Scott Wilson, Paul Fletcher, Stephen Pumfrey, Fred Botting, Jonathan Munby, Nick Gebhardt, Patrick Hagopian, and Michael Heale, have offered insights that have very much improved the book. Besides driving out the cold and damp of a Lancashire winter evening, our talks at the John O'Gaunt have helped particularly to sharpen this book's engagement with the concept of "modernity."

Preliminary versions of parts of this book have appeared in the following publications. Portions of chapters 2 and 5 as "'Mania Americana': Narcotic Addiction and Modernity in the United States, 1870–1920," *Journal of American History* 90 (March 2004): 1269–94. Portions of chapter 3 in "Heroin Chic: The Visual Culture of Narcotic Addiction," *Third Text: Critical Perspectives on Contemporary Art and Culture* 16 (June 2002): 119–36, and in "Drugs and Race in American Culture: Orientalism in the Turn-of-the-Century Discourse of Narcotic Addiction," *American Studies* 41 (Spring 2000): 71–91. Portions of the introduction and of chapters 4 and 5 in "The Double Meaning of Addiction: Habitual Narcotic Use and the Logic of Professionalizing Medical Authority in the United States, 1900–1920," in *Altering American Consciousness: The History of Alcohol and Drug Use in the United States, 1800–1997*, ed. Sarah W. Tracy and Caroline J. Acker (Amherst: University of Massachusetts Press, 2004).

The Secret Leprosy of Modern Days

Introduction

The Modernity of Addiction/
The Addiction of Modernity

Owing to the present advance of medicine, new words are being rapidly coined, therefore, if you desire to keep abreast of the times, keep your dictionaries and encyclopedias at your elbow: patronize them freely, and, when your reading or musing entices your curiosity on any subject, or in any direction, turn to them and be informed. They are both convenient and useful in looking up facts and meanings when you have but a few moments to devote to an inquiry, and will save you from many mistakes and uncertainties.

—D. W. CATHELL, M.D., and W. T. CATHELL, M.D.,
*The Book on the Physician Himself and Things that
Concern his Reputation and Success* (1913)

DESPITE ITS ASSOCIATION with Asian cultures, narcotic addiction gained little public attention in the West before the publication of Thomas DeQuincey's *Confessions of an English Opium Eater* in 1821.[1] De-Quincey's text was popular on both sides of the Atlantic, and its conclusions about the "pains" derived from breaking off regular opiate use were echoed by frequent reports from nineteenth-century physicians whose otherwise cured patients were sometimes unable to stop taking their narcotic medications. Nonetheless, few antebellum Americans felt themselves or their society to be particularly threatened by narcotics. The vast publicity created by the anti-alcohol campaigns of the various temperance movements helped to generate popular anxiety over the widespread personal and social consequences of heavy drinking, but the public imagination was not similarly gripped by the use of narcotics. This relative complacency, however, slipped away during the last third of the nineteenth century.

After the Civil War, several factors combined to force the drug habit out from the shadows and to recast it in the guise of a pressing social problem. First, the medical knowledge and use of narcotics had grown throughout the nineteenth century, especially after the hypodermic syringe came into broad use during the 1860s and 1870s.[2] Though the popular belief that Civil War battlefield medicine was the chief cause of subsequent narcotic use has been disproved, a general increase in the prescription of narcotics during the Civil War era created a taste for them. The actual number of narcotic addicts during this period is notoriously difficult to establish, but the most reliable estimate is that the rate of addiction probably peaked in the mid-1890s at about 4.59 per thousand and then began to decline. Various reformers and entrepreneurs exaggerated the figures and also their trend, convincing much of the public that 1 million or more addicts were on the loose during the second decade of the twentieth century—about 10.9 per thousand—and that their numbers were increasing. In any case, beginning in the 1870s, both medical and popular writers escalated their discussion of what they characterized as a spiraling national drug problem. The changing composition of the drug-using population further helped focus negative attention on the practice, as the constituency for drug use slowly shifted from upper—and middle-class white women, whose habits started on the prescription of their physicians, to lower-class urban men on the fringes of the underworld. The historian David T. Courtwright has argued that this demographic shift aided the task of painting narcotic use as a threatening and deviant practice.[3]

Politics likewise favored the emergence of the narcotic habit as a public threat. David F. Musto's *The American Disease* shows that drug policy has never been a transparently scientific solution to an unambiguously medical problem. In the early chapters of his book, Musto examines the influence of a group of diplomats, entrepreneurs, and reformers on the passage of the Harrison Narcotic Act, which in 1914 limited access to narcotics to licensed wholesalers, physicians, and patients in possession of a valid prescription. Yet as Courtwright points out, demographics and politics are not by themselves sufficient to explain the genesis of American attitudes toward the habitual use of narcotics. They do not, in and of themselves, explain why public attitudes and policy turned so unequivocally against unsupervised drug use in the first part of the twentieth century.[4]

The Secret Leprosy of Modern Days explores another of the necessary conditions in the emergence of a narcotic menace: the resonance of the concept of addiction within its turn-of-the-twentieth-century cultural context. Social, medical, and political historians such as Musto and Courtwright have noted that "culture"—the contested field where meaning and value are generated, assigned, and disputed—has also played an important role in shaping the nation's drug problems. Typical is Musto's explanation of how racial prejudice influenced American drug policy and its enforcement, especially in the South and in the West.[5] In a similar vein, Courtwright showed that our opinions about drug addiction have everything to do with our attitudes toward those whom we call addicts.[6] But despite those (and other) contributions to the historical study of drug use and policy in the United States, most researchers have not pursued the approach taken in this book, which offers a close analysis of the way that the addiction concept figured its broader cultural context. Cultural history, which draws its critical energy from literary and linguistic approaches to the close reading of primary texts, is beginning to have an impact on research in this field, and this book is a contribution to that project. It is part of a growing literature that adds to our understanding of America's "drug problem" as an important part of a much broader and historically contingent cultural context.[7]

To achieve public prominence as a social menace, an idea or a practice—*any* idea or practice—somehow has to resonate, to make sense, to integrate itself into the texture of everyday life as it is experienced by those who live it. These historically specific experiences are diverse, just like the people who have them, but there are nonetheless ideas and concepts that in some manner cut across those differences to seize a prominent position on the horizon of interpretive possibilities. Put quite simply, they catch on. They capture the public imagination through a combination of explanatory power and flexible application that allows them to operate as broader metaphors for what a variety of people perceive, though often only dimly, to be in some way threatening in their lives. Discovering and excavating these sites of cultural gravitas, these dense gathering points of meaning, value, and power, offers an opportunity to examine how ideas and concepts both reflect and help to produce the context within which they are embedded.[8] Such gathering points produce vivid images of their specific historical and cultural moments, and their study helps us to understand the past in terms that also illuminate the present as both a constituent and consequence of that past.

Narcotic addiction is such a concept. It has served as a means to describe and to interpret a vast and varied field of practices and behaviors ever since it emerged at the turn of the twentieth century. Today one can be "addicted" to just about anything. The term has become a commonplace—a familiar expression that we use to explain other, more confusing events and practices. This recent popular usage indicates the term's rich cultural resonance but simultaneously obscures it in a haze of dull familiarity. By recontextualizing the addiction concept, repositioning it in its original setting, I hope to rescue it from its current banality—to reinvigorate the expression and to excavate some of the cultural and historical presuppositions that made it thinkable in the first place.[9]

In this book I argue that the addiction concept of habitual narcotic use embodied what historians have long identified as the cultural crisis of modernity, which means that the addiction concept did not simply name a distinct condition that was discovered by bright, hardworking medical researchers. Neither can we fully understand the addiction concept by treating it as an unproblematically empirical development in the social and political history of medicine. It means, rather, that the addiction concept—the set of ideas that comprise "addiction"—was embedded within its broader cultural context. It means that the addiction concept simultaneously *reflected* what I describe as the cultural crisis of modernity and helped to *produce* that crisis by describing habitual drug use as a historically distinctive threat to the independent, rational, and autonomous individual—a figure that had long served as the fundamental building block for dominant constructions of American middle-class political and economic culture. The discourse of addiction, which was given legal teeth by the 1914 Harrison Narcotic Act, inscribed the threat carried by the historical changes that constituted turn-of-the-century "modernity" upon the bodies of those who were identified within that discourse as *addicts*.[10] That operation had distinct costs for many individuals and also for American society as a whole, as the addiction concept became a major justification for the nation's seemingly endless "war on drugs."

The Cultural Crisis of Modernity

To understand the cultural resonance of the addiction concept, we need to locate its ever more frequent appearance in the public discourse of what many historians have identified as a time of cultural crisis. This description has a long and distinguished pedigree.[11] It holds that an important part of late nineteenth- and early twentieth-century cultural life involved a struggle to redefine the terms of human agency in the face of rapid technological, economic, and political change. This formulation has been controversial, both for its frequent focus on the intellectual elite and for what some scholars influenced by the ideas of Michel Foucault—have argued is its inherent disregard of the fact that identity has *always* been under construction. From that perspective, formulations of cultural crisis as the failure or disruption of the coherent assertion of self reify the concept of a stable, autonomous identity by suggesting that, once upon a time and before the fall (usually before industrialization and capitalism), we *were* centered, independent, and rational subjects. Furthermore, such formulations tend to construct the immediately preceding period as one of stability and certainty, something hard to sustain in light of the massive upheavals capped by the Civil War, the abolition of slavery, and large-scale industrialization. In other words, much of the recent scholarship suggests that the crisis model valorizes precisely what it should critique: the autonomous, rational subject.

Merit exists in both the older and the newer approaches. As recent cultural histories have shown, identity is always in construction, and its perceived moments of stability tend to be the ideological projections of powerful hegemonic groups. Turn-of-the-century cultural production, however, does seem to have been more than usually obsessed with the renegotiation of a challenged notion of the self. "To immerse oneself in the documents of the period is gradually to come to recognize the depth of [these people's] sense of confusion and danger and to respect the historical specificity of their reported discomfort," according to the literary critic June Howard.[12] But I would add that we cannot hope to respect that specificity unless we also understand that a kindred sense of confusion has appeared at multiple historical times and places. On the one hand, the profoundly disconcerting experience of historical change, the sense of crisis that typifies the culture of modernity, might be located in any number of texts, drawn from a variety of historical periods and sites. On the other hand, the experience has taken specific and novel forms according to the time and place of its appearance. Modernity, therefore, is simultaneously a particular and a general experience of the passage of time. This is neither a contradiction nor a logical flaw. It is, rather, a paradox.[13]

Matei Calinescu examined that paradox in his 1987 book *Five Faces of Modernity*, in which he traces the history of the concept of modernity from the coinage of the late Latin word *modernus* in the fourth century of the common era.[14] He associated the term with a sense of the linear passage of time evident in early Christian eschatology, contrasting it with classical notions of time as a permanent cycle of old and new. Calinescu showed that a general sense of linear time has been central to Western intellectual and aesthetic culture, offering a

" DELIRIUM, OF COURSE, BUT SO REAL!"

Dan Beard's illustration for Mark Twain's A Connecticut Yankee in King Arthur's Court *(1889) exhibits late nineteenth-century "modernity" as a cultural crisis. The image posits the present as a profound and irreversible breaking away from the past. It is strikingly gendered, defining the modern as masculine and tradition as both antiquated and feminine. It also suggests that the hope for a fertile, procreative marriage of modernity and tradition was the product of a "delirium," forever banned by Father Time. Reprinted from a version with a variant title: Mark Twain,* A Connecticut Yankee at the Court of King Arthur *(London, 1889).*

means to assert the novelty of its own, particular historical present by positioning that present against a recent but now closed past, while also keeping an eye on a not yet realized future. The sense that we are hurtling along an arrow of time—the sense of *modernus*—has been reasserted under various names, in various guises, and with differing degrees of intensity for much of the intervening period. The Renaissance, Enlightenment, romanticism, historicism, modernity, and finally postmodernity are all names that have been deployed at times of particularly intense cultural ferment. Those attempts to assert the novelty of the present by naming it as a distinct period have depended on comparisons with the past and future, seen as discrete periods that are nonetheless related to one another in varied and complex temporal narratives. Calinescu's study thus shows modernity to be a chronic and recurring historical condition. It offers a framework that might move scholarly practice away from debates over which period really was modern or whether there really was a crisis, to more productive attempts to describe the differing strategies and techniques that people have employed to produce and make evident the *sense* of modernity for themselves and their contemporaries.

This description of modernity as a paradox meets the demands of Foucauldian cultural history by admitting that people have faced challenges to the definition of the self in *every* historical epoch, but it does not surrender the specificity of a late nineteenth—and early twentieth-century "modern cultural crisis." It may well be that texts recovered from *various* periods are noteworthy in their profound consciousness of their own modernity as a crisis, of the sense that today is radically different from yesterday. Some historians may want to speculate about the material causes of this sense, but for cultural history what becomes most interesting are the multiple and conflicting ways that these crises have been enunciated, negotiated, and, sometimes, resolved. Further, the historically specific ways of thinking, saying, and doing had, and continue to have, important consequences. Addiction is certainly a concept with consequences, but as with modernity, one needs to trace the concept's origins to understand the distinctiveness of its emergence at the turn of the twentieth century.

The Double Meaning of Addiction

To argue that the concept of addiction was embedded in a turn-of-the-twentieth-century cultural crisis is to suggest a modification to what is perhaps the most influential study of the concept of addiction. In an important 1978 essay, the sociologist Harry Gene Levine argued that the concept of addiction was the product of a change in medical thinking about alcohol at the end of the eighteenth and the beginning of the nineteenth centuries. He claims that "this new paradigm or model defined addiction as a central problem in drug use and diagnosed it as a disease, or disease-like." [15] The chief symptom of this "disease" was the loss of control over drinking, and thus the habitual drinker was relieved of the moral responsibility that seventeenth-century theorists and theologians had assigned the drunkard for his or her drinking.

Levine further argues that this new paradigm was consistent with what he terms "the ideology of the Temperance Movement" and was first worked out by physicians "whose orientation led them to look for behavior or symptoms beyond the control of the will and whose interests lay precisely in the distinction between Desire and Will." [16] He thus finds a cultural and social basis for this new explanation of habitual drunkenness and demonstrates the way that allegedly value-free medicoscientific descriptions of human behavior are often sociocultural productions of their historical moment.

Contrary to Levine's assertion, however, the disease concept of drug and alcohol use and the concept of addiction are not the same thing. He cautions his audience that "the modern reader translates the behavioral description of the habitual drunkard into modern terms—into the alcoholic," but he makes the same move himself when he quickly translates the older disease concept into the modern notion of addiction, which is something that did not appear until years later. [17] He argues that the seventeenth—and eighteenth-century view, which held that "habitual drunkards simply loved to drink and get drunk, and that they could stop at any time," did not simply die out but "continued to exist alongside the addiction—that is, the temperance—model." [18]

Yet the words "addict" and "addiction" were only rarely used before the turn of the century to denote drug users or their condition. Most nineteenth-century authorities preferred more colorful words such as "habitué," "morphinist," "morphinomaniac," "opium eater," and "opium slave." Though Levine finds the word "addict" occasionally employed in the sermons of eighteenth-century Puritan theologians as well as in antebellum medical texts, it is never used as a noun in his examples. It is not used to identify a condition called "addiction," nor is the word "addict" invoked as a name for a person who suffers from that condition. [19]

This is not a quibble. Levine shows convincingly that the disease concept signaled a shift in the medical paradigm of the late 1700s. In much the same way, the general adoption of the addiction concept, manifested in part by the growing use of the term itself, was a part of a shift to the paradigm of organized, professional, scientific medicine in the first years of the twentieth century. An important element of the addiction concept was the supposed scientific knowledge of the condition that use of the term implied. To use the word "addict" was to turn away from the older, more dramatic phrases that became far less common in medical discourse after the turn of the century. [20] Its use offered doctors a way to identify themselves as a part of a professional/scientific/legal community, and as we will see, the term's popularity coincided with the increasing power and prestige of organized medicine marked by the rise to dominance of the American Medical Association at this time.

Levine's association of the disease concept with that of addiction misses the addiction concept's chief distinction. "Addiction" did not "exist alongside" an older, voluntary notion of habitual drug use, because the term contained both concepts within itself. This is, quite literally, its definitive feature. We can better understand these two contradictory concepts and the way that the term "addiction" contains them both by examining the earliest English uses of the word.

Originally, addiction signified the assignment of a status or condition by a court of law. The *Oxford English Dictionary* lists the word "addict" as deriving from the Latin *addictus*, meaning "assigned by decree, made over, bound, or devoted." The word first appeared in English around 1529 as a legal adjective, describing the state of someone who was "formally made over or bound *(to* another); attached by restraint or obligation; obliged, bound, devoted, consecrated." This usage soon was made obsolete by a related verb *(to* addict or to have been *addicted),* whose most recent manifestation is the one that we still use today. Its first meaning was "to deliver over formally by sentence of a judge *(to* anyone). Hence, . . . to make over, give up, surrender." This definition was paired with a second, reflexive meaning that emphasized a greater degree of volition than the strict *juridical* sense of the legal term: "To bind, attach, or devote *oneself* as a servant, disciple, or adherent *(to* any person or cause)" and also "to devote, give up, or apply habitually to a practice." [21] Both of these contradictory senses of the word first, the notion of addiction as an assigned or *juridical* condition and, second, of addiction as a self-willed or *volitional* condition are at play in the noun "[drug] addict," a designation that became the dominant name for a habitual drug user (someone who suffered from an "addiction") sometime around 1910.

The discrepancy between the voluntary and the compelled—which, following etymological precedent, I will call the volitional and juridical definitions of the words "addict" and "addiction"—is of central importance in this book. [22] In the first years of the twentieth century, this double meaning of "addiction" was put into play within the context of the turn-of-the-century cultural crisis. The resolution of addiction's contradictory double meaning, which was signaled in part by the general acceptance of the term "addiction," was an affirmation of the concept's status as paradox: the addiction concept contained *both* meanings of the word within itself. Most important, the addiction concept provided a formula for the assessment of moral culpability for the addict's condition that held dire consequences for those who were left without an excuse for their drug taking.

Many turn-of-the-century medical authorities believed that the necessity of living with modern social, technological, and economic pressures caused mid-dle—and upper-class Americans—who were still, at least physically, creatures of "nature"—to become particularly susceptible to the seduction of narcotics.[23] This move greatly reduced the volitional sense of the word "addict" by mini-mizing the role of individual choice for middle-class drug users and thus spared them the moral responsibility for their condition. These people were *juridical* addicts because they were addicted *by* the conditions of a changing world.

The *volitional* meaning of the word was generally reserved for those whose class—and often racial—position was deemed inferior to that of white, middle-class America. It also served to illustrate the depths that beckoned the more re-spectable members of society should the drug hazard go unchecked. Nonwhite and demimonde others were supposedly free of the commercial and cultural strains of modern life and were, with few exceptions, denied an excuse for tak-ing drugs. They were thus assigned a greater degree of moral responsibility for their habit than were juridical addicts.

The Harrison Narcotic Act affirmed the addiction concept's double meaning in that it provided a solution to the problems posed by both groups of addicts. By 1920, volitional addicts came to be defined as *criminals* and were thus proper subjects of the penal system.[24] The juridical addicts, on the other hand, were de-fined as innocent *patients*, something that was shown in part by their willing-ness to place themselves under the authority of professional medicine. The Harrison Act thus carved up the addict population and divided the spoils be-tween medical and penal authorities, who in turn reinforced one another in their pursuit of the act's goals.

THE ORDER OF PLAY

This book, then, is best understood as an attempt to read two concepts—addic-tion and modernity—into one another at a specific moment in American his-tory. My intention is to show how the concept of narcotic addiction, a pressing and seemingly endless social problem, was an important element of the broader cultural moment from which it sprang, but I also offer an important example of the way that the so-called cultural crisis of modernity achieved effective, tangi-

ble form through its medicolegal inscription upon the bodies of those unfortunate enough to be vulnerable to the normative claims that it helped to generate.

To accomplish this task, I have divided the book into five chapters. The first
provides an examination of the period directly preceding that which will be
the central focus of the study. The chapter opens with a reading of Thomas
DeQuincey's 1821 memoir, *Confessions of an English Opium Eater*, and then looks
at the specifically American iterations of this fundamental and opening moment
of the discourse of addiction. Finishing with a reading of several pieces by "the
American DeQuincey," that is, by the journalist Fitz Hugh Ludlow (1836–70), I
show how the vocabulary of the temperance and abolition movements merged
with DeQuincey's romantic Orientalism to create a rhetoric of drug use, both
pro and con, that continues to inhabit the discourse of addiction today. De-
Quincey's description of narcotic *intoxication* as an escape from the fetters of
Western reason continues to attract followers, but his portrayal of the narcotic
habit as the narrative displacement of self-willed, effective agency from the user
to the drug was particularly worrying within the bounds of a nineteenth-
century American culture that prided itself on its (incomplete) commitment to
individual liberty. The chapter thus shows how the emergent discourse of addiction absorbed and accommodated the languages of temperance and abolitionism as it developed a rich vocabulary with which to condemn drug use as an
example of the mastery of the individual by tyrannical forces outside the self.

The second chapter moves directly into the concepts of modernity and addiction, exploring how a variety of writers described the rising incidence of
narcotic addiction as a product of, as well as a breaking away from, the medical
history that had produced it. In other words, I examine their description of narcotic addiction as a marker of radical historical change—as a sign of modernity
as cultural crisis. The logic of that description lay in the way that it situated narcotic addiction within the context of the profound social and cultural transformation that was a part of post-Civil War industrialization and technological
change. Swiss researchers isolated morphine, which is the active alkaloid of
opium, in 1805, and the process was widely known by the 1820s. Other powerful chemical compounds and syntheses, such as codeine, cocaine, and heroin,
joined morphine by the end of the century. Their use had grown quickly, particularly after the hypodermic syringe came into widespread medical use in the
1860s. This seemingly rapid transformation of medical technology was striking to its observers, but it was not unique. Many commentators described narcotic medication—the chemical agent itself and also its means of delivery—as a
part of the broader technological transformation of American society that ac-

companied swift industrialization. They depicted the narcotic habit, which they ever more frequently called "addiction," as a paradigmatic example of modernity's worst-case scenario.

Chapter 3 continues this cross reading of modernity and addiction with a consideration of how these concepts were inscribed upon the bodies of individual users, that is, upon the bodies of the addicts themselves—particularly those marked by race and gender difference. The chapter shows how the discourse of addiction took part in other cultural logics, principally those of Jim Crow, Orientalism, and Domestic Sentimentality, and thus situates the menace of narcotic addiction more firmly within the specific context of its historical moment of emergence. The association of addiction with stereotypical representations of Asians, African Americans, and women of any race offered many writers a way to personify the otherwise ambiguous concept of addiction. That strategy reflected broader cultural assumptions about these people, but it also helped to reinforce and reproduce those beliefs, adding a "natural" tendency to become addicted to the set of clichés that already marked their otherness.

The book's last two chapters turn away from the problem itself in order to look more closely at its medicolegal solution: the Harrison Narcotic Act and its subsequent interpretations. They indicate that the debates and testimony which surrounded the act's passage and implementation were saturated with the language examined in the first three chapters but also that the act proposed its own, typically turn-of-the-century solution to the problem when it suggested more thorough medical professionalization, backed by the authority of the state, as the solution to the challenges posed by the newly constituted drug menace.

Chapter 4 therefore provides a consideration of the stakes of antinarcotic legislation within the context of the rapidly organizing medical profession, while in the final chapter I sum up the book's argument by showing how subsequent interpretations of the Harrison Act divided the addict population along the lines of what I described above as the double meaning of addiction. The Harrison Act prescribed medical treatment and psychological counseling for the "patients" of the better, "juridical" class and incarceration for the obstinate "criminals" of the "volitional" group. Though the legal armature established by the Harrison Act was dismantled and replaced in 1970, its division of the addict population into groups of patients and criminals remains with us today. With this book I aim to show that this division is inherent in (the double meaning of) the concept of addiction itself and that its particular, 1914 formalization in the Harrison Act had everything to do with the historically specific concerns of the individuals, institutions, and forms of expression that weathered the turn of the twentieth century.

Finally, having explained what I aim to accomplish in this volume, it might be helpful to note what the book will not do. First, this book does not engage the question of whether there actually *was* a concrete, existential crisis of modernity, nor do I claim to have unearthed new documentary evidence that will fundamentally alter the basic narrative of events that dominates the history of drug use and policy. The book is, instead, about what people *thought*, and I engage those ideas through a close reading and analysis of the words that many of them *wrote*. As such, the book is meant to build upon and to add another distinctive facet to the archive of historical writing on America's troubled historical relationship with narcotic drugs. The texts that I have chosen to analyze are drawn from the best-known and most influential writings on addiction of the late nineteenth and early twentieth centuries. They are, indeed, canonical and will be familiar to those who already know that history. That is the advantage of using them. What is new is the close reading and rigorous contextualization of them. I believe that the contribution which these texts can make to our historical knowledge is far from exhausted, and I hope that the analysis performed in this book bears that out. Accordingly, one of the book's main objectives is to make recent work in the history of narcotics visible to a wider cultural history audience while also exposing the history of narcotics to some of the insights of contemporary cultural history.

Second, this book neither catalogues nor claims to exhaust the resonance of the notoriously flexible addiction concept at its moment of enunciation—or at any other historical moment. I do not attempt the impossible task of documenting and accounting for the myriad variations in the thoughts of everyone who participated in that immense discourse. Instead, *The Secret Leprosy of Modern Days* follows one particularly rich and suggestive strand through the intricate textual fabric that it both weaves and unravels. That strand, which I believe is the most significant, suggestive, and influential of the lot, identifies addiction as a condition that was peculiar to and emblematic of its moment of appearance. In other words, and once again, the addiction concept appeared in these texts as the epitome of the cultural crisis of modernity. Whether or not the concept's logic remains valid, convincing, or useful for twenty-first century society, I leave to the reader's discretion.

CHAPTER 1

Opium Eating and Political Subjectivity before 1870

Man who man would be
Must rule the empire of himself, in it
Must be supreme, establishing his throne
On vanquished will, quelling the anarchy
Of hopes and fears, being himself alone.

—PERCY BYSSHE SHELLEY, "Political Greatness" (1824)

Such a self-conquest may reasonably be set off in counter-balance to any kind of degree of self-indulgence.

—THOMAS DeQUINCEY, *Confessions of an
English Opium-Eater* (1821)

OPIUM IS AMONG the very oldest medications, and descriptions of its early history are abundant. Egyptian physicians recommended it to quiet crying babies and to relieve headaches as early as the sixteenth century BCE. Theophrastes and Dioscorides noted its ability to bring sleep and relief from pain to their ancient Greek patients. Opium was well known to the physicians of Rome, and after its introduction by Arab traders in the thirteenth century, it became a mainstay of late-medieval European medicine. Since the beginning of medical practice, the opiates have never dropped out of the world's medicine cabinet.[1]

There was, however, little mention of *habitual* drug use until the early nineteenth century. Earlier medical discussions of the drug focused on its ability to cure and relieve pain rather than on its potential to form a habit in its user. There were, of course, exceptions to that rule. As early as 1701, British physician John Jones, for instance, noted something like what later physicians would call withdrawal symptoms, writing that among the "effects of leaving off the use of opium" were to be found "great and even intolerable distresses, anxieties and depressions of spirits, which in a few days commonly end in the most miserable death, attended with strange agonies, unless men return to the use of opium; which soon raises them again and certainly restores them."[2]

Others also observed what would around 1910 come to be defined as an "addiction" to narcotics, but these early references were anomalous. They did not become paradigmatic until the late nineteenth century. Perhaps ironically, it was not a medical text but a personal memoir that first drew broad public attention to the habitual use of narcotics in the Western world.

THOMAS DEQUINCEY'S *Confessions of an English Opium-Eater* (1821)

No other text did as much to acquaint the general reading public with the pleasures and pains of opium as did Thomas DeQuincey's *Confessions of an English Opium-Eater*. Published first as a serial in *London Magazine* in 1821, *The Confessions* was the first detailed, widely circulated description of English opium eating, according to British historian Virginia Berridge, who explains that the book's significance lay in its break from a tradition that depicted regular opium use as a "peculiarly eastern custom."[3] DeQuincey's text was the West's introduction to the prospect of habitual narcotic use, and it set a tone that writers felt compelled to address for at least a century after its initial publication. Its influence persists even today.[4]

DeQuincey's description of an Englishman's opium habit is divided into several sections. After some "preliminary confessions" about his education and his youth, DeQuincey moved to a long discussion of the "pleasures of opium," which has chiefly to do with the opium-eater's perception of enhanced intellectual power while under the drug's effect.[5] He then explored the "pains of opium" through a narration of the opium-eater's growing dependence on the drug. His rich description of opium intoxication as a spur to the philosophical imagination seems to have painted an attractive picture for many of his readers—something that is evidenced by the obligatory denunciations of DeQuincey that one finds in the writings of former drug users and antinarcotic reformers in the later part of the century.

Though he made it plain that an Englishman was perfectly capable of developing an opium habit, it is important to remember that DeQuincey's text nonetheless maintained a vital connection between opium and the "Orient." In an 1824 review of *The Confessions*, Samuel Morewood explained that "In Great Britain, opium has been more used as a medicine than as an exciter of the spirits, although its infatuating influence is not altogether unknown in these countries, since the reveries of Asiatic luxury and effeminacy have in too many instances infected the manners and habits of the British people."[6] Morewood praised DeQuincey's work and recommended it as a demonstration of the extent to which "an Englishman may be brought to take this opiate."[7] His description of opium intoxication as an effeminate, Asiatic luxury relied on drug use as a sign of what he perceived to be a broader moral decline, wherein the "Asiatic" represented everything that was not properly masculine and British. As such, Morewood sought to assert his own racialized and gendered definition of authentic Britishness by casting Asiatic drug use (or, the drug-using Asiatic) as its opposite. His reading was based on a set of politically inflected concerns that were not strictly within DeQuincey's text, but its extratextuality does not mean that the review was groundless. Morewood's writing draws our attention to the status of *The Confessions* as a prime example of Orientalism, which the cultural theorist Edward W. Said defined as "a way of coming to terms with the Orient that is based on the Orient's special place in European Western experience." That special place is a distant point of otherness, an exotic, imaginary landscape where the cultural borders of European rationalism are threatened by the supposedly irrational, unenlightened, and sensuous Orient. This highly seductive, oriental counterpart to European reason was both a product of and a source for Orientalism, which served to legitimate "a western style for dominating, restructuring, and having authority over the Orient."[8]

DeQuincey's maintenance of the connection between opium use and a romanticized oriental otherness is particularly clear in a memorable scene where a "Malay" chances upon the opium-eater's cottage near Grasmere, in the picturesque and quintessentially English Lake District. "A more striking picture there could not be imagined" than that which meets the opium-eater as he first spots his uninvited guest standing next to the daughter of his house servant. The girl's "beautiful English face," set off by her "erect and independent attitude," greeted the opium-eater with a vision of "exquisite fairness." DeQuincey juxtaposed that image with the Malay, whose "sallow and bilious skin" drew attention to his "small fierce, restless eyes, thin lips, slavish gestures and adorations."[9] These parallel descriptions operate to sketch the Malay as the summation of everything that the English girl is not. The Malay's "sallow and bilious" complexion only emphasizes the English girl's "exquisite fairness." More important, his cringing slavishness draws attention to her erect independence, making it profound and unmistakable. The comparison makes absolutely clear the Malay's position as oriental within this text. His image is subaltern, it supports the definition of the occidental as commanding and dominant. Independence is a trait of the occidental, slavishness of the oriental, qualities that *The Confessions* associates with English and Malayan bodies, respectively.

Adding to these visual markers of oriental otherness, DeQuincey emphasized the Malay's amazing tolerance for extremely large doses of opium. Relying on an expertise acquired "as an Orientalist," the English opium eater offers his guest a piece of opium, explaining that any Malay would certainly be familiar with it, an assumption that is visually confirmed by "the expression on [the Malay's] face."[10] The Malay, in fact, immediately "bolted the whole" of the gift, causing his host to worry that his visitor might die of an overdose. To his great relief, though, the next few days brought no news of dead Malays, and the English opium-eater soon forgot his fears.

The significance of this episode lies in the way that it establishes a relationship between the Malay, the drug, and the English opium-eater. The Malay's tolerance for large doses suggests a physical affinity far beyond what even an experienced Englishman might expect—something signaled by the opium-eater's disbelief. The Malay is more accustomed to the drug than the opium-eater expected, but the text marks this notable tolerance as an exotic trait that further differentiates the Malay from his hosts. It is perhaps the most important entry on the list of attributes that designate his otherness. The episode with the Malay maintained a common association of opium with the Orient while locating this allegedly foreign practice within the walls of an English cottage. DeQuincey's text thus modified the older equation, suggesting that opium was a substance whose use could open an exotic, oriental world within the more familiar landscape of the English Lake District. While some readers found these images intriguing, others imagined opium use (and its oriental practitioners) as a potential threat to their native culture. In Morewood's terms, it was an infatuating, effeminate, Asiatic practice that could indeed take hold and proliferate in the West.

DeQuincey's text clearly associated more than the mere *practice* of opium use with the Orient. It also equated the *experience* of opium intoxication with the explicitly oriental visions whose rich descriptions are the book's most strik-ing and memorable element. Opium was more than a simple intoxicant in DeQuincey's text. It served as an inspiration to the imagination, as a creative muse, as a gateway to a state of consciousness that DeQuincey described, al-most exclusively, in oriental terms. But despite such exuberance, DeQuincey qualified the elaborate nature of his opium experience by noting that it was en-tirely idiosyncratic. He warned readers that his visions and dreams had every-thing to do with his own peculiar temperament and little to do with the opium itself. He wrote that "if a man 'whose talk is of oxen,' should become an Opium-eater, the probability is, that (if he is not too dull to dream at all)—he will dream about oxen: whereas, in the case before him, the reader will find that the Opium-eater boasteth himself to be a philosopher; and accordingly, that the phantas-magoria of his dreams (waking or sleeping, day-dreams or night-dreams) is suitable to one who in that character, *Humani nihil a se alienum putat.*"[11]

DeQuincey's caveat could not be stronger, but nonetheless, his vividly de-scribed opium dreams caused trouble for antinarcotic reformers for years to come. The suggestion that opium use produced lush visions of philosophical grandeur, that it somehow freed the mind from duller, everyday concerns, made a great impact. DeQuincey's readers, in fact, seem to have been remarkably se-lective in their reading. Though his text is unambiguous in its assertion that the person rather than the substance is responsible for a particular state of in-toxication, one frequently finds DeQuincey cited as the key influence and inspi-ration for what would, fifty years later, become a major public concern.

In the second part of *The Confessions,* "The Pains of Opium," DeQuincey fo-cused on both the growth of the habit and on the increasingly threatening world of dreams that gradually envelop the opium-eater. As the dreams become unbearable, the image of the Malay returns, conducting the unwilling En-glishman's journey to a terrifying new world. The opium-eater explains that "the Malay has been a fearful enemy for months. I have every night, through his means, transported into asiatic scenes. I know not whether others share in my feelings on this point; but I have often thought that if I were compelled to forgo England, and to live in China, and among Chinese manners and modes of life and scenery, I should go mad."[12] It is hard to imagine a clearer statement of a fictionalized Orient as a threat to the maintenance of this terribly occiden-tal character's sense of self. Opium threatened the opium-eater with a journey to a place where, bereft of his familiar markers of identity, there was nothing left but to tumble into the incoherent, irrational prattle of the madman—a mutter-ing that served particularly to highlight the expository clarity of the writing in

The Confessions but also to identify that particularly incoherent language as Chinese.

DeQuincey described the central aim of *The Confessions* as the production of a text that might "display the marvelous agency of opium." If we take that claim seriously, then the book's definitive moment comes when the narrator declares that "not the opium-eater, but the opium is the true hero of the tale and the legitimate centre on which the interest revolves."[13] DeQuincey thus described the opium habit as a reversal in the relations of center and periphery, of narrator and narrative, of author and text, of subject and object. The opium-eater was unable to maintain his position at the "legitimate centre" of his narrative and was instead placed under the controlling influence of a force external to himself—a power supposedly embodied by the opium. The English opium-eater's confession, then, was that luxuriant, oriental self-indulgence had triumphed over rational self-conquest and that this path led to all the other "pains" of opium use.

Once again, however, DeQuincey's readers seem to have been remarkably selective in their reading. In 1842, for instance, the American William Blair explained his decision to begin using opium in an essay for the *Knickerbocker* titled "An Opium-Eater in America." He wrote that "the strange confessions of DeQuincey had long been a favorite," but he made his own embarrassing confession when he explained that "the latter part, the 'Miseries of Opium,' I had most unaccountably always neglected to read."[14] Blair went on to describe his own miseries, but DeQuincey's *Confessions* would have to wait for at least another twenty years to find a group of readers whose experience might authorize a closer, more attentive reading—one that would generate a description of habitual narcotic use as a significant public threat.

DESIRE, REASON, AND POLITICAL SUBJECTIVITY

DeQuincey's writing was a part of a more general Romantic challenge to an Enlightenment insistence upon reason as the highest of all human faculties. If DeQuincey's text put opium use—and the dreams that it allegedly produced— at the service of a broader Romantic critique of Enlightenment reason, we must also note that the Romantic challenge itself was embedded in a much longer intellectual history. Philosophical discussion of the antagonistic relationship between reason and desire, or the "appetites," is nearly as persistent as the use of opium in the history of Western culture. To trace this opposition, one might only *begin* with Homer, Plato, Aristotle, Augustine, Descartes, and Locke, all of whom devoted considerable time to establishing the necessity of mastering the body's appetites to ensure the proper operation of the mind. A survey of this opposition is beyond the scope of this book, but we need to remember that the mastery of the body and its desires has long underlay the notion of an independent, rational, and autonomous subjectivity in Western culture.

In the United States, the assertion of an autonomous, independent subject has authorized both republican and liberal theories of political behavior since at least the eighteenth century. The liberal version of this autonomous subject pursued his self-interest in the public sphere and came to know those interests by situating himself in relation to other subjects—all within the world of objects that surrounded him. This self-conscious acknowledgment of one's identity as an independent agent requires, first, that the subject is in possession of his own faculties of perception. Because he is independent from the object world that surrounds him, he is (theoretically) able to perceive and locate himself within that world. In his classic 1961 study of the foundations of liberal thought, C. B. Macpherson wrote that "the central difficulty" of "original seventeenth-century individualism . . . lay in its possessive quality . . . [which] is found in its conception of the individual as essentially the proprietor of his own person or capacities, owing nothing to society for them." Macpherson further explained that in liberalism, "the human essence is freedom from dependence on the wills of others, and freedom is a function of possession." [15]

Thirty years later, the historian Gordon S. Wood located a similar definition of political subjectivity in the American Revolutionary and Early National periods. He described the "classical republican tradition" as the belief that "man was by nature a political being, a citizen who achieved his greatest moral fulfillment by participating in a self-governing republic." To fulfill one's humanity was, by definition, to follow the virtuous path, but "to be completely virtuous citizens, men—never women, because it was assumed they were never independent— had to be free from dependence and from the petty interests of the marketplace. Any loss of independence and virtue was corruption." [16] The "virtuous citizen" was thus both autonomous and his own master. The notion of republican autonomy, then, like liberal independence, rested in the more fundamental assertion of self-possession. To surrender or to lose one's "possession" was to relinquish independence and to corrupt the essence of the whole. The maintenance of autonomy from forces outside of the self was thus the key to both public and private virtue.

Within the context of the individualist culture of the United States, a society

that prided itself on its (incomplete) commitment to the exercise of independence and individual liberty, opium's ability to assume the position of agent, to
commandeer what DeQuincey called the "legitimate centre" of personal narrative, held a potential threat to the enunciation of some of the culture's central
images of itself. DeQuincey's formulation of the habit undercut the very possibility of the independence that guaranteed both liberal and republican political
visions, thus threatening the authority of the bourgeois subject. Opium *dis*possessed its user of himself. The opium-eater's displacement to the margins of
what was theoretically his own text made clear that he no longer possessed
himself. The opium habit could therefore be envisioned as a threat to the foundation upon which rational, autonomous bourgeois subjectivity was based.

THE INFLUENCE OF THE TEMPERANCE MOVEMENT

The impact of DeQuincey's romantic reflections upon the pleasures and pains
of opium use was, however, dwarfed in the United States by the much more
visible debate about alcohol, exemplified by the anti-alcohol campaigns of the
temperance movement. Though opium was readily available in American phar-
macies, expert estimates found only one opium-eater for every thousand liquor
drinkers in the 1820s.[17] Historian William J. Rohrbaugh explains further that
economic conditions between 1790 and 1830 caused the market to be flooded
with cheap whiskey.[18] Antebellum American drinkers rose to the challenge, and
by 1830, consumption levels for people over fifteen years of age had reached an
all-time high of 7.1 gallons of pure alcohol per capita, more than double the
rates of the late twentieth century.[19] Many people blamed heavy drinking for
increases in domestic assault, family desertion, and public violence. At the
same time, cities and towns were forced to meet the growing cost of support
for "drunkards" and their families, leading many influential members of society to try to control drinking itself in order to reduce its socially disruptive
consequences.[20]

This combination of social and cultural impulses contributed to the growth
of the temperance movement, which began in the first twenty years of the nineteenth century and soon became what was perhaps the most persistent and
influential political movement of the next one hundred years. Other important nineteenth-century reform movements, most notably abolition and the
women's movement, burst forth from roots that were established and nurtured
in the fertile soil of temperance. The link that bound these movements together

was their insistence on the autonomy of the individual, based on his (or some-times even her) self-possession. Though the reformers who challenged sub-servience to a Southern slave master or an imperious husband were less numerous than those who battled the tyranny of the whiskey bottle, all three groups shared a libratory rhetoric that celebrated the sanctity of the individual over and against any surrender to powers or agencies extrinsic to the self. As the first and most popular of these movements, temperance helped to define a discourse that envisioned the habitual use of an external, intoxicating sub-stance as a threat to the maintenance of individual liberty.

A young legislator named Abraham Lincoln made clear the connection be-tween individual liberty and the habitual use of intoxicants in an 1842 address to the Springfield, Illinois, chapter of the Washington Temperance Society. Founded in 1840, the "Washingtonians" were a national association of recover-ing drunkards who had turned away from other temperance groups in their re-jection of the clergy and other self-appointed experts in their efforts to quit drinking. They spoke to and for each other, thus anticipating the various twelve-step programs of the twentieth century which would also base their ef-forts on the outreach work of other "alcoholics." The Washingtonian phenome-non was brief—by 1847 most groups had stopped meeting—but in that short period as many as six hundred thousand men had participated in the group's activities.[21]

Speaking on Washington's Birthday, Lincoln celebrated the temperance movement by situating it within the broader individualist traditions of Ameri-can political culture. He explained that true independence was grounded in reason's triumph over the passions, which could, in turn, generate the kind of self-possession that empowered a society of free individuals. Because the drunk-ard labored under the tyranny of drink, seen here as a coercive, extrinsic power, his situation was not unlike that of the slave who toiled under the whip of his Southern master. Though Lincoln was not an abolitionist, his speech in praise of the temperance movement associated its promises of freedom for the drunk-ard with abolition's promise of liberty for the slave. Lincoln brought these ideas together by insisting on the necessity of self-possession for the production and maintenance of what he saw as a fully functional and distinctively American po-litical subjectivity.

Lincoln's speech offers a striking demonstration of a logic wherein the habit-ual use of an intoxicating substance stands as an example of the defeat of reason at the hands of passion. He invoked the nation's revolutionary heritage in order to transform its emphasis on self-government to a preoccupation with the governance of the self, declaring that "of our political revolution of '76, we all are justly proud. It has given us a degree of political freedom, far exceeding that of any other of the nations of the earth. In it the world has found a solution of that long mooted problem, as to the capability of man to govern himself." The final phrase in this passage was crucial, because it laid the foundation that would enable Lincoln's transition from the particularities of what he termed *political* freedom (self-government) to broader reflections on the terms of *human* freedom (the governance of the self). Moving quickly, he shifted to the more general question and raised the stakes when he said that the Revolution of 1776 sowed "the germ which has vegetated, and still is to grow and expand into the universal liberty of mankind." [22]

Having thus moved beyond narrower definitions of political freedom ("the germ"), Lincoln asked his audience to "turn now to the temperance revolution." He insisted that in abandoning alcohol, "we shall find a stronger bondage broken; a viler slavery manumitted; [and] a greater tyrant deposed" than those encountered in the political revolution of 1776. In terms that we might more plausibly attribute to a transcendentalist poet or philosopher than to a future American president, Lincoln made clear the connection between freedom from intoxicants and political freedom by grounding them in their lowest common denominator, the domination of the passions by reason: "And what a noble ally [is temperance] to the cause of political freedom. With such an aid, its march cannot fail to be on and on, till every son of earth shall drink in rich fruition, the sorrow quenching draughts of perfect liberty. Happy day, when all appetites controlled, all passions subdued, all matters subjected, mind, all conquering mind, shall live and move the monarch of the world. Glorious consummation! Hail fall of Fury! Reign of Reason, all hail!" [23] Lincoln's reliance on what I identified above as the long-standing Western antagonism between reason and passion is clear in this passage. Control of the appetites, or freedom from desire, could be made equivalent to the freedom from political tyranny by resolving both into a relationship with the more fundamental concept of self-possession. Alcohol thus threatened individual liberty, just as royal prerogative and parliamentary tyranny had done sixty-six years before.

Having identified self-possession as the necessary condition of American political subjectivity, Lincoln concluded by offering his audience what was then a more contemporary metaphor—the comparison to racial slavery. Adopting a position much closer to abolitionism than to the antislavery platform with which he would later become associated, Lincoln thundered his conclusion: "And when the victory shall be complete—when there shall be neither a slave nor a drunkard on the earth—how proud the title of that Land, which may truly claim to be the birth-place and the cradle of both those revolutions, that shall have ended in that victory. How noble and distinguished that People, who shall have planted, and nurtured to maturity, both the political and moral freedom of their species."[24] Lincoln's considerable rhetorical skills were much in evidence here. His conclusion brought together the causes of temperance and abolition under the banner of more traditional notions of American political liberty while completing the organic metaphor begun earlier. In his speech, Lincoln showed how the habitual use of alcohol could signify the domination of the individual by extrinsic forces, thus equating the whiskey bottle with royal despots and Southern slave masters. With its arguments based on the domination of the appetites by reason, Lincoln's address also illustrated a powerful strand of temperance thought that was to reemerge in the ideas of antinarcotic reformers.

FITZ HUGH LUDLOW: A MINOR DEQUINCEY

These elements of mid-nineteenth-century American culture came to bear on the emerging narcotic question in the eclectic works of journalist Fitz Hugh Ludlow (1836–70). Ludlow held numerous literary positions, including the editorship of *Vanity Fair* from 1858 until 1860. He traveled extensively within the United States, most famously as a companion to the landscape painter Albert Bierstadt, and was a frequent contributor to *Harper's Monthly*, the *New York World*, and the New York *Evening Post*. He wrote essays, fiction, poetry, and even college songs. Becoming a habitual opium user late in his short life, Ludlow dedicated his final years to finding and writing about a cure for what he characterized as a spreading narcotic habit. Ludlow's work brought together the full range of influences explored in this chapter, from DeQuincey's Orientalism to the individualist rhetoric of the American abolition and temperance movements. Ludlow died in 1870 at the age of 34, but his writing stands as the culmination of the first phase of (relatively light) concern about the dangers of the narcotic habit. His texts crystallized many of the themes that would come to dominate the turn-of-the-century discourse concerning narcotic addiction.[25]

Ludlow first came to public attention with the publication of an 1856 article in *Putnam's Monthly* titled "The Apocalypse of Hasheesh." The article's success encouraged the young author, and he quickly followed this first piece with a book-length memoir called *The Hasheesh Eater: Passages from the Life of a Pythagorean* (1857). The book's Orientalism was immediately evident as

Ludlow discussed his fascination with "oriental stories" in its introduction. By asserting that the powerful foreignness of such stories defied his Western readers' sense of plausibility, that their deviation from narrative convention marked them as intellectually other, Ludlow defined the tales as part of a fundamentally non-Western way of thought. The oriental story helped to distinguish Ludlow's "them" from his "us." It served as an element and indicator of an extraordinary culture of the other and also sought to establish a connection between the writer and his audience. He wrote that "our minds can find no clew to [the oriental story's] strange, untrodden by-ways of speculation; our highest soarings are still in an atmosphere which feels heavy with the reek and damp of ordinary life." [26]

Ludlow, however, found a clue to the origins of the oriental story in the use of the cannabis derivative "hasheesh." He argued against attempts to explain away these "fields of weird experience" by criticizing what he felt were scholastic attempts to attribute the oriental story's exoticisms to the Eastern climate or to Asia's ancient traditions. Ludlow also disagreed with those who might claim that the stories proceeded from the "semi-civilized" oriental imagination, "unbound by the fetters of logic and the schools." Ludlow substituted his own explanation for the oriental story's peculiarities, arguing that "the difference can not be accounted for by climate, religion, or manners. . . . The secret lies in the use of hasheesh." [27] Much as opium had served DeQuincey's English opium-eater, "hasheesh" opened a gateway to Ludlow's fanciful world of the oriental story. It was a passport to an exotic land that was free from what Ludlow had described as the damp, reeking ordinariness of the West, an entrance ticket to a place of imaginative freedom where one was released from the fetters of Western logic.

Because of its pronounced Orientalism and its focus on drug use, critics immediately compared Ludlow's writing to that of DeQuincey. An 1857 reviewer in *Harper's New Monthly Magazine* wrote that Ludlow was "unequal to De-Quincey in literary culture and in the craft of book-making, [but he] compares favorably with him in the passion for philosophical reflection, in the frankness of his personal revelations, and in preternatural brilliancy of fancy. In point of compact and orderly method in the narration of his story he has a decided advantage over DeQuincey." In a passage notable for its lack of the hyperbole that would soon come to mark the public discussion of drug use, the same reviewer noted that "the comparative merits of hasheesh and opium as a stimulant to the intellect and the source of wild, imaginative dreams, may be learned from a comparison of the two volumes." [28] The books thus served not only as descriptions but also as user's manuals for those interested in drug use and philosophical speculation.

The association of Ludlow's work with DeQuincey's would persist over years. Writing for the *North American Review* in 1862, D. W. Cheever noted the frequency of the comparison, concluding that "we are not among those who believe [*The Hasheesh Eater*] a fiction, based on the reading and admiration of the *Confessions of an English Opium-Eater.*"[29] In 1925, a physician reviewing Ludlow's work for the *Medical Journal and Record* called Ludlow "a minor De-Quincey."[30] In 1939, literary critic Franklin Walker wrote of the pleasure that the *San Francisco Golden Era* literary circle (e.g., Bret Harte, Mark Twain, and Joaquin Miller) felt at the presence of "the famous drug-addict, the DeQuincey of America," in their midst for a brief period in the 1860s.[31] Such references secured Ludlow's now largely forgotten position as the American DeQuincey.

Ludlow devoted *The Hasheesh Eater*'s entire preface to an explanation of his debt to DeQuincey. He declared that the association of the two authors was obvious, but he felt that this was a great compliment to his own work. Writing that "I know no master of style in whose footsteps I should more earnestly seek to tread,"[32] he praised DeQuincey effusively: "The path of DeQuincey led beyond all the boundaries of the ordinary life into a world of intense lights and shadows—a realm in which all the range of average thought found its conditions surpassed, if not violated. My own career, however far its recital may fall short of the Opium-Eater's, and notwithstanding it was not coincident and but seldom parallel with his, still ran through lands as glorious, as unfrequented, as weird as his own, and takes those who would follow it out of the trodden highways of mind."[33] As we have seen, this was not Ludlow's first reference to the "trodden highways of mind." He had earlier noted the oriental story's departure from such dull tracks, enforcing the opposition between what he characterized as the oriental landscape of narcotic use and the narrow limitations of Western logic.

Moving beyond the praise of DeQuincey's style or the depth of his vision, Ludlow addressed the most obvious connection between the two authors: their drug use. Noting the resemblance of the two works, Ludlow explained that "we both saw the same thing. The state of insight which he attained through opium, I reached by the way of hasheesh. . . . The vision is accessible to all of the same temperament and degree of exaltation."[34]

But Ludlow brought more than this secondhand version of DeQuincey's Orientalism to his own descriptions of drug use. His writing is also striking in its engagement with the rhetoric of mid-nineteenth-century American reform.

His father, Henry G. Ludlow, was an abolitionist preacher and his grandfather Daniel Ludlow was an early activist in the temperance movement.[35] The influence of both movements is clear in Fitz Hugh's writing.

In 1865 Ludlow wrote a piece for the *Atlantic Monthly* titled "If Massa put Guns into our Han's," which offered Ludlow's abolitionist childhood "as a representative experience, capable of explaining all enthusiasms for liberty which have created 'fanatics' and martyrs in our time."[36] After explaining how his family had been driven out of its house by an anti-abolitionist mob shortly before his birth, he reflected on his childhood: "Among earliest stories which were told me in the nursery, I recollect the martyrdom of Nat Turner, . . . and all the things which Toussaint did, with no white man, but with the whitest spirit of all to help him."[37] At the age of four he "learned that my father combined the two functions of preaching in a New England college town and ticket-agency on the Underground Railroad."[38]

Ludlow took this early experience, as well as a passion for evangelizing, with him to the schoolhouse, where "among the large crowd of young southerners sent to this school, I began preaching emancipation in my pinafore. Mounted upon a window-seat in an alcove of the great play-hall, I passed recess after recess in haranguing a multitude upon the subject of Freedom." Whether or not young Fitz Hugh actually spent his school days haranguing an unsympathetic audience on the subject of emancipation is unimportant. What matters is the way that this story situated the rest of his writing within the broader context of the abolitionist movement. Near the story's completion, Ludlow tells of a conversation he had with a slave on a journey to the South. When the slave inquired about Northern politics, Ludlow came out with his confession: "I then said openly that I was an Abolitionist—that I believed in every man's right to freedom."[39] His concern with individual liberty was nurtured from an early age, and the emancipatory rhetoric of the abolitionist movement would later inhabit and accentuate his writing on the opium habit.

This autobiographical piece also hints at Ludlow's interest in the temperance movement. He made a common association between the two movements in the memoir, claiming that every traveler to the South was sure to see "sons of the first South Carolina families" lounging about "some low grog-shop" with "their Negroes' earnings running down their throats."[40] Three years later, Ludlow further pursued the theme of Southern drinking in an 1868 *Harper's Bazaar* serial called "The Household Angel," a sentimental temperance story about a Northern family that was nearly ruined by drink after they moved to Reconstruction Kentucky to claim their inheritance.[41]

Ludlow's Orientalism, his abolitionist devotion to individual liberty, and his apprehension of intoxicants came together in his writings about the opium habit. Family letters make it clear that Ludlow, who had long struggled with his own heavy drinking, had developed a severe opium habit in the latter years of his life.[42] It is not surprising, then, that he brought the strength of his abolitionist rhetoric to bear when he described one of his life's "ruling passions" as "a very agony of seeking to find—any means of bringing the habituated opium-eater out of his horrible bondage."[43]

In 1867, *Harper's Magazine* published Ludlow's essay "What Shall They Do to be Saved," which illustrates many of the themes that would come to dominate the discussion of habitual narcotic use late in the century. The article was anthologized, along with several other pieces, including DeQuincey's *Confessions*, in Horace Day's 1868 compilation *The Opium Habit*. Day's book was an attempt to collect the most important writing to date about the opium habit "for the benefit of opium-eaters," but he also hoped that the volume would appeal "to moralists and philanthropists to whom its sad stories of infirmity and suffering might be suggestive of new themes and new objects upon which to bestow their reflections or their sympathies."[44] Day's assertion of the novelty of the opium habit should not be overlooked. The book's purpose was to bring what he, and many others, saw as a new affliction to broader public attention. Day feared that, because of the influence of the Civil War, the opium habit was a rapidly spreading problem.[45] His anthology is thus an important marker in the elevation of the drug problem to a level of major social importance. Day's hope that reformers might find "new themes and new objects" in its pages makes clear the relative obscurity of the drug problem, but it also suggests that the time was right for change. Ludlow's inclusion in the anthology testified to the importance and the influence of his ideas about the opium habit. It also guaranteed that his beliefs would remain in print and therefore influence future discussions of the habit.

In "What Shall They Do to be Saved?" Ludlow characterized opium use as a compromise of the freedom and independence of the will. He felt, however, that an adequate discussion of the opium *habit* required a break from his former literary idol: "The totality of the experience is only conceivable by adding this physical torture to a mental anguish which even the Oriental pencil of DeQuincey has but feebly painted." Ludlow sought to paint the picture anew, deepening its chiaroscuro. He explained that the habit was "an anguish which slays the will, yet leaves the soul conscious of its murder . . . and either paralyzes the reasoning faculties which might suggest encouragements, or deadens the emotional nature to them as thoroughly as if they were not perceived."[46] Opium thus turned against the user by paralyzing his reason and deadening his emotions. What Ludlow first viewed as an invigorating escape from the "trod-den paths" of Western reason was here reconceived as the entrance to a mad-dening labyrinth—a dense, cognitive tangle that offered no apparent return to that dull but reassuring occidental track.

Paralyzed reason and deadened emotions also produced a particular species of hopelessness, an inability to encourage oneself in order to resuscitate the slain will. This, for Ludlow, was the force that opium exerted on its habitual users—they were dominated at the level of the will. Put another way, the desire to take the drug overruled their will to avoid it. Ludlow described poet Samuel Taylor Coleridge's well-publicized opium habit as "a force despotizing it over his will, a degradation descending on his manhood."[47]

Ludlow expanded on this notion of opium use as a slayer of the will, convert-ing the abstraction into physiological terms by arguing that the opium user "is suffering under a disease of the very machinery of volition; and no more to be judged harshly for his acts than a wound for suppurating or the bowels for con-tinuing the peristaltic motion."[48] Here Ludlow hoped to shift the consideration of the habit from a moral to a purely physiological question. The notion of physical necessity, of a purely mechanical process, aided this move, but it com-plicated the explanation of the place of the will—of the role of the user's voli-tion *not* to use the drug. Ludlow found a way out of this problem when he wrote that the habit "slays the will, yet leaves the soul conscious of its murder." Thus remaining cognizant of its lost capacity to exercise control over the body, the "soul" was reduced to the status of observer as the body's mechanical desires overrode its subjective volition.

Yet in reconciling the relationship between mechanical bodies and immate-rial faculties such as the will or volition, Ludlow inadvertently reintroduced what he had earlier described as DeQuincey's inadequate representation of the narcotic habit. He further developed the idea that habitual narcotic use was a "disease of the volition" when he described the withdrawal symptoms of a habit-ual user: "The abandonment of opium brought on an agony which took his ac-tions entirely out of voluntary control, eclipsing the higher ideals and heroisms of his imagination at once, and reducing him to that automatic condition in which the nervous system issues and enforces only those edicts which are coun-seled by pure animal self-preservation."[49] The problem of habitual narcotic use was thus that the corporeal (finite, mechanical) substance overcame the intelli-gent (infinite, spiritual) essence of the sufferer. Actions became automatic, beyond the control of a central, orchestrating consciousness. Like DeQuincey's English opium-eater, then, the habitual narcotic user in Ludlow's text was unable to maintain the "legitimate centre" of the narrative that might structure and give coherence to his actions. In Ludlow's terms, the mechanical functions of the user's body eclipsed "the higher ideals and heroisms of his imagination." Ludlow's attempt to improve on DeQuincey's description of the habit by putting it into physical terms reinscribed what the English writer had earlier posited as the chief problem of opium use: "Not the opium-eater, but the opium is the true hero of the tale." In a move from the literary to the literal, Ludlow merely transcribed DeQuincey's narrative affliction into physiological terms.

Ludlow's description of the opium habit echoed DeQuincey's mingled fascination and horror at the experience of narcotic intoxication as the antithesis of Western reason and subjectivity, but it also recast his English predecessor's concerns in the more familiar and accessible idioms of American abolitionism and temperance. The hazard of habitual narcotic use could thus be sketched as particularly threatening to American individualism—as a menace to the liberty and independence born of self-possession. Ludlow's upbringing in an abolitionist household equipped him with the language and the habits of thought that animated much of his description of the opium habit. The abolitionists championed the freedom of the individual, but this rhetoric alone was not sufficient for Ludlow's purposes. The sense that an intoxicant might do the same work as a Southern slave master had to be drawn from another source, and as we have seen, that source was the temperance movement.[50]

Ludlow, however, wanted not merely to describe the opium habit but also to cure it. In addition to the languages of abolition and temperance, Ludlow mobilized images drawn from contemporary physiology in his description of the opium habit. Because the opium user suffered from a *disease* of the volition, it followed that "such a man is a proper subject, not for reproof, but for medical treatment. The problem of his case need embarrass nobody. It is as purely physical as one of small-pox. When this truth is as widely understood among the laity as it is known by physicians, some progress may be made in staying the frightful ravages of opium among the present generation."[51] This was partially the case because he felt that opium was "the most complicated drug in the Pharmacopoeia." This complexity was increased because the drug itself was composed of "the most complex compounds known to modern chemistry."[52] And its action was just as complex as its composition, attacking the nervous system "with as much intensity, and [changing] it in as many ways as its complexity would lead us to expect."[53]

The intricacy of this challenge required the attention of an expert, and Ludlow therefore introduced a theme that, especially after the beginning of the twentieth century, many proponents of medical professionalization would use to justify their leadership in attacking the problem: "Though the most untechnical man, he must already know the disorder which has taken place in his moral nature and his will. For a knowledge of his physical condition he must resort to his medical man." [54]

Finally, Ludlow made a point that would be critical in a debate which would rise to national prominence soon after his death. He was among the first to introduce the notion that there was something peculiarly contemporary, unambiguously *modern* about the narcotic habit. For Ludlow, habitual narcotic use was unequivocally a disease of its historical moment: "The terrible demands, especially in this country, made on modern brains by our feverish competitive life, constitute hourly temptations to some form of the sweet, deadly sedative. Many a professional man of my acquaintance, who twenty years ago was content with his tri-diurnal 'whiskey,' ten years ago, drop by drop, began taking stronger 'laudanum cocktails,' until he became what he is now—an habitual opium-eater." [55]

Ludlow believed that the threat was "gaining fearful ground" among all classes of American society, "from the highest to the lowest"; people "who a generation ago took gin" were "yearly increasing their consumption of the drug." [56] Habitual narcotic use respected no class boundaries, and according to Ludlow, it was rapidly replacing the old enemy of the temperance movement—alcohol—as a public menace.

Fitz Hugh Ludlow died in 1870 at the age of 34. But the themes that would emerge between 1870 and 1920, the crucial years of the antinarcotic movement, were clear in his writing on the narcotic habit. His texts brought together DeQuincey's Orientalism with the rhetoric of the abolition movement. He also shared the fears of temperance reformers who battled the liquor bottle, sensing that the drunkard's desire was an opponent of Western reason and the self-mastery required to make sense of American political subjectivity. As we will see, these themes and their attendant variations would be enunciated more fully over the next fifty years.

CHAPTER 2

Narcotic Addiction

"The Secret Leprosy of Modern Days"

> The ancients paid sacred homage to Morpheus, god of sleep
> and dreams; and now, in the midst of an age of intelligence
> and advancement, we find a vast army of men and women
> bowing at the shrine of the arch-fiend Morphia, named after
> the classic deity of old!
>
> —LESLIE E. KEELEY, M.D., quoted by HENRY G. Cole,
> *Confessions of an American Opium Eater* (1895)

W E HAVE SEEN THAT a variety of mid-nineteenth-century scientific and popular writers noted that narcotic use was potentially habit forming, but their texts failed to generate the intensity of public concern produced by widespread discussions of many other social problems, particularly those associated with heavy drinking. Beginning in the 1870s, however, the narcotic habit became much more visible. As I discussed in the introduction, this emergence can partly be explained by the increasing use of narcotic medication, especially after the popularization of the hypodermic syringe in the 1860s. Likewise, a gradual shift in the makeup of the drug-using population, away from middle-class women and toward lower-class and demimonde men, helps to explain the growth of public concern. These transformations are well documented, but historians agree that empirical accounts alone cannot explain the emergence of habitual narcotic use—termed narcotic *addiction* by the second decade of the twentieth century—as a matter of public concern and an apt target for federal intervention and regulation.

So that we can understand its emergence more fully, in this chapter I situate the addiction concept within a menacing, contemporary vision of turn-of-the-century historical change: the sense of modernity as cultural crisis. This powerful and frequently recorded perception derived its threatening tone from the way it undermined the articulation of nineteenth-century bourgeois identity, grounded as it was upon "the autonomous individual, whose only moral master was himself," according to the historian T. J. Jackson Lears.[1] Coherent assertions of self-mastery both underwrite and require the unambiguous delineation of responsibility and obligation, but if one is unable to identify or claim responsibility for one's own acts or is unable to determine where one's own obligations lie, then claims of independent, self-willed action—claims of self-mastery—are, by definition, incoherent. This was exactly the problem experienced by many of the (mostly white and mostly male) beneficiaries of the quickly incorporating end-of-the-century economy. Corporate, managerial capitalism lightened the burden of economic risk and personal responsibility borne by individual businessmen, but the new system often seemed to behave of its own will, independent of human cause and certainly beyond the mastery of any individual actor or agent.[2] Because it seemed that "individual will and action were hemmed in by the emerging iron cage of a bureaucratic market economy," Lears argues that "bourgeois culture entered . . . a 'weightless' period, marked by hazy moral distinctions and vague spiritual commitments." He concludes that "personal identity itself came to seem problematic" in the waning years of the nineteenth century.[3]

Relentless mechanization and technological expansion were both a consequence and a cause of the incorporating economy, and they further complicated the assertion of human agency in a world of machines, electricity, and the rudiments of mass communication. Between the end of the Civil War and the beginning of the new century, total railroad track increased from thirty-five thousand to nearly two hundred thousand miles.[4] In 1880 Thomas Edison made electric lighting practical, and in 1882 New Yorkers thrilled as the new bulbs illuminated Wall Street. Communication technology also boomed. Both the multiplex telegraph and the telephone debuted at Philadelphia's 1876 Centennial Exhibition. Steam-powered printing presses contributed to the proliferation of inexpensive magazines, which often carried newly viable half-tone photographs, and the circulation of big-city newspapers increased dramatically.[5] These few examples help to explain why the historian Thomas Haskell has claimed that the close of the nineteenth century represented the culmination of what was "undoubtedly the most profound and rapid alteration in the material conditions of life that human society has ever experienced."[6]

The technological and economic expansion that was creating a corporate world of railroads, telephones, and electrical circuits further complicated the assertion of human agency by increasing the public's perception of regional and individual "interdependence," according to Haskell, who argues that "as society became increasingly interdependent, we may speculate that the effect, as experienced by sensitive persons within the society, must have been a tendency for efficient causation to recede from the observer." Haskell thus describes the sense of turn-of-the-century cultural crisis as a widely perceived decline in the efficacy of human intention, derived from perceptions of the formerly *in*dependent subject's entanglement within a newly *inter*dependent society. Like Lears, Haskell finds that "the individual, the irreducible atomic constituent of society," was "devalued" within the context of a transformed society that was typified by its perception of increased interdependence.[7]

This context already helps explain why habitual narcotic use was perceived as a threat to the notion of an identity based on self-mastery and the independent, autonomous subjectivity that it authorized. The drug addict, whose condition was often described as an affliction of the will, exemplified the way that modern technology threatened older formulations of individual human agency. Many addiction experts found in narcotics a product of modern (medical) technology that, rather than fulfilling optimistic predictions of a world made better by science, turned its human subjects into the slaves of human discoveries. Narcotic addiction's modernity, its emergence at a specific time and place, further distinguished it from habitual alcohol use, which had a much longer history as a controversial social practice. Alcohol was an integral part of Western society in a way that narcotics were not.[8] The Romans drank wine, and Christians could scarcely imagine Jesus inviting his disciples to remember him over a shot of morphine. Narcotic addiction was comparatively novel, much more emphatically a product of its moment than was heavy drinking. Its historical specificity gave the addiction concept its metonymic clout, its capacity to represent an era. It underwrote addiction's embodiment of the otherwise abstract threat that stalked the autonomous individual in a changing society whose modernity was marked, at least partly, by new perceptions of interdependence. Narcotic addiction signified the annulment of the bourgeois subject's autonomy, willpower, and self-mastery. The unregulated use of narcotics thus presented many experts and reformers with a concrete example of modernity's worst-case

This William Dalrympie image, "The Age of Drugs," appeared in Puck *in 1900. Its original caption reads, "The kind of drunkard I make is going out of fashion. I can't begin to compete with this fellow." Drug use here serves as a signification of its historical moment—it is a question of changing style, of a new fashion, of being up-to-date. Habitual drug use is thus shown to be a thoroughly modern affliction. The cartoon further marks a shift from the old foe of the temperance movement, the superbly visible saloon keeper, marked by a flashy mustache, apron, spats, and stripes, to the new villain, a pharmacist who is drawn as more sinister precisely to the degree that he blends in. Philadelphia Museum of Art, lent by William H. Helfand.*

scenario. It offered them a tangible contemporary issue from which to launch their antimodern critique.

NARCOTIC USE AND MODERN MEDICAL TECHNOLOGY

The status of narcotic drugs as a part of modern technological progress had first to do with the substances themselves. Morphine is the active alkaloid of opium, and the means to isolate it were widely known by 1820. Medical use of it grew throughout the nineteenth century, especially relative to the use of older preparations of opium such as laudanum, an alcohol-based tincture in which opium was mixed with spices. In 1898, Germany's Bayer Chemical Company introduced a still more powerful, semisynthetic opium derivative, a cough medication it marketed under the name of "heroin." Writers frequently included cocaine, which was isolated from the coca plant in the 1850s, in the same category as the opium derivatives. The emergence of such powerful chemical medications within a matter of decades led many to praise them as examples of the advance of modern, scientific medicine. T. D. Crothers was a leading addiction-cure doctor who in 1902 described these new and powerful distillates as a part of the nineteenth-century success story of physiologic chemistry. Crothers wrote that the discovery of these alkaloids, "the active principles of the plants wherein they are found," was the result of "the indefatigable researches" of the nineteenth century's "best and most eminent physiologic chemists." He described these people as "pioneers in the field" and believed that "the medical world owes [them] a great deal of gratitude." For Crothers, narcotics stood at the cutting edge of modern medical science. [9]

Crothers's insistence on the modernity of narcotic use echoed and reinforced an argument made thirty years previously by his friend and colleague George Miller Beard, the well-known physician who, in 1869, gave the name "neurasthenia" to the age's most representative neurological disorder. In 1871 Beard wrote that drug use "has greatly extended and multiplied with the progress of civilization, and especially in modern times." [10] Like Crothers, Beard found that drug use had spread through "the discovery and invention of new varieties [of narcotic], or new modifications of old varieties." [11] Alongside this assertion of technological and scientific progress, Beard found another cause for the growth of drug use in "the influence of commerce, by which the products of each clime became the property of all." He thus felt that a new economic interconnectedness had increased both the knowledge and availability of the world's various, regionally specific intoxicants. He wrote that "the ancient civilizations knew only of home made varieties; the moderns are content with nothing less than all of the best that the world produces." [12] Beard blamed modern progress for increased drug use and identified technological innovation and economic interconnectedness as the essence of modernity. Those were, of course, two central contributors to the modern cultural crisis. As we shall see, many experts believed that this particular form of (narcotic) interconnectedness produced a condition of interdependence, that it quite literally reduced those on the receiving end from having even a nominal state of independence to an abject dependence on these chemical products and their suppliers.

The second aspect of habitual narcotic use that situated it within the changing turn-of-the-century technological environment was the growing use of the hypodermic syringe. Several inventors claimed to have built the first syringe, but it is most often credited to Scotland's Alexander Wood, who maintained that he developed it for use in his Edinburgh practice in 1843. It was first used in the United States in 1853 by a New York physician who brought a syringe home with him from a visit to Scotland.[13] Within 25 years, thanks in part to a prolific and expanding medical press, it became one of the principal items in every doctor's medical bag.

Many commentators believed that this example of modern technology greatly exacerbated the emerging drug problem. Recognizing its use was crucial in differentiating the "opium-eaters" of the early nineteenth-century past from the "morphinists" and "morphinomaniacs" of the fin de siècle present. The figure of the syringe thus helped to delimit the boundaries of the modern. Its mobilization established the present as distinctive, novel, a sharp break from the past. The paradigmatic "opium eater" was, of course, Thomas DeQuincey. Remembering the status of his 1821 *Confessions* within the discourse of narcotic addiction helps us to recover the significance of Crothers's 1902 observation that "DeQuincey was able to use at one sitting a quart of laudanum. This habit he could abandon at times without assistance, resuming it again readily. Had he used morphin with the needle, the quantity required would have been less, but he never could have abandoned it."[14] Here, Crothers conjured DeQuincey's ghost to aid in the textual production of the present as a profound breaking away from the past that had produced it. Crothers's identification of the recent past as antiquated, as closed, as *passed* marked the distinctiveness of the present, distinguished by its addictive chemical and mechanical technologies, as modern.

Indeed, the syringe, a *machine* employed in the drug's delivery, stood near the center of the modern discourse of addiction. Philadelphia physician Roberts Bartholow made its role clear in the five editions of his *Manual of Hypodermic Medication*, written between 1869 and 1891. This user's guide for physicians who hoped to master the relatively new technique was quite popular, as its run to five editions helps to show. In the third edition (1879) Bartholow claimed that his manual was the only book of its type available in English. In it, the author consistently described hypodermic medication as a medical technology: part mechanism, part knowledge, and part practice.[15]

In the first two editions of the book, published in 1869 and 1873, the opening section is dedicated to "history, technology and therapeutics." Here, Bartholow offered his readers the standard history of the instrument's invention by Alexander Wood while also situating hypodermic medication within a histori-

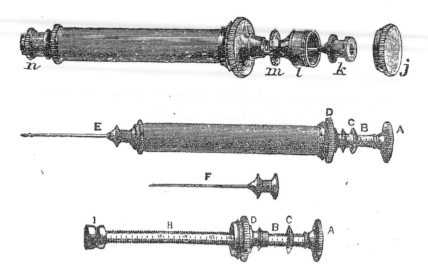

These images present the syringe as a modern mechanical implement. Reprinted from H. H. Kane, The Hypodermic Injection of Morphia *(New York, 1880).*

cal moment typified by its many technological advances. Bartholow described hypodermic medication as, first, a therapy made possible by a recently invented mechanism and the syringe in explicitly technical terms, writing that "the piston works, with or without a screw, by means of an auxiliary screw attached, not to the mountings, but to the piston itself. It contains two gold-plated needles, differing in size, and they fit to the barrel accurately by a socket-joint, and do not screw on."[16] These words describe a modern mechanical device built from machine-tooled parts.

Bartholow also described hypodermic medication as a special knowledge, which required an understanding of the machine's technical elements: "Nothing is more certain, however, than that carelessness will render useless the best instrument. . . . The leather packing must be kept well oiled, and so spread out that when the piston is forced down, the orifice of exit being closed, air cannot pass the piston."[17] For the physician who understood its operation and its proper maintenance, this machine could produce marvelous therapeutic results, and Bartholow's book was written in hopes of collecting, assembling, and disseminating this special knowledge to a broader medical public. Finally, Bartholow described hypodermic medication as a *practice*. The entire book is a manual, offering practical tips for the use of the syringe.

What is perhaps most striking, however, is that the first two editions of the manual devote less than two pages to the "morphia habit." Bartholow noted the potential for habitual use to develop but did not find hypodermic medication to be much riskier than oral. He wrote that "after long-continued hypodermic injection, the brain and nervous system become accustomed to the influence, and demand its repetition," which was quite the same "as when morphia is administered for a lengthened period by the stomach." [18] Though Bartholow noted the possibility of developing the habit, he believed that it was a relatively minor side effect of a very successful medical technique.

That would change with the publication of the book's third edition in 1879, which featured the expansion of the earlier editions' two-page section on the "morphia habit" into its own seventeen-page chapter. It is difficult to imagine a clearer illustration of habitual narcotic use's emergence as a public threat. After noting the medical advances made possible by the discovery of the hypodermic method, Bartholow waxed philosophical, explaining that "no good can exist in this world without a corresponding evil." Thus "the usefulness of the subcutaneous medication is embarrassed by a most serious abuse in the employment of the hypodermic syringe for the purpose of narcotic stimulation." The doctor warned that "this abuse is becoming a gigantic evil." It was crucial for the medical profession to be aware of the threat, because "if the habit be formed, the mental and moral degradation which ensues will always be referred to as the blunder or the crime of Dr. so-and-so." [19] Bartholow was right. As we will see in chapter 4, doctors *were* often blamed for spreading the drug habit. Here it is most important to note the change in emphasis in Bartholow's manual only ten years after its debut. Making his new emphasis absolutely clear, Bartholow wrote that "the introduction of the hypodermic syringe has placed in the hands of man a means of intoxication more seductive than any which has heretofore contributed to his craving for narcotic stimulation. So common now are the instances of its habitual use, and so enslaving is the habit when indulged in by this mode, that a lover of his kind must regard the future of society with no little apprehension." [20] Bartholow was so concerned by this turn of events that he "questioned whether the world has been the gainer or the loser by the discovery of subcutaneous medication." One must ask this question, he argued, because "every remote village has its slave, and not infrequently several, to the hypodermic syringe." Bartholow worried that "lamentable examples are daily encountered of men and women, regardful only of the morphia intoxication and indifferent to all the duties and obligations of life, reduced to a state of mental and moral weakness most pitiable to behold." He warned his readers that users might become "slaves to a vice beyond their control." [21]

Bartholow continued to revise his manual, publishing two more editions, due largely to what the doctor might have described as the cutting-edge modernity of his subject. In the 1882 edition of the book he explained that the rapid progress of therapeutic science made frequent revision necessary, something that he thought was "especially true of hypodermatic therapeutics, which deals with the active principles . . . the newest products of chemical research, which may be made available for this method of administration."[22] This fourth edition of the text offered little modification of the doctor's ideas about the habit, but the fifth and final edition (1891) made two small but significant changes.

First, Bartholow noted what would become medicolegal gospel by 1920: "There are really two classes of morphine consumers." He identified the first group as "those who take the drug as a means of intoxication." These were people who chose to use narcotics. They were guilty of making an immoral choice; they willed their own habit and were therefore *volitional* drug users. The second group was comparatively innocent and consisted of "those who have had morphine prescribed as a remedy."[23] In other words, their drug use was *assigned* to them, as if by a judge who had issued a binding court order that compelled them to take drugs. They were therefore users who met a more *juridical* aspect of the term "addiction." This crucial logic follows what I identified in the introduction as the double meaning of addiction, and it would, after the turn of the century, allow medicolegal theorists to sort the drug-using population into groups of criminals and patients.[24] I will pursue this logic more thoroughly in the chapters to come, but for now we should note that Bartholow's second modification was the addition of an ambivalence of tone. He explained that "in accordance with the usual practice, I have stated the evils of opium-taking in the strongest colors, that what influence so ever I possess may be thrown against the formation of the habit." But he had come to the conclusion that there was more to the narcotic story than ringing condemnations. He continued: "It must be admitted, however, that there is another side to the question; that examples exist in considerable numbers of men and women who have only been benefited by the habitual use of morphine or opium."[25] Bartholow's change in tone tells us that by 1891, the description of the evils of opium in the "strongest colors" had become the "usual practice," but it also displays his ambivalence about being a part of the mounting chorus of censure and hysteria surrounding the spread of the drug habit after 1870.

Among his examples of those who were benefited by the long-term use of opium, people who over many years "carried on business, and have carefully performed all of the duties of life incumbent on them," and who were "rather more free than their neighbors from the maladies and disabilities usual to advancing years,"[26] we find an old friend: "DeQuincey died at 74 . . . he achieved an immense amount of literary work, which seems to be increasing in reputation, and is now more read than during his lifetime." Bartholow added that DeQuincey's description of the drug's effects was "as little like the reality of ordinary experience under opium as can be conceived," but DeQuincey, who thought himself anything but "ordinary," would have agreed. It less clear that he would have agreed with Bartholow's conclusion: "It cannot be doubted . . . that DeQuincey had done no better had opium never crossed his path at all."[27]

Even though Bartholow felt what he described as a professional obligation to state "the reverse side of opium-eating," it would be incorrect to conclude that he became an advocate of the moderate use of narcotics. He tempered his deviance from what he identified as the "usual practice," writing that "the interests of his patients" demanded "refraining from the use [that is, the prescription] of narcotics when it can properly be done."[28] Whatever Bartholow's personal beliefs, the several editions of his manual mark the trajectory of the discourse of addiction across the years of its elevation to the status of a public threat. They also helped to establish the menacing novelty of the present as *modern* by distinguishing it from a recent and more benign past, now seen as irrevocably closed. Finally, Bartholow's texts share the ambivalence of those written by Beard and Crothers. They all celebrate the rapid progress of modernity while bewailing its threat to the autonomy of the human subject.

NARCOTIC USE AS A SYMPTOM OF MODERNITY

If narcotic use was a product of modern technology, then it also served as a symptom of modernity itself. To many experts, the desire to take narcotics was emblematic of the time in which they lived. The claim that habitual narcotic use was a specifically "modern" affliction—that it was produced by and was symptomatic of its historical moment—was among the most common assertions in the discourse of addiction.

There was probably no more influential authority on the relationship between a historical moment and a physical condition than George Miller Beard. In 1878 Beard defined "neurasthenia," as the "lack of nerve strength" that he believed was "a functional nervous disease of modern, and largely, though not entirely, of American origin."[29] He had made his vision of modern America clear in 1876, writing that "three great inventions—the printing press, the steam engine, and the telegraph, are peculiar to our modern civilization, and they give it a character for which there is no precedent."[30] He warned that a direct consequence of the growing predominance of these inventions was that "the methods and incitements of brain-work have multiplied far in excess of average cerebral developments."[31] Neurasthenia was therefore "a malady that has developed mainly during the last half century."[32] It was, in short, "the cry of the system struggling with its environment."[33]

Beard thought that neurasthenia had many symptoms. After producing a list that extended for nearly two pages in his 1881 book *American Nervousness: Its Causes and Consequences,* he explained that a comprehensive catalogue of symptoms was impossible because "every case differs somewhat from every other case." He found, nonetheless, that among the symptoms "especially worthy of attention" was a "susceptibility to stimulants and narcotics and various drugs." This increased sensitivity was "as unprecedented a fact as the telegraph, the railway, or the telephone."[34] Beard's claim suggests that scholars might fruitfully set narcotic use alongside other diseases of "overcivilization," including suicide, premarital sex (for women), and homosexuality. As Dr. W. F. Waugh wrote in 1894, the reasons for the emergence of the drug habit "are to be found in the conditions of modern life, and consist of the causative factors of suicide and insanity." Waugh described those afflictions as "the price we pay for our modern civilization."[35]

Though Beard was most concerned with decreased tolerance—people seemed more vulnerable to intoxication and its side effects than they had been—he also worried that the changing modern environment contributed to the development of the drug *habit.* Beard explained that a person whose nervous system had become "enfeebled" by the demands of modern society would naturally turn wherever she could for "artificial support," and thus "anything that gives ease, sedation, oblivion, such as chloral, chloroform, opium or alcohol, may be resorted to at first as an incident, and finally as a habit." Not merely to overcome physical discomfort, "but for the relief of exhaustion, deeper and more distressing than pain, do both men and women resort to the drug shop."[36] Neurasthenia came on "under the press and stimulus of the telegraph and railway,"[37] and Beard believed that it provided "the philosophy of many cases of opium or alcohol inebriety."[38]

This identification of drug use with modernity was ubiquitous in the writings of turn-of-the-century specialists, and examples are easy to find. In 1881 Dr. H. H. Kane began his book *Drugs That Enslave* with the declaration that "a higher degree of civilization, bringing with it increased mental development among all classes, increased cares, duties and shocks, seems to have caused the habitual use of narcotics, once a comparatively rare vice among Christian Nations, to have become alarmingly common." [39] In 1895 the journalist and recovered addict Henry G. Cole explained in his *Confessions of an American Opium Eater* that "rapid development in school and collegiate enterprises and sciences," in business and politics, and also in "our mechanical inventions" had created a mental strain that was "too much for the physical system to bear." This led many to "find rest in the repeated use of opium or morphine." [40] In a particularly evocative passage from 1915, Dr. L. L. Stanley offered a name other than "neurasthenia" for the condition that led to drug use, writing that "there is a nervous strain of modern life, or the 'Mania Americana,' which is temporarily relieved by the soothing effects of opium, but which is subsequently made worse by continued use." [41]

As Cole's statement suggests, former addicts often agreed with the experts that modern progress had contributed to their habit. Further examples of the convergence of opinion between medical and popular writers can be found in the confessional memoirs of other middle-class drug users. We have already seen, for instance, that in his *The Hasheesh Eater*, Fitz Hugh Ludlow used a similar strategy, and it will be apparent again in my analysis in the next chapter of William Rosser Cobbe's 1895 memoir, *Dr. Judas: A Portrayal of the Opium Habit*. It is probably not surprising that recovering middle-class addicts such as Ludlow, Cole, and Cobbe shared ideas—and their mode of written expression—with the medical writers. Very often such former drug users promoted or endorsed recovery schemes themselves. As the historian Carolyn Jean Acker has shown, however, working- and underclass drug users were not always as likely to agree with medical opinion. It is difficult to recover the voices of the truly marginalized drug takers, but Acker's work with hospital transcripts shows that it is not impossible. It also seems to suggest that these people were less able or less willing than the middle-class addict/writers to articulate their problems in broader social terms, opting instead to describe their struggles within the narrower horizons of their own immediate experiences.

In 1910 the theory that habitual drug use was a side effect of modernity received its greatest stamp of approval when it was submitted to Congress in support of the Foster Bill, an ill-fated first attempt at federal antinarcotic legislation. The bill, which was ultimately killed by the large pharmaceutical companies, was written in the State Department after American representatives to the 1909 Shanghai Opium Conference discovered, much to their embarrassment, that the United States lacked the kind of strong antinarcotic legislation that the delegates hoped to convince the rest of the world to adopt.[42] Dr. Hamilton Wright was a member of the American delegation to Shanghai, and his extensive report to Congress, which was relayed as a message from President William Howard Taft, provided a comprehensive overview of "the opium problem" in both its domestic and international aspects. Wright led the State Department's efforts to secure federal domestic antinarcotic legislation, and though later known as an ambitious careerist who longed for political advancement through his participation in antinarcotic legislation, his influence in its creation cannot be overestimated.[43] Wright's report to Congress is the crucial starting place for any study of government attitudes and policy regarding narcotic addiction in the early twentieth century.[44]

Wright argued both that drug use was on the rise in the United States and that the phenomenon was recent. He reminded the congressmen that "there is nothing to show that up to 1860 there was a serious misuse of opium or other habit-forming drugs in this country, bar the practice of opium smoking by the Chinese." But he lamented that "following our Civil War an abuse of crude or medicinal opium and its chief derivative, morphia, set in and spread over the entire country." Wright did not say that battlefield medicine or addicted veterans were the problem, only that the problem appeared across the population in the war era. Nonetheless, the popular belief would grow that the "the army disease" was to blame for the post-Civil War growth of drug use. Wright further argued that, since the war, the country had experienced a "persistently larger per cent increase in our importations of crude or medicinal opium than in our population."[45]

Dr. Wright thus emphasized the historical specificity of the drug threat, a strategy that showed the influence of Dr. Beard. Wright argued that there was "abundant evidence that one of the prime causes of the misuse of opium and morphia in the United States was the physical and mental overstrain or breakdown of a large number of our population during or immediately following the Civil War." He was certain about the threat's timing, though his attribution of cause remained ambiguous. On the one hand, he seemed to suggest that the war was a "prime cause" of increased drug use; on the other, he blamed general conditions "during and immediately following" the war. Wright believed that the initial group of Civil War-era drug users had "some real use for the drugs" but that they often extended their use "as an unnecessary and pernicious habit to younger members of families or associates."[46] Most important for my purposes is Wright's use of the war as a temporal marker. It offered a fixed historical referent, a point after which everything seemed to change. This was a strategy common to all sorts of late nineteenth- and early twentieth-century writing, but in Wright's case the war marked a break between a drug-free past and an addicted present. He used the war to show that habitual drug use was a contemporary issue, a thing of the moment—to assert the *modernity* of what he described as a looming drug menace. It is not surprising, then, that for Wright and many others, habitual drug use came to serve as a symptom of modernity. It marked the novelty of the historical present in which they lived.

THE AMERICAN ASSOCIATION FOR THE STUDY AND CURE OF INEBRIETY

Others saw addiction as more than a symptom. They viewed it as a disease. George Miller Beard's use of the term "inebriety" to describe habitual drug and alcohol use highlights his connection to a group of physicians who in 1870 organized themselves as the American Association for the Cure of Inebriates. This association, which by the 1890s had changed its name to the more scientific and disinterested-sounding American Association for the Study and Cure of Inebriety (AASCI), hoped to bring the power of modern medical science to bear against habitual drunkenness, long the domain of the moral reformers of the temperance movement.[47] As such, the group's first principle and aim was to define inveterate drunkenness as a disease, which they called "inebriety." More important for the group's own financial and professional interests, they sought to define inebriety as a disease that could be cured.[48]

The association's forum, the *Quarterly Journal of Inebriety (QJI)* was published between 1876 and 1906, continuing as the *Journal of Inebriety* until it ceased publication in 1914. Though the group's primary concern was with alcohol, there was scarcely an issue of the *QJI* across its thirty-five-year run that did not contain at least one article or review that addressed the narcotic habit. This combination of interests is reflected in the proliferation of terms that we find to describe various habits. Though the writers in the *QJI* most often referred to chronic drinking as "inebriety," drug habits could be called any number of names, including "morphinism," "morphinomania," "opium poisoning," "opium inebriety," and "morphine disease." In the 1880s, however, we begin to see the more frequent use of the word "addiction"—a term that would come to replace all the others over the next thirty years. In 1885 Dr. J. B. Mattison wrote that "opium addiction is a *disease*—a well-marked functional neurosis, and deserving recognition to a greater degree than it has hitherto received." He argued that "the term 'opium habit' is a misnomer—implying as it wrongly does, an opiate using under individual control."[49] Though doctors continued to use the other terms, narcotic "addiction" gradually replaced them, becoming the most popular term shortly after the turn of the century.

The group's concern with intoxicants other than alcohol was evident in the AASCI's first organizational meeting, thanks to the presence of Dr. Alonzo Calkins, author of *Opium and the Opium Appetite* (1871). Calkins's book, along with Beard's 1871 *Narcotics and Stimulants* and Horace Day's 1868 anthology *The Opium Habit*, helps to mark the opening of the modern discourse of addiction. Calkins's text wrested the discussion of the problem away from those who set its terms during the earlier period. He declared that "the history of opium eating did not have inception in the epistolary revelations of Coleridge and the Confessions of DeQuincey, though well it were could such history, with their memories, die out."[50] Calkins sought to replace those antiquated romantic memories with the modern realism of science, first by providing an "authentic" history of the use of opium and, second, by offering an exhaustive catalogue of clinical observations. Calkins's book is long-winded and tedious, but the serious and growing threat he saw in the habitual use of narcotics was clear when he asked if it was not yet time to "throw up some wall of circumvallation around our beleaguered city that shall more effectually shield us against those noxious invaders that are, year by year, floated to our shores from the lands of the prolific Orient?" Calkins declared that "in the warfare here inaugurated, we have for our antagonist a power subtle in his contrivings, stealthy in his approaches, dangerous as he is insidious, mischievous as he is plausible and seductive."[51] That declaration may be the opening salvo in the more-than-a-century-long "war on drugs."

Despite Calkins's presence at the first meeting, the first essay produced under the aegis of the AASCI which dealt specifically with the opium habit did not appear until the fifth (1874) meeting. Here, the president of the association, Dr. Joseph Parrish of Baltimore, wrote that "many persons who become enslaved by the drug" slipped into the "depths of demoralization" and indulged "with the same *abandon* of self, and the same disregard of public sentiment, that distinguishes the confirmed alcoholic sot."[52] Though the members were usually careful to distinguish between the effects of alcohol and those of the opiates, an easy slippage from one intoxicant to the other is clear in this passage.[53] Much of this obscurity would remain, but members of the AASCI would nonetheless struggle to define the drug habit more clearly over the run of the *QJI*. Many writers took part in this enterprise, but none were so prolific or influential as

Thomas Davison Crothers, who set out to explain how narcotic addiction, seen as a peculiarly modern disease, progressed by undermining the effective volition of the independent, autonomous human agent.

HABITUAL DRUG USE AS THE CORRUPTION OF HUMAN AGENCY

Dr. T. D. Crothers was the AASCI's leading figure. Born in 1842, Crothers earned a degree from Albany Medical College in 1865 and became the proprietor of a Hartford, Connecticut, inebriate asylum in 1878. He was the editor of the *QJI* over its entire run and served as secretary of the association after 1876.[54] Over the years he wrote hundreds of essays, reviews, and editorials that appeared in the *QJI*, many of which were reprinted in other medical journals. Though he also wrote about habitual drinking, he was among the most published turn-of-the-century writers on the hazards of narcotic use.

Like Beard, Crothers spilled a great deal of ink to promote his belief that "morphinism as a disease is due in a large measure to modern civilization associated with the rapid exhaustion following changes of life and living."[55] In 1902 he published *Morphinism and Narcomanias from Other Drugs*, a book that summarized his views on narcotic habits. Crothers opened the book by noting that "historically, opium mania is a very old disorder. Morphinomania is the modern form of the same disease, and the various drug narcomanias which are associated with it are the new psychopathic forms due largely to modern civilization." Further, he felt that "there can be no question that these diseases are increasing, as they are certainly becoming more prominent in every section of the country."[56] Crothers's distinctive contribution to the drug debate, however, was his work on the medicolegal aspects of morphine addiction. The crucial question in the many pieces that he wrote on this topic was whether drug users were responsible for their crimes. Crothers was thus concerned with the status of the drug user as an *agent*, with his ability to act as a *subject* despite the challenges of a modernizing world.[57] Though such writers as DeQuincey and Ludlow had addressed similar issues long before Crothers did, the latter's work differed by bringing the language of modern science to earlier metaphysical speculations. Crothers's writing offers a glimpse of the way that modernity, in the guise of narcotic medication, threatened to corrupt the autonomy of the independent subject.

Crothers did not believe that the inebriate, morphinist, or addict—by 1902 he used the latter two terms interchangeably—was responsible for his crimes. The doctor's interest apparently dated from 1883, when he discussed the case of a criminal drunkard in the pages of the *QJI*. He cited an appeals court judge who based a guilty verdict on his belief that "drunkenness in no condition is ever an excuse for crime or the consequences of a criminal act." Crothers objected, arguing that "half a century ago such interpretations of law would have excited no comment. To-day they are simply dogmatic statements contradicted by all teachings of science, experience, and the common justice of humanity." [58] Crothers established the enlightened modernity of his own scientific enterprise by relegating the judge's verdict "to the literature of the dark ages." [59]

In another piece published in the same issue of the journal, Crothers tried to illuminate the benighted judge's medieval thought, explaining that the important question to ask in such cases was "whether the inebriate was able at the time of committing the crime to exercise control over his actions." Crothers rephrased the question, asking whether the alcohol-intoxicated brain's "consequent disturbed activity; interrupting the normal flow of ideas; stimulating the imagination with its phantasies, images, and delusions, is sufficient ordinarily to break up consciousness of the present, and his knowledge of the normal relations of himself to the external world." [60] Answering in the affirmative, he concluded that the drunkard's consciousness was indeed impaired and thus that "the inebriate is not responsible for his acts, but is a mental waif, without helm or sail." [61] Drifting freely with the current, the inebriate was in no way responsible for the course of his actions; his capacity to act as a subject—as a captain navigating a sea of objects—was hopelessly compromised by the action of the drug.

This failure of effective volition had to do with what Crothers believed was a fundamental disordering of the senses, which was, he felt, a key symptom of the disease of inebriety, wherein "there is always a more or less complete disorder of the senses, in which false impressions prevail." The consequence of this disordering was that the inebriate's "thoughts and acts are unknown to himself." He was thus in a state "beyond his control." [62] Over the next nineteen years, Crothers would refine this initial interest by applying his findings to narcotic users. [63] By the time he published *Morphinism and Narcomanias* in 1902, Crothers had developed an entire neurophysiology to account for morphine's corruption of its user's power of reason, thus isolating the source of the alleged irresponsibility. He had come to believe that "continuous narcotism and blunting of the sensory centers impairs the power of reasoning by obscuring and narrowing the impression of the senses." Consequently, "the morphinist, as well as the opium-taker, always has diminished and disturbed powers of seeing, hearing, taste, and smell."[64]

This was a daunting problem. The production of reliable sense data is important in the most tenacious and influential Western formulations of reason. The meaningful assertion of subjectivity rests on the subject's ability to determine his interests in an object world and then to act reasonably upon them. The consequence of the drug user's sensual disordering, then, was that "the objective world is not correctly seen." As a result, habitual drug users "cannot have a clear recognition of the nature and consequences of acts and conduct."[65] Put another way, the addict was unable to assess relations of responsibility or obligation because "the relation of both subjective and objective conditions and events is confused and misunderstood." Addicts "act automatically, repeating what has been done before, but when confronted with new sets of facts and conditions, are not quite able to realize the relations of right and wrong." Crothers's conclusion was adamant: "It may be stated as a fact which clinical experience will amply sustain, that morphin used either in large or small doses, depending on the case and the conditions, always alters the reasoning powers and changes the sensory activities, and is always followed by intellectual weakness, with diminished moral sense and consciousness of right and wrong."[66]

Dr. J. L. Bowman agreed with Crothers, writing in 1908 that when a person took morphine "the individual is changed . . . not only as others know and recognize the change, but the 'I,' the subjective self, is changed." As a consequence, "the objective becomes prominent" at the same moment that "the question of taking drugs ceases to be one of will, but [becomes] one of necessity."[67] Dr. Henry Freeman Walker wrote in 1896 that "the greatest evil of the morphine habit is the perversion of the moral sense. It obliterates in the victim's mind the distinction between truth and falsehood, right and wrong." Hence habitual morphine users could not be trusted at their word, and an addict's "testimony on oath is worthy of discredit in legal matters."[68] Asa P. Meylert had written in 1885 that the opiates wrought "shipwreck" upon "the moral nature of those habituated."[69] The result was that the drug user "lives in an imaginary world of his own creation. He is its central figure." Most interestingly, Meylert argued that a splintered perception of the passage of time was a consequence of drug taking: "Every nerve of the body seems to take on conscious thought. . . . There is no past but that separated from the present by the great gulf,—fixed, impassable. There is no future save the bottomless pit of eternal despair—everlasting." For Meylert, consciousness literally became disintegrated as each nerve gained a mind of its own, causing the drug user to lose track of the progressive flow of time. Addicts found themselves suspended in an eternal, unchanging present: "a thousand years of agony in a single night!" [70] This was indeed a modernity to be feared.

Crothers believed that morphine disordered the senses and therefore corrupted the user's power of reason, leading to his 1916 description of the habit as a "paralysis of the ... centers of volition." [71] Likewise, Alexander Lambert, future president of the American Medical Association and a personal physician to Theodore Roosevelt, wrote in 1914 that morphine use, "a development of recent years," had been spread and exacerbated by the use of the syringe. Its consequence was that "the will power is enfeebled." Though the patient remained ostensibly clear minded, Lambert claimed that for drug users "the sense of responsibility is wiped out and is replaced by the indifference of perfect egotism." [72] Such explanations may well have resonated with broader cultural concerns over the fate of the independent subject in a rapidly changing, modern society. Crothers's writing therefore shows one way that persistent concerns with independence, autonomy, and subjectivity might find expression in seemingly distant debates, in this case over the effects of narcotics. Crothers's texts make it easier to conceptualize the otherwise vague sense of peril that was essential to any formulation of a turn-of-the-century cultural crisis. Most important, his writing helped to produce that sense of crisis by inscribing it on the bodies of real people through its expression as a medicolegal concept. Crothers offered his readers a detailed description of drug addiction as a threat borne by modernity at the same time that he produced a thoroughly modern character— the drug user/addict—to carry the threat.

THE PHYSIOLOGICAL ECONOMY OF DR. LESLIE E. KEELEY'S GOLD CURE

Though their special interest was not widely shared by the mainstream medical community, the physicians of the AASCI were proud of their status as medical "regulars," subscribing to the protocols of scientific medicine and eschewing the practices of some of the fin de siècle's less orthodox practitioners. Medical licensing and regulation were not as strict or as formalized in the late nineteenth century as they would become in the twentieth, and after 1870, a multiplicity of addiction cures and cure doctors proliferated throughout the country. [73] While the regulars wrote for one another within the bounds of their arcane medical journals, popular cure doctors were busy making fortunes by prescribing specific cures, often by mail order, for drug and alcohol habits. They also helped to publicize the drug problem to a broader population who had neither access to nor interest in professional journals. The fact that both regulars and popular doctors subscribed to the same underlying modernist etiology of addiction suggests its resonance within the broader cultural context.

Though many practitioners filled the back pages of late nineteenth-century periodicals and newspapers with their advertising, one towered over the others. Leslie E. Keeley, promoter of the "bi-chloride of gold cure," was the period's best-known cure doctor. Born in 1832, Keeley received his medical degree at Chicago's Rush Medical College in 1864. Immediately after, he entered the Union Army's medical service, where he became interested in curing habitual drunkenness.[74] He began experimenting with potential cures after the war, and in 1879 he and a partner opened the first Keeley Institute in rural Dwight, Illinois. The institute, which Keeley soon expanded to a nationwide and even international franchise, was a great financial success. Between 1892 and 1900, the Keeley Company made more than $2.7 million, according to William L. White, who notes further that over five hundred thousand alcoholics and addicts took the Keeley cure between 1880 and 1920.[75] Likewise, H. Wayne Morgan has argued that "Keeley's name became almost a household word" during this period and that "the billboards and wall sized signs proclaiming the presence of a Keeley Institute were almost obligatory for a city to be up-to-date from the 1890's to the first world war."[76]

It was probably, therefore, equal parts jealousy and scientific principle that earned Keeley the status of bête noire with T. D. Crothers and the AASCI. Beard, who died before Keeley achieved his greatest popularity, believed that "specifics for constitutional disorders are only looked for by those in whom survive the superstitions of our ancestors."[77] By this measure, Keeley's therapy—which offered a specific remedy for drug and alcohol addiction—was superstition rather than science. Worse, it was a relic from an archaic past, a hindrance and a barrier to the progress of modernity. Keeley also kept his formula a secret, which was a violation of the American Medical Association's code of ethics. In a scathing 1895 *QJI* editorial, Crothers wrote that the gold cure was "an inebriate's theory for the cure of inebriates; a scheme of degenerates for the restoration of degenerates; an insane man's treatment for the cure of the insane."[78] Because of his very visible financial success and advertisements featuring effusive testimonials by his "graduates," Keeley was a target of the regulars' scorn, even after his death in 1901. To them, he was the consummate quack.

Though much of the medical profession held Keeley's cure (and his success) in contempt, his description of the condition to be cured did not vary much from mainstream accounts. In 1897 Keeley wrote *Opium: Its Use, Abuse and Cure; or, From Bondage to Freedom.* His description of narcotic addiction as a growing and peculiarly modern malady that disordered the senses and precluded the proper positioning of subjects and objects is exactly in line with the more "respectable" theories put forth by such "regulars" as Beard and Crothers. Keeley was a colorful writer who followed the popular sentimental conventions of his day. Like the others, he emphasized the modernity of the drug problem, but his vividly embellished prose differed from their more conventional accounts. Keeley called opium "the Mephistopheles of the Age."[79] In a particularly rich phrase, he referred to narcotic addiction as "the secret leprosy of modern days," an affliction "which permeates the body, mind and spirit of its victim."[80] Like Crothers, Keeley believed that his addicted patients suffered from an "absolute deception," that "in body, soul and spirit there remains not one sensation, not one power by which an actual, true perception of the real world can be obtained."[81] Again like Crothers, he felt that users were unable to separate reality from its representation and were thus unable to judge the accuracy of that representation. Addicts became dependent on a substance that situated them in a dream world of ungrounded representations, an epistemological house of mirrors where they could not accurately assess the causes and effects of their own actions.

Keeley claimed further that the primary object of the addict's confused perception lay precisely in the assertion of self-mastery and independence. He explained that the addict "thinks himself to be still his own master. . . , not knowing that the feeling of liberty with which he quiets himself is but the 'stuff that dreams are made of.' "[82] Keeley's linkage of self-mastery with "the feeling of liberty" was in perfect accord with the assertions of autonomous selfhood already discussed in this book. He argued, however, that the addict could never claim the prerequisite self-mastery required to enable the autonomy that underlay such a concept of subjectivity. This was the case for Keeley because the drug user's feeling of liberty was not grounded in the clear and distinct ideas of reality enjoyed by the unafflicted but rather forged from "the stuff dreams are made of," and this "stuff" was narcotic. He believed that the feeling of liberty that it provided was an unreliable basis of self-knowledge. Keeley called addiction an "autocracy," a figure that he enhanced in phrases that declared it to be "a servitude the most enslaving upon earth; a bondage to a soulless merciless tyrant; a captivity whose daylight is despair, and whose hope is death."[83] He depicted narcotic addiction as a case of the formerly independent subject's surrender of his or her presumed autonomy to an implacable master—a jealous tyrant whose seat of power lay somewhere outside the violated borders of the addicted body.

Yet Keeley's greatest and most suggestive contribution to the discourse of addiction lay in his triumphant claim that the drug user could "be delivered from his bondage into perfect liberty" thanks to the "double chloride of gold."[84] Keeley's addiction cure (and its advertisement) relied on the therapeutic and rhetorical mobilization of gold—a substance that, when compared with the paper dollar, served as perhaps the turn of the century's preeminent, though controversial, figure for grounded authenticity and representational accuracy. Though the medical regulars branded Keeley a "quack" and respected nothing but his ability as a salesman, one must go beyond medical science before rendering a verdict on Keeley's gold cure by first understanding the cultural logic of the gold standard.[85]

Keeley's description of addiction as a disorder of perception merged smoothly with the discourse of the gold standard because entrapment in a modern world of illusion was a hazard equally feared by proponents of hard currency, who enlisted gold as a figure for authenticity. For these so-called goldbugs, the metal stood for solid, grounded value that was derived and mined from the earth itself. Goldbugs juxtaposed their precious metal to a mass-produced, highly decorative piece of representational paper, the greenback dollar bill. David Wells, in his 1876 goldbug manifesto titled *Robinson Crusoe's Money; or the Remarkable Financial Fortunes and Misfortunes of a Remote Island Community*, argued that advocates of paper dollars were subject to a "mere fiction of speech and bad use of language," because paper could only *represent* money. He felt that granting greenback dollars the status of money was equivalent to declaring that "a shadow could be the substance, or the picture of a horse a horse, or the smell of a good dinner the same as the dinner itself."[86] For Wells, real money was gold coin, and he argued that paper currency lacked "the really most important quality of good money; inasmuch as it ceased to be . . . *in itself an object of value.*"[87] For Wells, paper money was at best a representation, a shadow or a picture of the value that *was* gold; it could never hold value *in itself* but was instead dependent on an arbitrary assignment of value from a source outside of itself.

Gold possessed value, according to Wells, because it had "always been, of all material things, the one which most men have desired most."[88] Its value lay in what Wells described as its inherent desirability, but more important, its sta-

This handbill contested the claims made by those who imitated Dr. Leslie E. Keeley's treatment for drug and alcohol addiction. The handbill not only testifies to the popularity of the Keeley gold cure (which inspired imitation) but also suggests that the Keeley Company and its advertisers recognized the power of gold to signify authenticity, as it did in the currency debates. William H. Helfand Collection, New York, and the National Library of Medicine.

tus as "substance" rather than "shadow" meant that it could also *satisfy* the craving that it inspired. It was anchored in its simultaneous representation and satisfaction of human desire. Paper money, in contrast, could signify desire but never satisfy it. It was *"a representative of a debt to be paid* [rather than] *a means of paying a debt."*[89]Greenbacks represented the want of real money, or the lack of gold. To adopt paper currency was therefore to build an economy on the irresponsible dissemination of desire, which could lead to the goldbug's greatest fear: runaway inflation and a massive supply of paper that outstripped the world's ability to back it up in gold. Thus, to champion paper money was to be trapped in a representational house of mirrors—all surface with no substance. It threatened a condition of incessant exchange, the permanent circulation of values made worthless by a radical rupture of the *sign* of value from its referent. Wells and his fellow goldbugs argued that only gold provided the solid ground of substance that might halt a tumble into the bottomless pursuit of insatiable desire.

Like Wells, Keeley thought that gold could appease and satisfy the invading force of desire that besieged his patients. His specific cure for the narcotic habit was the introduction of gold *into* the addict's body through a red, white, and blue syringe called the "barber pole." Keeley believed that his cure worked in a manner similar to opium but to exactly the opposite effect. By infiltrating the nerves of the patient's brain, gold "first brings the consciousness out of its stupor, and liberates the will." He claimed that, as a result, "one of the early effects of my preparation of gold is to give the opium user will power." Keeley's gold cure reversed the narcotic's spell, liberating the addict's "will power" by releasing "the consciousness" from its "stupor," born, as we have seen, of a drug-generated disordering of the senses. Keeley claimed that the gold cure defeated the "autocracy" of addiction, and by providing addicts "a strength of purpose that almost prepared them for complete renouncement of all desire," it gave the patient back the liberty to *be* himself.[90]

Restoration was a key concept for Keeley, who argued that gold had the power to return the addict to a golden age when the temptations of modern technology were still held in check. "The patient is placed back . . . to the days in which he had not tasted or longed for the intoxicant, and his life and his fortunes are once more subject to the control of his own will and judgment." The powerfully nostalgic statement imagined the present as a (no-longer-irreversible) break with the past. Keeley believed that gold had the power to "cleanse, renew and re-create" the user's poisoned system. Gold's restoration of the subject to himself reinvigorated his power of judgment and freed the patient from his house of mirrors. In an aside, Keeley claimed that "in nearly every case where there has been disturbance of the vision, the sight becomes perfectly adjusted and glasses are thrown aside."[91] The addict's restored ability to adequately perceive the world allowed him to put his "life and fortunes" back into the world of objects—a world once again under the control of a centered, rational subject. Gold stood for the restoration of human agency—the sign of autonomous subjectivity's conquest of the technological. The gold cure's great promise was to produce a subject as good as gold and, in so doing, to offer a cure

OFF FOR HOME.

This image of a group of "cured" Keeley patients shows the "graduates" comfortably and triumphantly returning to their homes via the railroad, perhaps the preeminent symbol of "modern" America. Chicago Historical Society.

not only for the drug habit but also for the cultural crisis of modernity itself. Is it any wonder that Keeley died a rich man?

All these texts, despite their differences in approach, tone, and audience, form a discourse of addiction that shared much besides its subject matter. They all sought to explain the historical appearance of the drug addict by turning to broader discussions of the way in which rapid changes in economics, transportation, and communications technology—even far removed debates about the gold standard—affected the agency of the human subject in a "modernizing" world. The writers cobbled together their notions of addiction from the cultural categories available to them in the years surrounding the turn of the twentieth century. Chief among those was the perception of a threat to the assertion of autonomous subjectivity that was borne by and emblematic of modernity. The texts explained the otherwise obscure idea of narcotic addiction by turning to more familiar, everyday experiences that their readers might have recognized. Still, this strategy tended toward a rather abstract concept. It offered a sense of addiction, but without the addicts. In the next chapter, therefore, I examine how addiction was often made comprehensible by associating it with people who were never accorded the status of autonomous subjectivity in the first place. We will thus see how a reliance on the race and gender clichés of the period helped to explain the notion of addiction.

CHAPTER 3

Subjects of Desire

Race, Gender, and the
Personification of Addiction

IN THE LAST CHAPTER, I argued that the addiction concept both reflected and helped to produce the broader sense of modernity as cultural crisis that resonated across much of America in the late nineteenth and early
twentieth centuries. In this chapter I turn toward what was perhaps the chief
means by which many addiction experts gave more tangible form to that concept. By identifying and naming certain people as "addicts," writers were able to
give human shape to the otherwise vague sense of dependence signified by the
modern term "addiction." Though there were nearly as many ways to personify
addiction as there were writers, certain themes appeared frequently enough to
have drawn scholarly attention. Most notable among these was how the discourse of addiction adopted and then modified stereotypical images of people
who allegedly lacked the self-mastery that underwrote independent, autonomous subjectivity in the first place. In other words, the discourse of addiction mobilized images of the centered subject's traditionally racialized and
gendered others in order to give physical form to the modern menace of narcotic addiction.

In this chapter I present a broad sample of the words invoked by various
writers who put themselves forward as experts on the topic of narcotic addiction. Rather than assess these words merely in terms of their mimetic accuracy,
my analysis draws out their affiliations within the culture more broadly, thereby
offering insight not only to the discourse of addiction but also to turn-of-the-

century notions of race and gender. My goal is not simply to catalogue the quite obviously racist and sexist language of the period, and still less do I claim to account for everything enunciated in this sprawling discourse. Instead, I have chosen representative samples from some of the period's prominent texts, several of which have already appeared in the preceding chapters, entering their logic of personification in an effort to understand the period's growing antinarcotic sentiment. In short, this chapter presents samples of the racialized and gendered language that typified much of the discourse of addiction in order to examine the way in which it inscribed the cultural crisis of modernity upon the bodies of those it identified and named as addicts. More specifically, I consider how the discourse of addiction both reflected and helped to produce the rhetorics of Orientalism, Jim Crow, and Sentimental Domesticity, thus connecting the threat of addiction with stereotypical images of, respectively, Asians, African Americans, and women of any race.

THE ORIENTAL ADDICT

As we saw in the first chapter, the equation of narcotic use with an oriental threat to the rational Western subject was an integral part of the discourse of addiction. Long after the 1821 publication of DeQuincey's *Confessions*, however, American medical theorists continued to use exotic, seductive, and degraded images of the oriental—attached to both the Middle and the Far East—as a means of demonstrating the perils of drug addiction.

Leslie Keeley's Orient

In 1897, cure doctor Leslie E. Keeley created an exotic, oriental landscape peopled with outlandish drug addicts. He wrote that " 'God's best gift to man,' is the Arab's favorite name for Opium. . . . The poor, worn nomad of the desert, battling against the elements as he toils across the dry and trackless waste, comes to his encampment as the evening shadows gather, suffering from an exhaustion overpowering. And as the stars gleam out from that Eastern sky like bolts of glowing steel fresh-forged from the furnace of Jove, and the sighing winds breathe out their requiem for the dying day, he finds in the all-potent 'drug,' 'surcease of sorrow.' " [1] This was an imaginary world whose lavish, romantic description served primarily to mark its distance from the world of Keeley's late nineteenth-century American readership. His references to the "eastern sky" and to a "dry and trackless waste" emphasized both the difference and the distance between the worlds while confining the metaphorized Arab within that desolate and forbidding landscape. Keeley's Orient was barren, god-forsaken, and uncivilized. In Keeley's writing, the Orient served as the antithesis of modern America, thus helping to assert the latter's novelty and to secure the identity of those who lived there.

Keeley described the exotic distinctiveness of this remote world still more explicitly when he argued that the Arab's "opium dreaming has no affinity for the life which palpitates in this new world of ours."[2] His association of "palpitating life" with the "new world" equated the forces of dynamism and growth with the new or novel. It produced a static, archaic "old world" but also assigned it to a global and ethnic location. On the one hand, this echoed common associations of progress, dynamism, and technology with modern American civilization. Andrew Carnegie, for instance, famously asserted in 1886 that "the old nations of the earth creep on at a snail's pace; the Republic thunders past with the rush of the express."[3] Keeley made a similar move but replaced one gastropod with another in his 1897 declaration that "the sluggish nations of the Orient may be content to let today be as yesterday, and tomorrow as today," but he gave the analogy a more explicitly exclusionary twist, adding that "the Present, our Present, so full of life and movement and throbbing energies, has no part in [the Arab's fireside tale]."[4] While the similarity between the two figures is apparent, it is important that we remember Keeley's ultimate strategy, which was the emphatic mobilization of the figure of the drug addict, tied fast to an image of the Oriental, as an example of what modern America was not. Addicts and Orientals—or oriental addicts—were the others against whom Keeley measured modern America's progress. They offered him a way to establish American progress in terms that were simultaneously spatial and temporal. Keeley's text thus reflected the broader discourse in which it was embedded, but it also modified that discourse, helping to produce and to reproduce it in new and varied forms as it fashioned new and varied others with which to give the discourse coherence.

Keeley's most striking argument comes at the conclusion to this section of his text, where he put the threat of narcotic addiction into explicitly ethno-racial terms. He wrote that the Arabs "live in the desert, and its monotony has passed into and become a part of their very souls." This association of an imaginary geography with a set of people described by racial or ethnic difference is typical of Orientalist writing, but for readers who had still failed to get the point, Keeley made the comparison clear: "And he who, in this mighty continent of the West, delivers himself over to a life of Opium torpor, falls from his high estate and passes into a world which, by contrast, is even more dreary and monotonous than that of the Arab tribes. . . . He passes from the living progressive world into a desert whose extent is limitless, and whose dry and dreary pathways have no end." [5] Here we see the threat of addiction put directly into terms more tangible for Keeley's turn-of-the-century readers. Addiction threatened modern Americans with a passage from West to East, a crossing that was a descent from high to low. This path downward was marked by the loss of one's "high estate" in what Keeley characterized as a bad trade—an exchange of the "living progressive" West for the "dry and dreary" East. Keeley suggested that narcotic addiction was an affliction that rendered its victims unable to participate in the "living progressive world" that modernity's boosters hoped the coming century promised. The narcotic addict, inextricably linked to racial difference, played the role of the other in this discourse.

Keeley, however, amplified the threat of addiction by locating it much closer to home. He accomplished this in his vivid depiction of the Chinese-associated opium den, writing that the "SMOKER . . . must devote time and money to compel the inspiration of his god, and he can only do so in a temple, known as a 'den' or 'joint,' prepared for his Satanic worship." Occasionally, wrote Keeley, within such an evil temple a white addict would arise, and "shaking himself back to consciousness, to the astonishment of the 'almond-eyed' coryphee, he steps down from his bunk, and, with a quick movement, passes out into the street, where the rising sun greets him with its beams of gladness and renewed life." [6] Keeley compared the darkness and decay of a fantastic East to a glowingly dynamic, ascendant West. Most important, this tiny splinter of the Orient lay only just out of sight, barely concealed in the cellars and the back alleyways of urban America. Keeley's recovered addict, however, left the astonished, "almond-eyed" Orientals behind in the dark, in a place where they were "lost to the world, consumers and not producers." [7]

A close reading of Keeley's writing thus offers the opportunity to recover much of the common linkage of the Orient and the addict, but it also highlights how those concepts helped to define the West in terms of its modernity. Keeley wrote that the addict often felt that he was "incompetent for any duty," which was especially problematic because "in the young and ardent West, where every man is in competition with his fellow-man, he needs a clear head, a steady nerve, a quick and active muscle, together with a freshness of mind that must be constantly available if he would achieve success." [8] This was, for Keeley, a key problem of drug use: the addict was unable to join the "honest workers, sons of toil," who, while drug addicts drowsed, were, "already, up and doing."⁹ The addict was therefore notable for his negative contribution to the progress that marked modernity. But because Keeley, like many others, chose human metaphors to illustrate this point, the metaphorized Oriental came to be positioned somewhere outside the main text of modern American progress. Its role in this story was to help make up the margin—a borderland at the periphery of the text, which also served the vital function of giving that text its shape. Keeley placed the Oriental and the addict outside the charmed circle of responsible modern identity in a gesture that helped to give coherence to that concept. He wrote that the addict's voice "could no longer bear its part in fireside song, even if the opium user cares to join in fireside singing, which he does not."¹⁰

Yet one of the paradoxes that typify the discourse of addiction lurches more plainly into view. While Keeley insisted that the present had no place in the "Arab's fireside tale," it is nonetheless clear that the Arab's tale, or perhaps tales of the Arab, had a place in the present. In other words, both the addict and the Oriental might play an important, even definitive role as the product and as the antithesis of modernity. In the last chapter, we saw that turn-of-the-century writers often invoked the emergence of habitual drug use and the presence of drug users as signs of the novelty of the present—as a sign of the present as *modern*. As Robert G. Lee has shown, the presence of "Orientals," in this case the Chinese in California, had, since the 1850s, offered a visible reminder of the capitalist enterprise that underlay the American occupation of California. As I have just discussed, Orientalist writing often works by marking and exaggerating an imaginary difference and distance between the West and the metaphorized Orient. When thousands of Chinese began to settle in California, however, that distance immediately collapsed, enabling the construction of racial difference as present and threatening. Especially for many working-class Californians, the face of modern economic change was oriental. The presence of large numbers of Asian immigrants who had come to California looking for work offered tangible evidence to native-born and Irish workers that their world was changing in fundamental ways which seemed quite beyond their control. Lee uses this insight to explain working-class animosity toward the Chinese as a misplaced reaction against the historically specific economic changes that they came to represent, something which only grew and helps one understand support for the Chinese Exclusion Act of 1882.¹¹ For my purposes, however, Lee's work shows how the mere presence of the Chinese in America might be taken as a marker of change, as a sign of the present—as a sign of modernity. The discourse of addiction mobilized this sign but linked it to its own special concerns, that is, to drug addiction and the drug addict. Chinese immigration may have been banned in 1882, but the rhetorical power of Chinese bodies as signifiers of contemporary social problems remained very powerful in the discourse of addiction.

Charles B. Towns, "the White Hope of Drug Victims"

The growth of Chinese immigration coincided with a period of greater, indeed global, economic expansion. Some elements of the discourse of addiction reflected and enhanced this growing, imperialistic longing for the economic rewards that entrepreneurs hoped to reap in the Asian market. Anti-addiction rhetoric sometimes served, among other things, to cloak economic considerations in humanitarian garb while aiding calls for the domestic persecution of Chinese immigrants and their descendants. This combination of impulses was particularly clear in the efforts of one "American citizen's direct and practical proposal to help fight the great monster right in its lair." [12] These were the words chosen in 1913 by Peter Clark Macfarlane, a journalist writing for *Collier's*, to describe entrepreneur Charles B. Towns's attempt to bring his addiction cure to the Chinese mainland.

A colorful and influential character, Towns was the "undisputed king, or, perhaps emperor," of the cure doctors, according to historian David F. Musto, and in terms of government influence, this may well be an apt title. [13] Based on approval and support from Cornell University's Dr. Alexander Lambert, Towns's influence registered at the highest levels of government and professional medicine, and as we will see in the next two chapters, it helped to shape the national regulation of narcotics. What is most interesting for now, though, is that his rise to domestic prominence came in China.

Towns's journey began on a Georgia farm, where his actions led Macfarlane to describe him as a "giant of will" in his 1913 *Collier's* biography. Such a characterization offered a strong counterpoint to the image of the drug addict, whose condition was often described as a failure or even as the loss of the power of will. Macfarlane was emphatic about the strength of Towns's resolve, making it overshadow all other aspects of his personality. He explained that Towns was someone who supposedly "breaks the horses and the mules and the steers that no other will can conquer . . . [he has] the coolest, strongest will and a courage that will take a dare from nobody." [14] Towns thus challenged the most stubbornly defiant of creatures in acts whose strength, courage, and conviction resulted in the domestication, domination, and control of the powerful natural forces they embodied. This power was something that Macfarlane quickly translated from the animal to the human, casting Towns opposite the weakened, enervated addict. Most important, and most unlike the narcotic addict, Towns was able to translate his willpower successfully to a modern argot.

Towns, like many other turn-of-the-century Americans, moved from the country to the city, but unlike so many of his contemporaries he was not forced to do so by financial necessity or declining agricultural prospects. Rather, he sought new challenges to meet and master. As Macfarlane put it, the farm became "too easy for Charlie," and he therefore sought new opponents against whom he might measure his boundless willpower. Tellingly, his next challenge was perhaps the preeminent symbol of modernity—the railroad—which "yielded somewhat to his aggressive disposition, but when transportation problems began to be halterbroken, his interest flagged and turned to life insurance." [15] Towns had the power to "break" the railroad if he wished, just as he had done with the stubborn horses and steers.

According to *Macfarlane,* he soon became the most successful life insurance salesman in his district, and thus the ever restless Towns sought a fresh challenge. While casting about New York City for a new project, he was supposedly approached by a man who claimed that he possessed a cure for the drug habit. Towns asked his personal physician about the feasibility of such a product, but when the doctor told him that the notion was absurd, Towns's interest was piqued. Taking up this new interest, Towns allegedly perfected his cure by experimenting on addicts who had answered the ads that he placed in New York newspapers. Soon Towns sought a larger market for his cure, and in 1908, with the support of Dr. Lambert, he took it to China,[16] where, as noted in *Collier's,* he faced the "yellow tide" single-handedly: "And this man on the soap box, with only a revolver in his lap and another on his hip, is just as much alone as he appears. . . . There is absolutely nothing between him and death for his American impudence, save his Georgia-born nerve. Yet there he sits, one lone white man, in the midst of four hundred million Chinamen, waiting for the soldiers of the Empress Dowager to come and try to take down his signs." [17] Towns appears in this passage as the consummate, self-possessed individual. The writer elevated him above the crowd and isolated him on a soapbox, emphasizing his individuality in implicitly political terms. The soapbox here served as a sign of the individual's right to hold unpopular beliefs and to make them heard—independently of the forces that might supply a lectern, pulpit, or platform and the institutional legitimation which these imply. Instead, Towns's resolution,

his adamant assertion of individual will, was backed by the power of the re-
volvers in hand and on his hip. He therefore appeared as a lonely and resolute
frontiersman, drawing on his experience with recalcitrant horses, mules, and
railroads in order to face down a pack of undifferentiated, threatening racial
others. The *Collier's* biography thus stressedTowns's individuality and his autonomy—his status as an independent subject—by measuring it against the
nondescript mass represented by the subjects *of* the Empress Dowager, whose
soldiers threatened to overwhelm Towns and dismantle the signs that, in this
case, helped to differentiate him from that mass.

It is important to note, however, that even though Macfarlane praised him as
an exemplary American, he also made it clear that Towns was not exceptional.
He was, rather, an "everyday American" who represented the strength of the
will over and against the surging tide of modernity and its threat to reduce the
white, American bourgeoisie to the level of their swarming racial inferiors.
Towns was everyman, but he was particularly flexible, strong, and dynamic.
Coming from Georgia and New York, he represented both North and South
and was a product of both rural and urban America. He had been a worker and
a manager, a laborer and a professional: "Formerly of Georgia, late of Manhattan, now of the Flowery Kingdom, once a farmer and horse wrangler, then a
railroad man, insurance agent and broker," Towns was, according to *Macfarlane*, "the White Hope of drug victims." [18]

Most decidedly, Towns *was not* Chinese. As Macfarlane waited outside the
office of the American consul to China, he claimed to see "Mr. Towns, himself
much angrier than his tones, issue from that same reception room and go
bouncing down the stairs with a stride as undiplomatic as it was un-Oriental." [19]
Painting Towns's profile upon the flat field of an oriental other, this passage
also suggested that Towns, who lacked "diplomacy," was able to maintain his
autonomy and independence against an expanding, bureaucratically administered corporate society. Macfarlane pictured Towns as a strong, self-willed, and
independent individual struggling against a faceless bureaucracy and an undifferentiated mass of racial others in an attempt to protect modern America from
the ravages of drug addiction.

*Racial Essence and the Double Meaning of Addiction in
William Rosser Cobbe's* Doctor Judas

Closer to home, in 1895, Chicago journalist William Rosser Cobbe, himself a
recovered addict, published *Doctor Judas: A Portrayal of the Opium Habit*, in

which he differentiated between various types of addicts according to the type of drug they preferred. He wrote that "[narcotic] users who take the drug into the circulation by the stomach or by injection, never form the habit by deliberate purpose; they are tied hand and foot by the physician or they are led into it by racking physical pain, at a time when they are not morally responsible for their conduct. The smoker of opium becomes such through wantonness of desire."[20] Here Cobbe distinguished between the volitional and the juridical notions of addiction that I explained in the introduction. Describing medical narcotic users as "tied hand and foot by the physician" invoked what I identified as the juridical definition of addiction. Cobbe argued that these *patients* were the responsibility of the physician because they "never form the habit by deliberate purpose." They were thus *assigned* their status of addict and were free of any personal guilt or blame. By this logic, they ought not to be punished for their condition.

He paired this version of addiction with that of the opium *smoker*, claiming that this kind of addict became "such through wantonness of desire." It is hard to imagine a clearer statement of the volitional definition of addiction. Cobbe described an addict who had willfully chosen his or her condition and was thus guilty of wrongdoing. He strengthened his differentiation, writing that "this distinction alone, the fact of independent action on the one hand, and irresponsible subjection on the other, must forever divide the smokers from the eaters of the drug. One habit is superinduced by physical infirmity; the other instigated by moral depravity."[21] By 1920, this distinction became the basis for the medicolegal resolution of the double meaning of addiction. On the one hand, the "patients," described by Cobbe as the innocent victims of "professional recklessness or physical suffering," were assigned a status that placed them under the authority of the medical profession. On the other hand lay the criminal opium users, whom he associated with opium smoking. These latter had a habit that Cobbe claimed was "entered into consciously, with the open purpose of finding forbidden delights."[22] They were addicted through their own volition and thus suffered from an "irresponsible subjection" that was a consequence of their own "moral depravity." Cobbe made the sources of both addiction and its control clear for these volitional addicts when he wrote that "the opium smoking habit comes of association with unholy persons and is entered into with deliberation. The surroundings are always repulsive and the inmates of these resorts are criminals or petty offenders against police regulations. They are ignorant, illiterate, vulgar, brutal, and wicked."[23] This type of addict had learned addiction from sources outside the medical and had freely chosen to enter into the company of criminals. The responsibility for control of such addicts was thus to be found in the penal system.

Cobbe went still further in his description of these addicts, insisting that "smoking is an Asiatic vice and one which can never gain favor among reputable people in this country."[24] His use of the phrase "Asiatic vice" operated, first and most obviously, to situate the problem in a particular place, far distant from American shores. At its most simple, the words merely declared that Asian people smoked opium. Yet Cobbe's phrase went beyond simple association, suggesting that something about opium smoking was fundamentally alien—that both the practice and its practitioners were essentially "other." Like Keeley and Towns, Cobbe thus described narcotic addiction in Orientalist terms.

Cobbe maintained that "opium smoking is rooted and grounded in the Chinese character."[25] He argued that opium smoking was embedded in the Asian character in a way that it could not be in the American and that it was integral to and symbolic of an essential Asian identity that was quite clearly oriental. To make his point, Cobbe painted a vivid picture of the opium den for his readers. He continued to use racial imagery but immediately extended the drug's threat to non-Asians when he explained that "the master of the prison-like place is a jaundiced Chinaman or an American mummy; in either case dried out, fleshless, wan, and worn."[26] Like Keeley, Cobbe described the opium den as a gloomy, morbid place. It was a place of imprisonment presided over by "fleshless" Chinese but, perhaps more significant, also by "American mummies." He thus expanded the racial constituency of the opium den, suggesting that this "Asiatic vice," which was, crucially, "rooted and grounded in the Chinese character," could indeed find a home in the contemporary United States; here, however, it threatened to mummify modern, native-born Americans. Cobbe's imagery therefore united both East Asia and the Middle East, both China and Egypt, in a threatening, Orientalist evocation of both exoticism and antiquity.

In further characterizing the race as well as the gender of the smokers in the opium den, Cobbe found within its walls, "besides Chinamen, young men, both whites and Negroes, from the lowest stratum of social life, and the most abandoned female outcasts of the streets. Now and then a male subject, never a female, is supplied from the higher walks of life; but, from the nature of the case, as will presently be seen, he is one whose pride and self-respect were cast aside before resorting to the stupefying pipe of the Oriental."[27] The opium den was a place where race, gender, and sometimes even class mixed indiscriminately. The "lowest stratum of social life" was well-represented, but one might also find an occasional male of the "higher walks" present. Cobbe explained these occa-

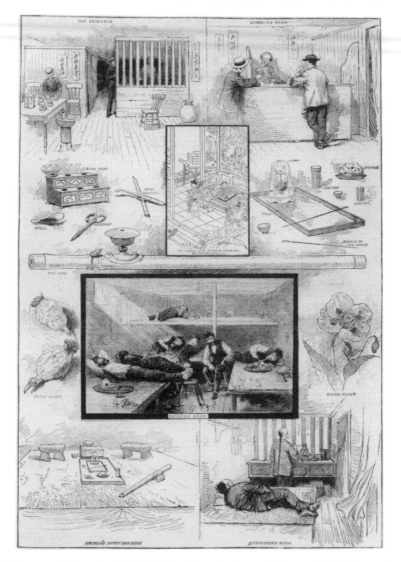

This image, which ran in the September 24, 1881, issue of Harper's Weekly, *made visible the hidden "truth" behind the degradation of opium use by associating it with recognizable types of people. By foregrounding the image of an opium den patronized by a rough-looking bunch of white males over a network of decidedly Orientalist images, it suggested that the truth behind the appearance of white opium use was unequivocally oriental. Its central juxtaposition of white degradation against a smaller image of relatively normal Chinese opium smokers suggested that what was relatively normal for one group was degradation for another.*

sional upper-class visitors as a sign of an already-completed process of degeneration—their decline was not, as far as the readers could tell, simply a product of the pipe. My point is that opiate addiction and the reduction of one's racial or ethnic status, depicted in strongly Orientalist terms, figured each other in Cobbe's text, just as they did in the work of other writers I have examined. The logic of this persistent pattern of associations was cemented in and by its tropic strategy—that is, by the tropo-logic of personification—a rhetorical tactic that these writers used to help explain the novel phenomenon of narcotic addiction to an uninitiated audience.

Cobbe further mobilized images of the opium den to illustrate the loss of individual autonomy implied by the concept of addiction. He claimed that, within the den's protective walls, smokers lay upon "little platforms, . . . three or four men and women, perhaps; there being no distinction of sex in these places and usually no consciousness of it, and no respect of age, or race, or previous condition—black, white, and Mongol, young and old, male and female." [28] Cobbe thus depicted one of the horrors of the opium den to be its lack of regard for class status or the racial and gendered borders that marked the limits of one's autonomous individuality. In this passage, the opium smoker was cast adrift in an ocean of sameness, a place where, for Cobbe, even the borders of the piled bodies became unclear, indistinct, stacked on "little platforms," one upon the other. Among the faults of the opium smoker, then, was the willful surrender of the consciousness of these markers of difference—markers of the boundaries that normally separated one person from another and served to reinforce the logic of autonomous selfhood characteristic of American bourgeois society.

That Cobbe held such autonomy as a sign of respectable selfhood was abundantly clear in his declaration that "opium smokers make no effort to conceal their sin, and hence have no objection to being thrown together; but it can easily be seen that if respectable members of society formed the habit, they would demand isolation." [29] This was the basis for Cobbe's belief that the respectable could never be found in an opium den—it violated the sense of propriety that they could find in the maintenance of distance from others, especially in terms of an otherness marked by gender, race, and class. To become an opium smoker was to surrender one's autonomy and to become swamped in an ocean of similitude.

We might then ask about the cardinal points of this otherwise monotonous seascape. Cobbe followed a route first mapped in 1871 by George Miller Beard, who claimed that opium had different effects on people according to race. [30] Cobbe wrote that "dark races, as the African and Asiatic, are not so easily affected by the pipe as the white peoples." Expanding on this seemingly innocuous claim, Cobbe noted that "Chinese are, as a rule, temperate in their smoking, and, accounts of travelers in China to the contrary notwithstanding, it does not appear that their lives are appreciably shortened by the habit. Unquestionably, though the general effects are present in all habitués; only that in the Chinese they are not so virulent." [31] But if this were the case, how could one account for the supposed depravity, degradation, and decay that Cobbe so extensively documented in his description of the Chinese-associated opium den? Such claims made sense only if one assumed that practices which were horribly degraded for one race might be much closer to normality for another. This is precisely the logic that we find in Cobbe's text.

Cobbe's claim that opium smoking did not alter the lives of the Chinese to the same degree that it changed the lives of whites was another way of saying that there was less difference between lives of the addict and nonaddict in Asian and Asian American cultures. In a telling passage, Cobbe reminded his readers that his book pertained primarily to habitual drug users who were addicted at the hands of their doctors, *not* to opium smokers: "It is here repeated that nothing said in these pages relating to the opium habit includes this class of slaves, who were slaves before they began the habit. The fact is emphasized, because the world in its ignorance confounds the latter with respectable people, who have been led into the other forms of indulgence through ignorance of the effects of the drug, or by physicians who did not consult their wishes in the premises." [32] Cobbe's point is important and bears repeating: Opium smoking was something enjoyed by a class who were "slaves before they began the habit." [33] Opium smoking was thus the outward and visible sign of a hidden condition—slavery—that existed *prior* to the actual smoking of opium.

Forty years earlier, advocates of racial slavery in the American South had defended it in a variety of ways, including economic necessity, religious duty, and historical precedent. But perhaps fundamental to all their arguments was the claim that the social, economic, and political status signified by the term "slavery" was a legitimate consequence of the racial inferiority of the slaves themselves. In Cobbe's 1895 text, slavery remained the consequence of an inferior identity, but this corruption only became visible in the individual's choice to smoke opium. He wrote that "opium smokers are bestialized by birth environment, or, by evil practices before the opium stage is reached." [34] The precise origin of the degradation was thus unclear, but Cobbe was strong in his assertion that, in the act of smoking opium, the smoker betrayed a slavery that was, or had become, essential. Put another way, the smoker became *himself*. If we further recall that, for Cobbe, opium smoking was "rooted and grounded in the Chinese character," then we must conclude that the Chinese opium smoker both realized and displayed his (essentially corrupt) racial essence in the act of smoking, whereas the white smoker displayed his degradation. Cobbe thus suggested that a condition of slavery, in this case a slavery to what he called the "wantonness of desire," was the true and original state of Chinese character. Slavery to desire was precisely the problem experienced by addicts, and thus we glimpse the operation of a logic that personified addiction by associating it with racial others. A critical element of this logic was its circularity. Cobbe's writing demonstrates how addiction could stand for the hidden truth of racial character: to be an addict was to be like the Chinese, but also to be Chinese was to be like an addict.

The final ominous conclusion to his argument emerged when he insisted that these volitional addicts could never truly be cured: "The serious question is, does it pay to cure such creatures? Absolutely devoid of moral sense they have no strength of purpose and no thought of disgrace, and consequently are as ready for a recurrence of the habit as they were originally for its formation." [35] Even if an addiction cure might be effected, simply attempting to stop their drug use amounted to little more than removal of the symptom because they were "slaves before they began the habit." In fact, such a removal could, in the long run, cause still greater harm. Cobbe argued that opium smokers were of such a low stature that any attempt at their redemption could well turn against the redeemers; even "if they remain healed of the desire for the narcotic, their vices, unrestrained by the subduing influences of the drug, are liable to break forth in passion of venal practices to the injury of society." [36] For this class of drug user, recovery was impossible, according to Cobbe. These users were beyond therapeutic help, leaving permanent incarceration or supervision as the logical solution to the threat that they posed to society. I will return to some of the policy suggestions derived from this logic in the final chapter of this book, but here it is important to note that, for Cobbe, a literal enslavement of those who were slaves before they began the habit offered a logical solution to at least one-half, the volitional half, of this turn-of-the-century drug problem.

"The Cocaine Nigger Is Sure Hard to Kill"

Cobbe's association of habitual drug use with slavery is but one example of a link that was very common within the discourse of addiction. We should, in the

This Frank Beard image, "The Slave Driver," appeared in the temperance journal The Ram's Horn *in 1896. It shows how the metaphor of slavery might help to illustrate the concept of addiction. The image depicts "appetite" as a ghoulish driver who wields the lash of "habit" over a variety of "slaves." The image invokes slavery as a metaphor, yet it makes no explicit connection to African Americans. It does, however, use a picture of a Chinese man—who appears to have seduced a white woman—to illustrate habitual opium use. As we will see below, the image of the vulnerable white woman, who is using morphine in this illustration, was an important way to make addiction more tangible for the general public.*

first instance, be careful not to make too much of this very familiar rhetorical strategy. The use of slavery as a handy metaphor for wider social problems was a commonplace, having a very long history. The historian David Brion Davis explains that "for eighteenth-century thinkers who contemplated the subject, slavery stood as the central metaphor for all the forces that debased the human spirit."[37] Any number of reformers used the metaphor during the nineteenth century, particularly advocates of temperance and the abolition of actual slavery. In chapter 1 we saw that the language of both groups had inhabited the emerging discourse of narcotic addiction from at least the 1860s onward. For such later writers as Cobbe, opium use continued to signify the degradation of the human spirit, and he unequivocally associated it—by way of the metaphor of slavery—with (Asian) racial identity.

The notion of an inferior racial identity, grounded in the "wantonness of desire" and signified by the words "slave" and "slavery," further resonates with formulations of racial difference found in other examples of late nineteenth- and early twentieth-century racist discourse, especially within that directed against African American men who were lynched for the alleged rape of white women. That racism, captured in texts left by a small but prolific group of racist whites, is some of the most distasteful material that American writers have ever produced. Typical of the genre were rants by the South Carolina governor and U.S. senator "Pitchfork" Ben Tillman, who raged against what he called "the damnable heresy of equality." [38] In 1909, Tillman stood on the floor of the Senate and declared that "we took the government away. We stuffed ballot boxes. We shot them. We are not ashamed of it." Tillman believed that emancipation had "inoculated [African Americans] with the virus of equality," and as a consequence, the "poor African" became "a fiend, a wild beast, seeking whom he may devour." [39]

Thomas Nelson Page agreed, explaining in a 1904 *North American Review* article that the combined influences of African American emancipation and civic education held a threat because, he believed, blacks made up a race whose overwhelming desire defined and determined its actions. In Page's words, the African American's "passion" was "always his controlling force," but with Reconstruction came "the teaching that the Negro was the equal of the white." The result was that, "since the new teaching," the object of that passion was "the white woman." [40] Fourteen years later, Winfield H. Collins wrote that "the Negro . . . had developed in him by nature, possibly stronger sexual passion than is to be found in any other race." He therefore felt that "when proper restraint is removed from the Negro he gets beyond bounds." [41] For Tillman, the proper mode of restraint was obvious: "Although I had taken the oath of office to support the law and enforce it, I would lead a mob to lynch any man, black or white, who ravished a woman, black or white." [42] Though some of his colleagues showed their displeasure with his tirades by withdrawing from the Senate chamber when he spoke, the historian Francis Butler Simkins argues that Tillman's popularity with the voters meant that "no southern politician dared make the Negro question a campaign issue against the South Carolina leader." [43]

Such thoughts as those above were frequently put into action. Between 1889 and 1946, nearly four thousand African Americans were lynched, very often as revenge for the alleged rape of a white woman.[44]

This racist discourse resonated with that of a newly emergent drug menace. We can begin to appreciate that resonance if we first note that racist writers depicted the alleged appearance of the black rapist in intensely historical terms. These writers described the liberation of what they saw as a "passionate" black essence as a marker of change, a threatening sign of the times in which they lived. Page noted that the "time was when the crime of assault was unknown throughout the South. During the whole period of slavery, it did not exist, nor did it exist to any considerable extent for some years after Emancipation." He explained that during the Civil War, even "on isolated plantations and in lonely neighborhoods, women were as secure as in the streets of Boston or New York." But this would soon change. He explained that with Reconstruction came those who taught African Americans to believe that they were equal to whites, resulting in "cases where members of the Negro militia ravished white women." Though he felt that the "redeemers" had briefly restored order, Page lamented the emergence of the new conditions, mourning the passage of the "old Negro," who knew his place. He felt that when the "old generation began to die out, the 'New Issue' with the new teaching took its place, [and] the crime broke out again with renewed violence."[45] Likewise, Collins argued that "the regulations adopted by masters for the control of the Negroes during slavery times may have served as a check upon their natural sexual propensities, however, since emancipation they have been under no such restraint and as a consequence they have possibly almost reverted to what must have been their primitive promiscuity."[46]

These writers believed that the immense historical transition marked by black emancipation had released what they felt was the racial essence of African Americans: the dominance of character by (sexual) desire. The idea that racial inferiority might partly be based on an alleged enslavement to passion was thus a relatively common, though controversial, concept at the turn of the century. As we saw above, writers such as William Rosser Cobbe used similar concepts to assert the inferior status of the Chinese, connected to the habitual use of opium. Other writers engaged in a comparable practice regarding African Americans, but for them it was cocaine, rather than opium, that prompted their fears.[47]

Thinking about the figure of the black cocaine user within this wider cultural context means that we need to listen closely when, for instance, in a powerful 1914 statement of the way that black cocaine use threatened whites, the *Literary Digest* quoted Dr. Christopher Koch, who stated that "most of the attacks upon white women of the south . . . are the direct result of a cocain-crazed Negro brain."[48] But most strikingly, writers like Koch did not envision *enslavement* as the threat held by black cocaine use but rather the threat of black *emancipation*. In a startling reversal that nonetheless harmonized with much of the racist writing I introduced above, many writers feared that cocaine emancipated a brutal, bestial, and predatory African American essence. Black cocaine use thus operated as a marker of the menacing novelty of its historical moment, and it did so in two ways. First, and in a manner similar to what we have seen with the opiates, cocaine often served as evidence of modern medical progress that simultaneously threatened those whom it was supposed to help. But, second, because African American freedom was among the period's most important and notable markers of change, racist writers found in cocaine use a powerful figure for what they believed was the threat held by black equality. Many writers feared that prolonged cocaine use might form a habit, but a vocal and influential minority argued that it inspired violent crime, particularly in African American users.

In the first place then, we should note that very much like the opiates, the presence of cocaine in a doctor's medical bag offered writers a means to mark the present as modern. The drug first came to broad medical attention in the United States in late 1884, when New York's *Medical Record* published an essay documenting an Austrian physician's use of it in the successful anesthetization of a patient's eye. American ophthalmologists adopted the practice in a matter of weeks, and soon its use spread to other fields of surgery. The historian Joseph Spillane therefore argues that cocaine, as a successful product of laboratory research, came to embody "the promise of modern medicine."[49] Dr. W. Scheppe-grell, for instance, noted in an 1898 edition of the *Medical News* that "when cocaine was first brought to the attention of the medical world it was heralded as an unalloyed blessing to mankind, and one which would revolutionize surgical methods."[50] The article established a sense of contemporary change as revolutionary, and the doctor further posited that cocaine's "application has become such a routine in practice that we but little realize that fifteen years ago this drug was practically unknown." But, in a typically ambivalent move, Scheppe-grell reminded his readers that "one must consider a more remote effect but one which is far-spread in its evil and which now offers a serious menace to society. I refer to the development of the cocaine habit."[51] In 1902 Dr. T. D. Crothers likewise declared that "cocainism is a new disease of civilization," and in 1912

Charles B. Towns still worried that "cocaine provides the shortest cut to the insane asylum. It takes them there across lots!" [52] Cocaine thus operated as an ambivalent marker of the modern, serving, at least partially, to define modernity as a threat, as a moment of cultural crisis. These brief samples of an already well-documented logical and rhetorical strategy rest comfortably alongside the writing about the opiates. It cast cocaine as a beneficial but potentially harmful development of modern medical technology and progress. Along with the opiates, cocaine served as an indicator of an emergent twentieth-century society that carried within itself the potential to ruin the human condition that it was supposed to foster.[53]

But more pertinent to the narrower concerns of this chapter is that many writers on the cocaine threat located it in the African American community. Schepegrell claimed, in the same *Medical News* article, that "a peculiar phase of the cocain habit which has developed in New Orleans and in a number of other cities in the South is the contraction of this habit by the Negroes." Continuing, he stated that "the extent to which this has spread can be easily verified by druggists and in police circles."[54] Contemporary experts often viewed cocaine use as a problem somehow based in the black community because drug experts associated black cocaine users with urban crime. In 1914, Atlanta police chief James L. Beavers requested that the city provide him with four police substations, forty new patrolmen, and additional equipment to support his "war on men who traffic in drugs." He justified this early call for a war on drugs by claiming that "if we could stamp out the drug evil . . . we would eradicate seventy per cent of all crime." Beavers made it clear that his officers were attempting to meet this goal when he declared that "the prison institutions of the city are being forced to make special provisions for the care of drug fiends." The supposed prevalence of cocaine use among the criminal population was particularly worrisome for Beavers because cocaine made its users into a sort of supercriminal. He lamented that "the drug fiend is oblivious to pain. Beaten almost into unconsciousness—even shot or cut near to death, the dope fiend has been known time and again to exert superhuman strength in making his escape."[55] Such evocative writing prompts wonder at the tactics of the 1914 Atlanta police force, but what is most important here is that this view of cocaine's effects was often shared by contemporaries of Chief Beavers.

On the weekend of February 7 and 8, 1914, Dr. Edward H. Williams simultaneously published articles in the *New York Times* and in the *Medical Record*. Besides demonstrating the convergence of medical, legal, and popular writing on the subject of cocaine addiction, these articles served to confirm the widespread dissemination of Beavers's fears. They contributed, at a cultural level, to the construction of a "worthy adversary" that might justify the use of what could otherwise be perceived as disproportionate use of police force. An important aspect of this operation was to emphasize what they believed was the racial aspect of the problem. In the *Record*, Williams wrote that "in the language of the police officer 'the cocaine nigger is sure hard to kill'— a fact that has been demonstrated so often that many of these officers in the South have increased the caliber of their guns for the express purpose of stopping the cocaine fiend when he runs amuck." [56] Again, one wonders at the circumstances around such brutal police performances. The point, however, is that we are not seeing an accurate description of "real" African American cocaine users but rather the construction of a racist figure. In the discourse of addiction, the "cocaine nigger" signified a particularly nasty side effect of modern medical technology and represented a threat to whites. The inscription of modernity as cultural crisis upon the bodies of these peculiarly modern characters worked by invoking the liberation of a latent, supposedly African American, bestiality, brought to the surface by a dangerous interaction with modern technology. To many, especially to African American commentators, modernity might signify the emancipation of black America, but the texts discussed here imagined this momentous transition as a decidedly menacing event. As such, extreme defensive measures were necessary, and as Williams and Beavers testified, police departments were not reluctant to take those steps.

Williams's *New York Times* article received a full page and banner headlines in the Sunday magazine section. He began his article by declaring that "stories of cocaine orgies . . . followed by wholesale murders, seem like lurid journalism of the yellowest variety. But in point of fact there was nothing 'yellow' about many of these reports." Williams expanded on his *Medical Record* article, adding that cocaine provided a "temporary steadying of the nervous and muscular system, so as to increase, rather than interfere with, good marksmanship." In other words, "cocaine-crazed Negroes" were better shots than were other criminals. Williams explained that "the deadly accuracy of the cocaine user has become axiomatic in southern police circles." [57]

In 1903 the "growing habit" prompted the *New York Tribune* to quote Colonel J. W. Watson, who declared that "cocaine sniffing . . . threatens to depopulate the southern States of their colored population." While this sensational claim was dramatic enough on its own, Watson's larger goal was to warn the citizens of the North that "the use of cocaine is not confined to the Negroes of the south by any manner or means." [58] In other words, cocaine addiction, like opium and morphine dependence, was spreading beyond its alleged base in the black population and was affecting whites as well.

In 1914 Harvey W. Wiley and Anne Lewis Pierce detected this spreading malaise and declared in the pages of *Good Housekeeping* that "the great part of the ⌜cocaine⌝ traffic is carried out by special agents dealing from state to state." For Wiley and Pierce, this was "an evil that only action by the national government can correct." They feared that an underground drug network was operating from state to state, and explained that these "special agents" jeopardized America's future by "selling cocain under the name of 'flake' or 'coke' to school children at recess time." Of particular note though, was the way that they described this as a racially based threat. Wiley and Pierce found an interesting conflation of the modern and the archaic hidden within the baskets of agents, who were "old colored men, presumably selling roots, barks, and herbs [who] conceal the drug beneath their wares, and sell it in white envelopes of twisted dirty newspaper packages." [59] Wiley thus conjured images of itinerant folk healers—practitioners of a traditional medicine rooted in the customs of a particular racial community—as interstate drug dealers.[60] Wiley and Pierce's root man leapt the temporal and technological gap between differing medical practices in order to threaten the children of those who read *Good Housekeeping*. Wiley linked archaic medications—"roots, barks, and herbs"—to the very modern cocaine, suggesting a connection between the antiquated and a chemical product of the new technology. Further, the peril of cocaine addiction was, for Wiley, Pierce and their cohort, spreading rapidly from the black to the white population.

The growth of cocaine addiction, however, had a different meaning for blacks than it did for whites because the latter supposedly took the drug out of medical necessity whereas the former took it merely for pleasure. Such differentiation once again exemplifies the double meaning of addiction previously discussed. These writers often reserved the juridical definition—that the conditions of modernity *forced* users into the habit—for their white, bourgeois patients while saddling minority others with the moral responsibility for what they envisioned as a volitional addiction. Such a distinction was clear when the *Medical News* wrote that narrow Caucasian nasal passages had a tendency to become contracted—a condition relieved by cocaine use—but that larger nasal passages offered African American drug users no such excuse.[61]

This ambivalent celebration of cocaine's medical potential thus reflected and reinforced such racist fears of black freedom as those mentioned at the beginning of this section. Writers who were uncomfortable with African American emancipation might point to alleged cocaine use in the black population in order to cast aspersions on that community's ability to cope with its freedom. Likewise, writers who were uncomfortable with unregulated cocaine use might bolster their arguments with lurid tales of "black brutes" unleashed upon southern femininity. The public discussion of cocaine, then, especially its alleged use by African Americans, like the discourse of addiction more generally, was embedded in a broader cultural logic that marked the distinctiveness of turn-of-the-century America as modern. At its worst, the debate tended to equate unregulated cocaine use with unrestricted African American freedom. It offers an example of one way that these two strands of thought, one medical and one social, might be woven together to produce an antimodern other. The black cocaine user, like the oriental addict, offered a negative, menacing image of the independent, responsible modern subject.

THE "FEMININE" ADDICT

The representation of women's desire also played a prominent role in the discourse of narcotic addiction. In the *Journal of the American Medical Association* for August 18, 1900, Dr. T. J. Happel declared that "whiskey has slain its thousands, but a vice of greater magnitude, . . . that is seizing hold upon the mothers and daughters of the day, will have to be faced and fought in the twentieth century." [62] In a familiar pattern, Happel marked the distinctiveness of historical change in terms of its shifting technologies of intoxication, but he sought to amplify the contemporary threat by assigning it more specifically to women. Happel was particularly disturbed because, in attacking women, narcotics were "an evil which is poisoning the very sources of all that ought to be good." The causes of women's drug use, he argued, were to be found in "the demands of modern society." [63]

One might assume, therefore, that there was cause to celebrate when, only seventeen years later, a special committee of the United States Department of the Treasury reported that "contrary to general opinion . . . drug addiction is not more prevalent among females than males." [64] While the committee's empirical findings might suggest that Dr. Happel and his colleagues had successfully turned back this modern threat to the nation's collective femininity, there remained a dissonant note in the committee's statement: it was unequivocal in its assertion that, despite demographic findings to the contrary, the *general opinion persisted* that women made up the majority of the addict population. Put another way, the committee made clear that most Americans who thought about the subject at all remained convinced that most drug addicts were women.

The tenacity of this belief ensured that women's drug use would become an important topic in the historical study of narcotic addiction. Though we now know that narcotic use among middle-class white women had been superseded by that of various disreputable men even before the 1914 passage of the Harrison Act, such demographic findings cannot deny or explain the persistence of the older, popular belief in the predominance of female addicts. There seems to have been a social investment in the idea that women were particularly vulnerable to narcotic addiction that outweighed inconvenient demographic findings to the contrary.

In the discourse of addiction, women's bodies figured as a dangerously vulnerable point in the configuration of bourgeois subjectivity. Of even greater concern was that Contemporary writers feared that female addicts might infect the home—the citadel of bourgeois identity. The discourse of addiction employed, modified, and reinforced common ideas of gender, constructed between the poles of feminine fragility and masculine fortitude, to explain the way in which temptations of modern technology threatened the self-mastery that underlay conventional notions of middle-class individuality. A similar, though not identical, operation was at work as a crucial constituent in the production of racial otherness, but here we see its operation in the construction of gender difference. As such, we find a resonance between the constructed positions of both women and racial others in the discourse of addiction. That similarity was crucial in making narcotic addiction more comprehensible as a threat to the white, middle-class family.

Prostitution offered the first and most obvious point where addiction theorists might link the characteristics of racial difference and female sexuality. As early as 1871, Alonzo Calkins explained that "in the division of sex the women have the majority," but added that "the cyprians who perambulate Broadway by gas-light are reliant upon laudanum in extremity. . . . Two-thirds of the class become habituated eventually to opium in some form. . . . A young man, an apothecary on Union Square, gives similar testimony regarding the courtesans of Savannah." [65] Though Calkins's references to laudanum and gaslight locate his writing at the very opening of the modern discourse of addiction, he nonetheless provided a powerfully lurid image of the sexual and narcotic seduction that threatened urban males in the late nineteenth-century city. He also suggested that an oriental decadence, carried by menacingly feminine "cyprians" and "courtesans," was a feature of urban life in both the North and the South.

The American Pharmaceutical Association conducted a three-year study of the drug problem between 1901 and 1903, and among its projects was a request that doctors and pharmacists from across the country report to the association on their narcotic-related experiences in the trade. The association received reports such as one from Georgia which stated that "almost every colored prostitute [is] addicted to cocaine." [66] Often, the respondents dispensed with the mediation of prostitution and associated the drug use of white women and African Americans more generally, as in an account from Indiana, which reported "that a good many Negroes and a few white women are addicted to cocaine." [67] In 1902 the association had received enough evidence that it felt confident to report to its general meeting that "the use of cocaine by unfortunate women generally and by Negroes in certain parts of the country is simply appalling." [68] One report to the committee claimed that "the use of cocaine seems to be rapidly supplanting in part the use of morphine among men and women of the 'under world,' and the writer knows personally of two cases of men who acquired the cocaine habit from lewd women they visited habitually." [69]

The problem was still in evidence in 1918 when L. L. Stanley wrote, in his study of addiction in the military, that fully "fifteen per cent [of addicted soldiers] were induced and educated to this addiction by women of the underworld, who perhaps took a fancy to the young man and persuaded him to go with her to indulge in this insidious vice." [70] Persuasion and seduction were the weapons of the immoral women who corrupted this otherwise honorable young soldier and others like him, but prostitutes were not the only feminine carriers of the affliction. Even in 1871 Alonzo Calkins felt the necessity to temper his argument, citing another physician who claimed that "the aggregate of instances [of addiction] among women in high place is incredibly large." [71] Likewise, Leslie Keeley wrote in 1889 that "the saddest fact of all is, that . . . the majority of the victims are women; not poor, degraded, outcast women, although this class helps to swell the array, but those occupying high positions in the world." [72]

While it is clear that a similar act of marginalization was at work in the linkage of addiction to lower-class women and racial minorities, it would be absurd to argue that the same operation applied to both groups and even more so to suggest that it applied to middle-class women. Medical theorists argued that women's vulnerability to narcotics, especially that of middle-class women, was different from that of nonwhites. Instead of locating the tendency to become ad-

The Chinese often received the blame for spreading the opium habit to an unwary American public. This cartoon, from an October 1888 issue of Harper's Weekly, *gave visual form to a common argument—that narcotic addiction might be transferred from Chinese to European American society through its allegedly weakest point, that is, its women.*

dicted in an identity that was dominated by desire, many experts found women to be at risk because of a sexual susceptibility that was aggravated by the refinement and growth of genteel civilization. Here we find traces of the sentimental domestic discourse that the historian Barbara Welter has called a "cult of true womanhood"—the popular, middle-class depiction of women as submissive, domestic, pious, and sexually pure. True women were expected to anchor the nineteenth-century bourgeois home by creating a wholesome environment for children and a cheery respite from the demands and temptations of the marketplace for weary men. Though the discourse held that a woman who left the safety of the marital hearth courted disaster, many women spent the nineteenth century doing just that. Reform-minded women used this domestic discourse, particularly its assertion of female moral authority, to justify political activism outside of the home, and thus the older formulation became ever more unstable

as the century progressed. By the time that narcotic addiction had become a
public issue, the decay of the older cult of true womanhood was well under way,
and large numbers of well-educated "new women" became more visible in a
public sphere that had earlier been reserved for their husbands, fathers, and
brothers. In its own way, the partial dissolution of gender-specific, separate-
sphere ideology was as much a marker of the distinctiveness of turn-of-the-
century life as was the emancipation of 4 million African American slaves.[73]

To many commentators, this limited female emancipation was a threat, and
to many narcotics experts, the (changing) status of middle-class women as
keepers of the hearth rendered them all the more dangerous as addicts. If the
bourgeois home was largely secure against the invasion of addicted *racial* others, modern middle-class women had seized the keys to the gate, threatening to
open a route into the stronghold. White, middle-class women were not as radically other as African American or Chinese men—or even prostitutes—and
thus narcotic addiction, a condition that might be carried into the home by vulnerable women, became more of a menace to male members of the white bourgeois family. The female addict figured a seductive, technologized, and thus
more potent contagion than did addicts whose difference was marked primarily
by their race. Women's bodies presented attractive targets for writers who
sought to create convincing scapegoats for their fear that narcotic addiction
might become widespread among middle-class homes. The female body offered
a convenient and familiar form with which to personify the addiction concept.

George Miller Beard imagined the vulnerability of the modern woman as a
historical phenomenon. In 1881 he argued that her delicacy and refinement
were products of temporal progress and of cultural growth, writing that a fine
nervous alignment "is the organization of the civilized, refined, and educated,
rather than of the barbarous and low-born and untrained—of women more
than of men. It is developed, fostered, and perpetuated with the progress of civilization." He declared that "the weakness of woman is all modern, and it is pre-
eminently American."[74] Explaining his insight by turning to its historicity,
Beard linked the expansion of women's thought with technological change in
a brilliant summary of the way that environment and biology combined to
produce a debilitating, modern, nervous disease—a disease whose symptoms
included the desire to use drugs: "The modern differ from the ancient civilizations mainly in these five elements—steam power, the periodical press, the telegraph, the sciences, and the mental activity of women. When civilization, plus
these five factors, invades any nation, it must carry nervousness and nervous
diseases along with it."[75] Beard contrasted modern America with ancient

Greece to illustrate his point in still more strongly historical terms. In *American Nervousness* he claimed that Greek wives "had no more voice in the interests of state, or art, or learning, or even of social life, than the children of to-day," which led him to conclude that "the mental activity of woman is indeed almost all modern." Beard believed that women had lost their childlike social position over the centuries, the consequence of which he explained quantitatively: "If the brain of the average American is tenfold more active that the brain of the average Athenian, the contrast in the cerebral activity of the women must be even greater." [76] He brought his point up-to-date for his readers with a contemporary metaphor that also defined modern feminine weakness as the consequence of an exceptionally American increase in mental activity: "In the brain of the American girl thoughts travel by the express, in that of her European sister by accommodation." [77] Railroad imagery linked history with biology to describe a modern threat to the American woman and, simultaneously, to denote the distinctive modernity of its emergence.

Leslie Keeley, writing in 1894, also lamented the modern prevalence of nervousness in women as a historical phenomenon that contributed to habitual drug use. He believed that many of the physical and psychological maladies suffered by "young girls . . . undoubtedly arise from an over-stimulation of the nerve centres, brought on by the pressure of the present educational system." Written during a period of expansion and growth in both the quantity and quality of women's educational opportunities, his argument echoed Dr. Beard's. Keeley clarified his attack on women's education when he sought "the cause of all this" and concluded that "a mere glance at the ordinary life of a woman will show us the secret. The present system of education must be held responsible in a great measure, as its tendency is to increase the activity and susceptibility of the nervous system by diminishing the nutrition of the brain and thus promote organic disease." Keeley conflated biology and history to describe the specificity—to insist on the *difference in kind*—of modern women's weakness. Other aspects of "the ordinary life of a woman" likewise contributed to her vulnerability. Keeley found that "the domestic cares and demands of society are another fruitful cause of nervous diseases among women, especially when they do not take sufficient care of themselves, as is generally the case." [78] Modernity thus required the vigilant supervision and care of women, who generally could not care for themselves in the face of society's demands.

Keeley led his readers into the bourgeois home, where he found the rejection of feminine social and domestic responsibilities among the symptoms of drug addiction: "The distaste for exertion and for society which it causes, results in neglect of social activities. Even household duties are in time postponed or carelessly performed. All that is truest, most helpful, and most winning is destroyed, affection sadly departs from the fireside and comfort from the home." [79] Habitual narcotic use struck at the sentimental heart of bourgeois domesticity, attacking what was simultaneously its anchor and its most vulnerable point. Narcotics destroyed "all that is truest, most helpful, and most winning" in the home by transforming its central figure into something like a fallen angel of the hearth. Addiction turned the true woman's truth into falsehood, which is why Keeley claimed that affection and comfort, the qualities that she was expected to exemplify for her children and her husband, had "sadly departed" from the fireside.

Keeley was not alone in his identification of domestic irresponsibility as a prime symptom of drug use among middle-class women. In 1885, cure doctor Asa P. Meylert wrote that the addicted woman's husband and family "notice that she is queer, that her memory is impaired, . . . that she sometimes invites friends to dine with her, but forgets to provide for them and is evidently perplexed at their coming; that she does not make calls, and is seldom prepared to receive; that her household duties are neglected, her children uncared for, her friends almost forgotten. But they say she has never been the same since she was sick some years ago and that accounts for it all." [80] Meylert alluded to a narcotic habit that began at the hands of an irresponsible physician, but more important, he agreed with Beard and Keeley on the effects of narcotic addiction on the home. This move reinforced gender stereotypes drawn from an older discourse of domestic sentimentality, but it also modified them by adding the threat of addiction to the list of bourgeois women's traits. It helped these writers to animate and vivify the menace that they believed narcotic addiction held for middle-class America.

Fin de siècle physicians believed that women's weakness was not merely cultural but also biological, a product of both physiology and environment. Beard argued that this modern psychological strain had its counterpart in a new *physical* weakness experienced by middle—and upper-class American women. He explained that "our women cannot endure such exposure to heat or to cold, and soon become unable to bear the muscular strain that such labor makes necessary." Most important, Beard followed many of his colleagues in associating feminine weakness, modern society, and new challenges for women's reproductive medicine: "Modern civilization demands prolonged rest for the parturient female; and how many there are in our own land, for whom the conventional nine days is extended to double that time; how many, also to whom the simple

act of giving birth to a child opens the door to unnumbered woes."[81] The trans-
lation of modernity into an affliction of female reproductive biology made it
much easier to inscribe the likelihood and the peril of narcotic addiction upon
her modern, middle-class body. Accordingly, many practitioners located a
woman's propensity to be addicted in a mysterious feminine nature, originating
somewhere in her reproductive organs.

The medical identification of a woman's essential character with reproductive biology has been widely noted by historians.[82] Addiction experts were thus
in perfect harmony with their colleagues when they, like Dr. T. D. Crothers, argued in 1902 that "capriciousness of mind, irritability, selfishness, restlessness,
and excitability are the natural characteristics of many women, who quickly become morphinists, especially if under treatment for disorders of the generative
organs."[83] Crothers claimed that the presence of what he depicted as natural
feminine eccentricity was multiplied by his certainty that "women are more
susceptible to morphin than men, and its sedative effects are more pleasing and
of longer duration [for them]."[84] In other words, while narcotics were a powerful temptation for men, they were an even stronger one for women who were
biologically less able to resist them.

The association of reproductive biology and narcotic addiction was nothing
new when Crothers made his 1902 claim. In 1878 another doctor had argued
that "the most frequent cause of the opium-habit in females is the taking of opiates to relieve painful menstruation and diseases of the female organs of generation." He added that "the frequency of these diseases in part accounts for the
excess of female opium-eaters over males."[85] Such hypotheses were persistent,
and thus we find another doctor, in 1915, writing that "it appears reasonable, . . . to ascribe to [the menopause period] of female life, no small portion of
the addiction among women."[86] These passages serve as temporal brackets to
Crothers's argument, and the connection made between women's reproductive
medicine and opiate addiction may well have been accurate in the sense that
physicians often prescribed opiates for women's reproductive disorders. But
that is not what was said in these texts.[87] Such writing demonstrates the widespread persistence of the biological linkage of femininity with addiction, the effect being to establish a biological tendency for women to become narcotic
addicts.

Multiplying the dangers still further, the American Pharmaceutical Association suspected that the traits of the nervous, addicted, middle-class woman
might be handed down to future generations. In 1903, the group worried about
the pharmacist's responsibility in spreading addiction and asked, "Shall we

carry this idea forward to the generation which follows?" The somewhat re-lieved answer was that "it is needless; the nursing babe absorbs medicine from its mother's breast as it draws its nourishment; it becomes an habitué from its birth. My mother takes this, and I will try a little of it, is another trend of the habit, as well as other associations in various walks of life."[88] The committee thus diverted, from pharmacists onto women, some degree of what it felt was the blame for the spread of addiction.

The notion of feminine contagion transcended the class-specific references to the "decadent," "lewd," or otherwise "immoral" women of the underworld. In the discourse of addiction, infectivity was a property of the constructed femi-nine—a way of stating its contagious relation to the centered self-mastery of an autonomous masculine subject. The association of addiction with femininity was thus a double operation. It affirmed a belief that women were weak and therefore vulnerable, but it also mobilized the feminine as a metaphor for vul-nerability to narcotic addiction. The assembly of this modern susceptibility was crucial to these writers' attempt to define drug addiction as a danger to middle- and upper-class women, but also to middle- and upper-class American men, who otherwise personified the strong, centered, autonomous self.

In 1897 Leslie Keeley provided powerful examples of this metaphorical fem-ininity, its linkage to drug addiction, and its relation to men when he wrote that "the palace of the siren and its delights are so wonderfully seductive that the sight of the grunting herd of those who have been the lovers of the temptress, and upon whom, in past days, her kisses have wrought swinish transformation, does not deter the flushed, eager new-comer, fresh landed upon the 'island of joyance.' . . . Alas for him, if even but once a flame be kindled in his blood by the fatal sweetness of the siren's kiss!"[89] This assertion of a "swinish transforma-tion" wrought by a "temptress" offered an unambiguously gendered image of masculine degradation. The man's role in this narrative was to emulate Ulysses, strapped to the mast in an act of heroic resistance to the Siren's song of desire. The logic of the text was that the Keeley gold cure could help this chal-lenged, modern Ulysses rise to his task, but my point is that Keeley figured opium and its attractions as an unequivocally feminine threat to men.

He also figured cocaine as feminine, writing that "as long as a man clings to Cocaine his life is like a misspent day; it cannot be recalled or reclaimed. The one time charmer changed into a fury persecutes and afflicts where once she held out only delights."[90] As was the case with opium, a seductive charmer turns into a wrathful fury in a demonstration of the powerful temptations that threatened the otherwise strong, but perhaps incautious, male. Additionally, images of misspending reinforced the efficacy of the gold cure as an appropriate way to restore the seduced male's squandered selfhood.

Finally, Keeley quoted Fitz Hugh Ludlow, who made the threat to men absolutely clear when he asked: "When the most powerful alleviative known to medical science has bestowed the last Judas kiss which is necessary to emasculate its victim, and, sure of its prey, substitutes stabbing for blandishment, what alleviation, stronger than the strongest, should soothe such doom?"[91] Ludlow's hyperbole—re-stated by Keeley—posited suicide as a tragic, though reasonable, alternative to the addict's writhing in the pain of his "emasculation." This ultimate and final reassertion of the addict's will in an act of self-destruction demonstrates the stakes of the opposition between masculine and feminine in Keeley's text. Keeley described addiction as a compromise of the user's masculinity, suggesting that narcotic addiction so jeopardized a man's existence *as* a man that his life would be inconceivable in such a state.

The threat of emasculation, the removal of an active, productive masculinity by a femininity whose aggressiveness lay in its seductive passivity, was widely feared in addiction literature. The American Pharmaceutical Association, in its 1902 report, called addiction a "man-destroying appetite" while also affirming that "honorable and manly pharmacists" admitted their share of the responsibility for the spread of addiction.[92] This passage demonstrates how addiction literature often constructed an image of a strong, functional masculinity at the same time as it assembled the addict as its feminine other. A "man" was an effective agent who *produced* his own actions and was *responsible* for those actions. Responsibility required self-mastery, which was, in this case, affirmed by not blaming others for the consequences of one's own acts. On the other hand, the association depicted addiction as a "man-destroying" appetite that compromised the possibility of self-mastery and thus of responsibility and honor. Such a suggestion mobilized, modified, and reinforced popular conceptions of masculine fortitude, which were inevitably measured against images of feminine fragility.

In 1918 Dr. C. B. Pearson argued that addiction attacked the male on two fronts, both physical and mental. He wrote that "the mental stress and depression are not only horrible in the extreme, but they also *unman* the addict to such an extent that he is in no condition to bear the physical suffering."[93] Again we see images of addiction as psychologically "unmanning," but in this instance the doctor adds a particular physical weakness to the mix. In such an assertion one hears echoes of George Miller Beard's association of the fin de siècle American woman's inability to bear physical suffering because of the advance of modernity. Dr. Pearson argued that men, too, faced a specifically modern weakness, but one brought on by narcotic addiction.

Other doctors followed their colleagues' linkage of female character and reproductive biology in their studies of the specific physical ravages of addiction on their male patients. This attention frequently concerned images of lost productivity and self-mastery due to addiction. In other words, addiction doctors often searched for physical evidence of "unmanning" in their male patients. Many researchers, such as Archibald Church and Frederick Peterson in 1914, associated impotence and drug addiction in a powerful demonstration of lost male productivity.[94] Another physician, who added a more general loss of sexual desire to diminished male performance, wrote in 1918 that "with the exception of a primary euphoria, those addicted to morphine have little or no sexual interest (in the narrower sense of the word). After withdrawal this usually returns, and with great intensity. There is, as a rule, an absence of spermatogenesis during morphine addiction. This disappears on withdrawal. During chronic morphinism the power of erection is often lost."[95] We should bear in mind that, physiologically, this may all be true. Heavy narcotic use may adversely affect many biological functions, such as sexual potency and spermatogenesis, especially while the user is under the influence of an intoxicant. My point, however, is that these images helped in the construction of a masculinity that was threatened *as* masculine by a power that was often depicted as feminine and was, crucially, transmissible through the agency of women. Drug addiction jeopardized the very possibility of autonomous, responsible, honorable masculinity, and the rhetorical strategies that experts employed to tell this story had serious implications for those whose imagined bodies figured threats and served as warnings of what lay in store for the addicted white male.

Doctors found sexual dysfunction to be a consequence of narcotic use in both sexes. In 1908 one researcher reported that "the generative functions are depressed by opium, and in chronic poisoning the menses cease and men become impotent while under its influence." As was the case with men, morphine abuse "may occasion atrophy of the female organs."[96] Addiction thus threatened its users with the loss of their productivity, an argument posed here in specific reference to human reproduction. But such assertions also played on more general images of a lost ability to produce or motivate one's own actions or what the American Pharmaceutical Association sketched as a negation of the terms of responsibility. The inability to resist the unchecked desire of drug addiction and to assert one's active agency—the impossibility of individual action as an effective, productive human subject—typified this gendered discourse and helps to account for its frequent and almost frantic attempts to construct its own versions of responsible selves and powerless others.

The peril of "unmanning" haunted the turn-of-the-century literature of narcotic addiction. We have seen how women in general and bourgeois women in particular were figured as both the representation and the embodiment of the danger of addiction. Women's alleged weakness, their biological inability to resist their desires, threatened to bring down the men around them by serving as a conduit for the introduction of narcotic addiction into the middle-class home.

The three cultural paradigms of Orientalism, Jim Crow, and Sentimental Domesticity underwrote and were themselves underwritten by the discourse of addiction. They provided the logical frameworks that helped all the writers that I have discussed explain the addiction concept by associating it with an array of premodern, not-quite modern, or pathologically modern (in the case of women) identities that menaced the assertion of a well-adapted, autonomous, and thus successful form of modern subjectivity. Because the notion of a strong, independent identity based on claims of self-mastery had long been restricted to white, middle-class males, writers had at their disposal a large and convenient archive of images from which they might construct a likeness of addiction that was familiar to their readers and to themselves. The trope they employed was personification, and they used images of the autonomous subject's traditional others to give recognizable form to the obscure addiction concept. The texts drew upon and modified older race and gender stereotypes to find examples of people who, through viciousness or vulnerability, were unable to master the powerful forces of desire that both animated and enveloped them. Such an operation did not simply suggest that addicts were like Chinese men, African American men, and women of any race but also inevitably turned back upon itself, adding force to the stereotypes by implying that to be Chinese or African American or female was to be like an addict. The discourse of addiction thus reflected, but also helped to produce, the logics of identity in which it was grounded.

Still, these operations were not identical for racial others and for women. Despite important similarities, these were not the same processes of marginalization. Distinctions were to be made within the addict population and classes of addicts to be identified, diagnosed, and cured. Herein lies the distinctiveness of the addiction concept, and it brings its double meaning once again to the fore. This task—differentiating between patients and criminals—was the challenge thrown down to those who sought to represent and to remedy the condition. This delicate balancing act is the subject of the next two chapters.

CHAPTER 4

Legislating Professional Authority
The Harrison Narcotic Act of 1914

For the last forty years the public press of this country has teemed with accounts, sometimes highly colored, sometimes trivial, but nearly always quick with the truth in regard to the spread of the vice of opium smoking from Chinese subjects of our own population.

> —DR. HAMILTON WRIGHT, U.S. Representative to the Shanghai Opium Commission, report in *Opium Problem: Message from the President of the United States*, February 1909

BY THE FIRST DECADE of the twentieth century, a growing coalition of reformers had come to believe that the federal government ought to take decisive national action to control what they described as an escalating drug threat. As we have seen, both the popular and the professional presses had framed narcotic use as a problem for over forty years, and this, combined with Progressive Era faith in legislative cures for modern social ills, helped to create a favorable climate for some form of federal intervention. Progressive journalists, sometimes called "muckrakers," also chimed in, enjoying a great deal of success in alerting the public to the dangers of an unregulated drug market. In October 1905, Samuel Hopkins Adams began publication of "The Great American Fraud," a series of articles in *Collier's* magazine that discussed the abuses and excesses of the patent medicine industry.[1] The spread of narcotic addiction to an unwary public was prominent among the abuses he cited. Over the next five years, the American Medical Association distributed over 150,000 copies of Adams's series, and along with Upton Sinclair's best-selling, fictional indictment of the meatpacking industry, *The Jungle*, it contributed to the passage and implementation of the 1906 Pure Food and Drug Act, which was among the Progressive movement's chief legislative accomplishments.[2]

We should remember, however, that the Pure Food and Drug Act was a truth-in-labeling law that sought to improve market efficiency by enabling more effective consumer choice. Though it required manufacturers to list narcotic ingredients on the label of a package, it did not prohibit their manufacture, sale, or consumption. Legislative attempts to reduce or prohibit narcotic consumption by individuals raised difficult questions about the extent to which the federal government had the right to intervene in citizens' private affairs, not to mention delicate issues of states' rights. Although many states had enacted laws to control the manufacture and distribution of narcotics, such legislation was generally ineffective, particularly because of the interstate nature of much of the drug trade. Put into the analytic language of this study, the economy that produced and was encouraged by new transportation and communications technologies had increased the interdependence of towns, cities, and states, which complicated the local control of the drug trade and, for many, highlighted the need for federal rather than state action. In this chapter I sample the language of the legislative debates that surrounded the passage of America's first federal, domestic antinarcotic law, the Harrison Narcotic Act of 1914. First, I will show that the cultural logic we have so far explored pervaded both the debate over and the outcome of the Harrison Act. Second, I will also examine the way in which a variety of individuals and organizations championed the authority of professional medicine, enhanced by federally mandated prescription laws, as the solution to challenges posed by turn-of-the-century narcotic use.

That choice of solutions—the resort to professional authority—further situates the discourse of addiction within the broader cultural crisis of modernity. In chapter 2 I cited Thomas Haskell's explanation of that crisis as the growing perception of interconnectedness and interdependence at the close of the nineteenth century. His claim that such perceptions undermined the assertion of independent, autonomous subjectivity—long a marker of middle-class identity—has animated much of this book. The point of Haskell's study, however, is to show that an emergent class of "professionals" justified its existence by offering expert solutions to the intricate problems of a complex, modern society.

Haskell defines professionals as "persons who claim to possess esoteric knowledge which serves as the basis for advice or services rendered to the public for remuneration."[3] He defines professionalization as "a measure not of quality, but of community," explaining that intellectual "work is professional depending on the degree to which it is oriented toward, and integrated with, the work of other inquirers in an ongoing community of inquiry."[4] Haskell argues that various groups of late nineteenth-century experts justified their professional status, as well as their consequent assertions of exclusivity, by claiming to possess the specialized skills and knowledge that might reconstruct coherent narratives of (human) causal agency for a society whose concept of the self was grounded on deeply imperiled notions of individual autonomy and self-mastery.

Medicine was far from immune to the allure of turn-of-the-century professionalization. In fact, medicine was in many ways the paradigmatic example of that process. The American Medical Association (AMA) was the leading voice of professionalizing medicine at the turn of the twentieth century. The first twenty years of the century saw the AMA, founded in 1847, rise from its disorganized and somewhat marginal nineteenth-century status to the place of dominance over the medical profession that it enjoys today. This was not, however, an easy victory. Nineteenth-century medicine was typified by squabbles and feuding, not only between the "regulars" and their sectarian rivals but also within the ranks of the regulars themselves, whose commitment to clinical and laboratory-based medical practice and research grounded their claims to the purveyance of "scientific" medicine. But using those claims to construct a gateway to the profession, or as a standard of medical legitimacy, sounded elitist and antidemocratic in the wide open medical marketplace of mid-nineteenth-century America. While some medical sects, homeopathy and eclecticism, for example, were eventually assimilated by the scientific regulars—sometimes called "allopaths"—others, such as Christian Science, osteopathy, and chiropractic remained outside the fold. The regulars further felt themselves besieged by the claims of patent medicine makers, who mocked and distorted allopathic findings in a flood of national advertising that also offered therapeutic advice to the lay public.[5]

Against this backdrop, the early twentieth-century growth of the AMA is striking. Between 1900 and 1910, AMA membership skyrocketed from 8,401 to 70,146. By 1920, total membership stood at 83,338.[6] Scientific breakthroughs, effective leadership, and growing professional cohesion among the regulars all help to account for the AMA's surging numbers and status, but simple

narratives of a scientific victory over superstition, or too close a focus on the intentions and strategies of the individuals and organizations that benefited from
enhanced professional power, cannot fully explain the phenomenon. "It seems
more reasonable to look for the origins of increased resort to professional advice in the new conditions of life at the end of the nineteenth century," according to the medical historian Paul Starr, who turns to the broader cultural
context—to the "profound changes in Americans' way of life and forms of consciousness" that we have so far called the cultural crisis of modernity—to explain the success of medical professionalization.[7]

According to Starr, an important effect of urbanization, of expanded communication and transportation technologies, and of scientific discoveries that
defied common sense was that "Americans became more accustomed to relying
on the specialized skills of strangers." In a world where "technological change
was revolutionizing daily life," he explains, "it seemed entirely plausible to believe that science would do the same for healing."[8] We've seen throughout this
book that narcotic addiction often figured modernity's worst-case scenario,
that it offered a convenient example of the way that turn-of-the-century Americans might become the slaves of the technological innovations that helped to
define their age. In such a context, and because narcotic drugs were, after all,
products of modern *medical* technology, turning to professional medicine to
remedy the condition made sense. Physicians were the people least likely to
miss the connection.

THE RESPONSIBILITIES OF THE PROFESSIONAL PHYSICIAN

In June 1900, near the beginning of its remarkable rise to power, the AMA
gathered in Atlantic City, New Jersey, for its fifty-first annual meeting. A future
president of the organization, Dr. John A. Witherspoon of Nashville, Tennessee, delivered the Oration on Medicine to that year's assembly, calling it "A
Protest against Some of the Evils in the Profession of Medicine." He used his
opportunity to explore a host of challenges that confronted the AMA's physicians at the beginning of the twentieth century. Witherspoon found "the indiscriminate use of narcotics" looming large among these problems, prompting
him to one his more excessive flights of sentiment: "Ah, brothers! we, the representatives of the grandest and noblest profession in the world, with the God-
given mission of making growth more perfect, life more certain and death more
remote, must shoulder the responsibility, follow in the footsteps of the Great

First Physician, and warn and save our people from the clutches of this hydra-headed monster which stalks abroad throughout the civilized world, wrecking lives and happy homes, filling our jails and lunatic asylums, and taking from these unfortunates the precious promises of eternal life." [9]

Witherspoon thus connected the control of narcotic addiction with professional responsibility and set very high stakes for the linkage. He asserted that the physicians of the AMA held proprietary responsibility for perfecting the growth of society, a notion which helped to anchor his claim that the AMA conventioneers were "the representatives of the grandest and noblest profession in the world." Yet Witherspoon feared the obstacles that could impede what he called professional medicine's God-given mission to perfect human growth. He noted that "there are but a few men here of wide experience who do not daily come in contact with practitioners whose panacea for everything is opium in some of its forms." [10]

Witherspoon worried that "the morphin habit is growing at an alarming rate" and blamed his audience for spreading the condition: "We can not shift the responsibility, but must acknowledge that we are culpable in too often giving this seductive siren until the will-power is gone, and a moral and physical wreck is sent down to shame and degradation." Patients were thus lured onto a downward path by an unambiguously feminine figure, a "seductive siren," ushered into the home by the physician. He further argued that "the same can be said of cocain, which is rapidly becoming a national evil, because of its indiscriminate use in minor surgical operations." But rather than simply censuring the medical use of these substances, Witherspoon followed popular medical opinion when he found the narcotic to be "a wonderful remedy, capable of great good when judiciously used," but he felt himself "bound to say that when used as it is by some doctors, it is productive of terrible results." [11]

Witherspoon thus made a crucial distinction when he accused his colleagues of spreading narcotic addiction. He blamed *some* doctors, not all of them. He did not indict the medical use of narcotics per se but rather their *indiscriminate* use, setting a standard based on the mastery of modern medical technology which might also measure the professional quality of a physician's care. His tone suggested that it was the responsibility of the properly professional physician to arrest the public's slide into narcotic addiction, but in 1900 this line of thought was no longer new. It had been plainly discernible as early as 1877, when one doctor claimed "that nearly all the cases of opium inebriety are produced by its medicinal use, and most commonly through the prescription of physicians." He was emphatic, declaring that "during a practice of twenty-four years, I have never known a single instance which did not thus originate." [12] The author of an 1880 article for the *Chicago Medical Review* used a familiar metaphor when he declared that "the truth must be confessed, that the greater number of men and women who are now completely enslaved to the different preparations of opium, received their first dose from members of our profession." [13]

Witherspoon's AMA oration offers evidence of the claim's persistence into the first years of the twentieth century, but this was hardly the end of it. In 1913 a physician writing in the *Pennsylvania Medical Journal* explained that he wished to bring his colleagues "face to face with the ugly fact that perhaps the majority of the morphinists in this country today were first prescribed their drug by a physician." He further worried about the technological means of the drug's delivery, arguing that "we find patients who have had given into their own hands the hypodermic needle. The use of the needle practically always insures the formation of the habit." [14] In 1917, Dr. Francis X. Dercum wrote in the *Pennsylvania Medical Journal* that physicians continued to bear "the great responsibility involved in the abuse of morphin." He lamented his perception that "some physicians are altogether too ready with the use of the hypodermic syringe." [15] But in 1914, medical researchers Archibald Church and Frederick Peterson offered what was among the strongest amplifications of these fears, writing that "it is a sad commentary on the heedlessness of some medical men, but the family physician is responsible in almost every case of development of the morphin habit and its far-reaching consequences. It should be looked upon as a sin to give a dose of morphin for insomnia or for any pain . . . which is other than extremely severe and transient." [16] The notion of a professional "sin" helps us to recapture the urgency that some medical writers assigned to what they described as the unacceptable prescription practices of their colleagues. Deviance from a set of broadly agreeable, standardized prescription practices—from the proposed norms of a professionalizing community—appeared in this passage as a measure of the apostasy of practitioners who deviated from the gospel of narcotic responsibility. It offers a particularly resonant echo of the frequent indictment of "some medical men" in the spread of addiction.

Witherspoon's AMA oration thus offers a convenient locus for several crucial themes in the rhetoric of medical professionalization that we find at work in the construction of the addict and of addiction at the turn of the century. First, while acknowledging the drug's therapeutic value, he warned that its potential for medical misuse was great and that physicians were often to blame for the growing prevalence of addiction. Second, by blaming only some physicians, his logic suggested that proper prescription practices might serve as a marker of professional aptitude—professional exclusivity and cohesion might be fostered by stigmatizing physicians who failed to meet a new narcotic standard. Finally, Witherspoon staked a claim for professional ownership of the esoteric knowledge of narcotic therapeutics. He felt that physicians often compounded their mistakes by sharing their pharmacological knowledge with their patients. By dispensing "the unnecessary and hurtful information too often given the laity of [the drug's] seductive influence on human beings," the physician contributed to the habit's spread.[17] He thus suggested that physicians take exclusive possession of their knowledge—a key marker of any professionalized occupation. These themes were repeated over and over, both before and after Witherspoon's oration. Taken together their inevitable conclusion was that responsible physicians must come to grips with and master this new form of technology in order to meet the demands and reap the rewards implied by the term "professional." By the same token, such themes implied that proper medical professionalization, especially if doctors were empowered to act with authority, might help to solve the paradigmatically modern challenges signified by narcotic addiction.

CRIMINALS AND PATIENTS

Doctors continued to blame themselves, each other, and modern conditions for unleashing narcotic addiction upon their middle—and upper-class patients across the first twenty years of the new century.[18] But many physicians paired the description of what they envisioned as a victimized middle-class addict with a drug user who became addicted or continued her drug use through channels outside the medical profession and was thus assigned the burden of responsibility for her own condition. These addicts, unlike their respectable counterparts, were not given the sanctuary of a condition *assigned* by their doctors or by the challenge of meeting the demands of changing social conditions. They were instead blamed for becoming addicts through their own *volition*.

In a 1914 study conducted in City Prison, Manhattan, Dr. Perry Lichtenstein cited findings that sit very uncomfortably alongside those discussed above. He wrote that "the number of victims who directly trace their addiction to physicians' prescriptions is very small; I have found but twenty such people out of 1,000."[19] Because so many of the addicts in his sample of prisoners learned to use drugs from sources other than medical ones, Lichtenstein concluded that the information regarding these drugs had spread independently of medical sources. He suggested that these addicts were responsible for their own situation, implying that volitional drug use be added to the list of criminal activities that had already put them behind bars. Contending that the medical doctor needed to protect his knowledge and to keep it from the public, Lichtenstein wrote that "the information given by physicians to patients, that they had been receiving morphine, cocaine, etc., is to be deplored. Patients should be kept in ignorance as to medication." [20]

The significance of Lichtenstein's study lies in its comparison with a contrasting account given by Dr. Alexander Lambert only one year before, in 1913. The powerful and influential Lambert described in the *Journal of the American Medical Association (JAMA)* "the striking fact that nearly 80 percent of those addicted to the use of morphine have acquired their habit through legitimate prescribing by their physicians or by self-medication." [21] At the time, Lambert was engaged in promoting Charles B. Towns's addiction remedy, and most of the addicts in his sample had come to him for a cure. Lambert therefore referred to those who, at least implicitly, acknowledged the physician's authority and trusted in his power to make them well—people who approached the physician in the role of *patient*. It is to these people that Lambert's assertion of medical responsibility applied. They had, by this logic, contracted the habit through the ministrations of a physician and were therefore free from personal responsibility for their condition. But, as Lichtenstein's study made clear, these were not the people in jail, where only "twenty . . . out of 1,000" could trace their habit to the family doctor.

The juxtaposition of these two studies, which are representative of the poles of early twentieth-century medical thought on the makeup of the addict population, illustrates the way that the Harrison Act would reflect and enhance these doctors' findings, dividing the control of the addict population between medical and penal authorities. Addicts who came to their condition at the hands of a doctor—in other words, patients—were considered to be proper subjects of medical rather than penal attention, whereas those who failed to acknowledge the authority of the physician—those who came to their condition by their own doing—would be regarded as criminals. This assignment of differing positions within the addict population follows what I have described as a contrast between the juridical and the volitional elements that constitute the concept of addiction. It shows the way in which drug use by people who were unable or uninterested in receiving professional medical attention could be classified as criminal, while defining a proper patient by her willingness to submit to the authority of her doctor. We see here a construction of narcotic addiction whose implied remedy required both classes of addicts to hand over their independence to powerful social institutions. Professional medicine might take responsibility for those who were willing to assume the role of patient—thereby proving their membership in the better, juridical class—while the correctional system lay in wait for the recalcitrant, unmanageable criminals of the volitional class.

Dr. Hamilton Wright's Report to the International Opium Commission (1910)

Alongside this medical debate, events arising in the distant Philippine Islands helped to push federal lawmakers toward antinarcotic legislation. When the United States seized the Philippines at the conclusion of the Spanish-American War—an act that was itself an important marker of modern historical change—it also acquired responsibility for a sizable population whose reported opium use had concerned Western missionaries for years. To deal with those concerns, the United States encouraged other world powers to participate in the first International Opium Conference, which was held in Shanghai in 1909. Because the members of the U.S. Opium Commission, which operated under the authority of the State Department, hoped to encourage the other nations of the world to regulate narcotics more aggressively, they were embarrassed at discovering that the United States also lacked such legislation.[22]

Before the 1909 meeting in Shanghai, Congress hurriedly passed the Opium Exclusion Act, which banned the importation of smoking opium into the United States. Crude opium, on the other hand, which was refined into its various medical derivatives by powerful American pharmaceutical companies, was not so regulated, and neither was cocaine.[23] Further, there was no regulation of the interstate shipment of narcotics, which made it impossible to trace the drugs to their sources if they had been carried across state borders and rendered local narcotic control unenforceable. By basing their efforts on the federal government's constitutionally assigned revenue-collecting powers—that is, on the power of taxation—and on the regulation of interstate trade, proponents of antinarcotic legislation avoided the questions of individual and states' rights that were broached by any attempt at the direct control of drug sales and use. The regulation of the interstate narcotic trade through a taxation measure, with the ultimate aim of reducing consumption, thus became an important issue at the State Department, offering its proponents an institutional base of support for their domestic legislative agenda.

As I explained in chapter 2, Dr. Hamilton Wright led the State Department's efforts to secure federal anti-addiction legislation, and his 1910 report, which detailed for Congress the U.S. Opium Commission's goals and tactics, is an important text for understanding the medicolegal aspects of the discourse of addiction. Because a perceived opium problem became a matter of government concern after the U.S. invasion of the Philippines, his report included a review of government policy in the islands. Soon after the islands' seizure, he explained, it became clear that "the vice of opium smoking was spreading rapidly [from the Chinese] to the native Philippine population, with the result that whole communities were becoming impoverished and rendered unfit for any part in the life of the islands."[24] Whether or not the presence of a Chinese ethnic minority in the Philippines had actually corrupted the islanders is beside the point. What matters is the way that the image operated in a congressional document produced in 1910 in Washington, D.C. As Wright reminded the congressmen, the press had been full of stories detailing a drug problem in the United States for the past forty years.[25] We have already seen that a great deal of that publicity had to do with Orientalist images of racial degradation at the hands of the Chinese. Wright's mobilization of that racial imagery in his description of the Philippine opium problem both reflected and reinforced that broader domestic context.

Wright's report also provided a sketch of the commission's supporters in the administration, making clear the source of the president's interest in the commission and in antinarcotic legislation more generally. Wright argued that American unease over Filipino opium use was a "continuation of our pronounced anti opium policy . . . as developed by President Taft when governor-general" of the Philippines. Secretary of State Hay's "sympathetic attitude" matched the president's concern, and thus the formation of the International Opium Commission became the responsibility of Secretary of War Elihu Root.[26] Federal antinarcotic legislation thus began as a foreign policy initiative, a consequence of the occupation of the Philippines and of the Shanghai Opium Conference. Perhaps this helps to explain some of the militarist rhetoric that remains a part of the discourse of addiction, but at the very least, it helped to define narcotic use as a foreign threat.[27] State Department involvement in domestic antinarcotic legislation further helped to reinforce much of the Orientalism that typified the discourse of addiction because it helped to sketch the problem not only as a menace borne by aliens but also as one that required fed-eral mobilization to combat it.

The commissioners expanded their investigation, according to Wright, when they discovered that "the opium problem was not confined to the Far East." He told Congress that "through the misuse of morphine and other opium preparations, several of the large western countries, including the United States, had become contaminated." The commission therefore decided, "on the suggestion of this Government," that it would consider "the opium problem, in all of its moral, economic, scientific, and political aspects, not only as seen in the Far East but also in the home territories of those participating." [28] This ration-ale explained the State Department's interest in domestic narcotic regulation for countries outside of Asia, including the United States.

Wright then moved to an explanation of the domestic situation. As we saw in chapter 2, he emphasized the novelty of the problem. By echoing and ampli-fying the terms that addiction writers had used since the 1870s, Wright reinforced the perceived modernity of the drug threat. He argued that the con-sequences of increased narcotic medication after the Civil War were staggering. Citing his own investigation of the drug trades, Wright reported "that from 70 to 80 per cent of the crude or medicinal opium imported into the United States is manufactured into morphia and that at least 75 per cent of such morphia is used by habitués." Wright thus warned the congressmen about a growing pop-ulation of habitual drug users, supplied by an industry whose primary market was found in meeting their demands. He summed up several factors, especially ignorance of the problem and the disregard of its consequences, when he lamented that the country had been brought "to the position where it may be accused, on some basis of fact, of being an opium-consuming country." [29]

Wright elaborated, explaining that "in ever-increasing proportion our sev-eral States have for fifty years, from lack of interstate aid, been reproducing within themselves the opium problem as it appeared until quite recently in China." He explained his comparison of the United States with China, focusing particularly on what he described as their interconnectedness with other states and nations: "It may be said in regard to the traffic in habit-forming drugs that each State in the Union in its relation to other States is much in the position that China found herself in her relations with opium producing and trafficking countries; for, historically and otherwise, it had been demonstrated that China could not control her internal production and abuse of opium without a large measure of interstate or international assistance." [30] Wright thus argued that China's interconnectedness with the rest of the world and inability to control the relations between the states within its borders contributed to China's status as an opium-consuming nation. He maintained that the United States was in a comparable condition, and thus he sought federal antinarcotic legislation, at least partly, as a way to monitor and control the effects of interconnectedness, especially its alleged tendency to produce and exacerbate a drug threat.

Wright went into greater detail in his description of what it was to be "like" China by opening a discussion of what it was like to be Chinese, thus turning to familiar racial imagery to explain the effects of narcotic addiction in the United States. He compared the influence of opium use on the American and the Chinese populations, writing that "opium smoking with the Chinese is a social, regular, and open custom. With Americans it is often social, seldom open and not regular, those of our people who indulge in it being largely of the outlaw classes, or others with irregular incomes and opportunities." [31] By this, Wright seems to have meant merely that Chinese classes other than the criminal commonly smoked opium, but his comparison of what was "open and regular" for each community led him to a position similar to that contained in William Rosser Cobbe's *Doctor Judas*, suggesting that what was normal for one was degradation for another. Wright contended that the "great majority of the Chinese residents in the United States" were "openly smokers" but that even they "recognized the moral and economic effects of the habit of opium smoking; that it emasculated and depraved them, and in the majority of cases led to economic disaster." [32] He tried to motivate the congressmen with many familiar turns of phrase, invoking threats to economic productivity and masculine autonomy (users were "emasculated") in conjunction with assertions of the opium smoker's general depravity. Wright's opinion of what was "regular and open" for the Chinese was clear. A condition of emasculated depravity, typified by economic ineptitude, was the regular and open mode of living for the Chinese, but it signaled degradation for Americans. Further, by pandering to fears of miscegenation, Wright added some of the contemporary gender clichés that I explored in the last chapter to the racial imagery of his report. He mobilized images of feminine vulnerability when he wrote that "one of the most unfortunate phases of the habit of opium smoking in this country is the large number of women who have become involved and were living as common law wives of or cohabiting with Chinese in the Chinatowns of our various cities." [33]

Wright hoped to convince Congress that this allegedly Chinese condition, that is, narcotic addiction—a consequence of the Chinese-associated practice of opium smoking—was spreading to the American population. As we have seen, he believed that the comparison of population and consumption figures showed "beyond a doubt the extension of the habit of opium smoking from the Chinese to Americans."[34] When he cited those statistics, he found that "for the decade 1880–1890 the percent increase in our total Chinese population was but 4 . . . , while the percent increase in the importation of smoking opium was 76.4." He concluded that this "marks the more active spread of the habit of opium smoking from our Chinese to our White and Negro population," and he used terms that implied the need for a medical response to the problem: "Primary infection was from the Chinese, but it soon spread from white to white and from black to black."[35]

Besides his use of medical metaphor in this passage, Wright also shifted the emphasis of his discussion from the relationship between the white and the Chinese to that between the white and the black populations. Though he worried about an increase of opium use in the African American population, his greater concern was with the spread of the use of cocaine.[36] He began his discussion of cocaine with a general warning to the committee: "In addition to the steady growth of the misuse of opium, an unforeseen and almost strictly American vice had sprung into existence during the last twenty years, adding its terrors to the drug problem which confronts the American people today. This has been brought about by the unrestricted importation of coca leaves and the unregulated manufacture and distribution of cocaine, a substance of no real use whatever except in the hands of the surgeon."[37] Wright thus paired what he described as a peculiarly American phase of the drug threat with the "oriental" menace of opium. He explained that "15,000 or 20,000 ounces of this drug are sufficient to satisfy the demands of surgery in the United States" but lamented that "to-day there are manufactured at least 150,000 ounces of this drug, the larger part of which is put to improper uses," adding that cocaine "is more appalling in its effects that any other habit-forming drug used in the United States." Wright exploited the fears of many congressmen when he explained *who* was putting the drug to improper use and how they were doing it. He began his argument by making clear "the unanimous opinion of every state and municipal body . . . that the misuse of cocaine is a direct incentive to crime, that it is perhaps of all factors a singular one in augmenting the criminal ranks." What was worse, he claimed, was that cocaine did not make ordinary criminals but rather produced a more menacing variety: "The habitual use of it temporarily raises the power of a criminal to a point where in resisting arrest there is no hesitation to murder."[38]

Wright claimed that this cocaine-related crime problem was principally regional and racially based. He thus carried a message that we encountered in

chapter 3 into the Capitol, writing that "it has been stated on very high authority that the use of cocaine by the Negroes of the South is one of the most elusive
and troublesome questions which confront the enforcement of the law in most
of the Southern States." [39] Particularly troubling for Wright was how "the cocaine vice, the most serious that has to be dealt with, has proved to be a creator
of criminals and unusual forms of violence, and it has been a potent incentive in
driving the humbler Negroes all over the country to abnormal crimes." [40]
Wright used an argument that was underwritten by older, pro-slavery, and
minstrel show stereotypes of African Americans as lazy and shiftless in order to
provide evidence of the interstate trade in cocaine. He wrote that "the use of cocaine among the lower order of working Negroes is quite common," but, as he
elaborated, "this class of Negro is not willing, as a rule, to go to much trouble or
send to any distance for anything, and for this reason, where he is known to
have become debauched by cocaine, it is certain that the drug has been brought
directly to him from New York and the Northern States where it is manufactured." [41]

Wright's primary concern, however, was that cocaine threatened bourgeois
whites. He warned the congressmen that cocaine had also "exhibited a strong
tendency to spread, corrupt, and ruin many who belonged to the higher ranks
of society" and that once cocaine had crept into those higher social ranks, "it
converts the useful, orderly citizen who has become a habitué into a dangerous
character. It wrecks him individually and jeopardizes the position of all who depend on him, and in the end drives him to crime." [42] Wright quite clearly felt that
the menace of drug use for respectable whites was one of degradation. He wrote
of a substance with the power to transform its victim from the status of
respectable bourgeois into a "dangerous character." The upper-class victim
would be "wrecked" and "driven" into crime because of drug use.

As was the case with opium, Wright suggested that cocaine was especially
threatening to the preservation of feminine purity. He claimed that he had "absolutely trustworthy information" that cocaine was "used by those concerned in
the white-slave traffic to corrupt young girls, and that when the habit of using
the drug has been established it is but a short time before the latter fall to the
ranks of prostitution." [43] Again we see the threat of degradation, marked here in
terms of the corruption of female sexual agency. As I noted in chapter 3, such
arguments served to situate antinarcotic rhetoric within a discourse of domestic sentimentality, suggesting that narcotics threatened both the virtuous center of the family as well as the family's ability to reproduce itself.

Wright summarized the threat held by the unregulated use of cocaine and began to introduce his suggestions for its containment, writing that "the misuse of cocaine is undoubtedly an American habit, the most threatening of the drug habits that has ever appeared in this country, and there is no uncertain feeling in every State and municipality of the country that the habit will continue to spread unless there is some coordination of state laws and federal control of the manufacture and interstate commerce in the drug by the Federal Government." Further, Wright equated congressional support of interstate narcotic regulation with a stand against the drug-borne threat of violent miscegenation, which recalls the racial logic explored in the previous chapter. He wrote that the state antinarcotic laws "can not be made really effective until there is interstate control of the traffic. It has been authoritatively stated that cocaine is often the direct incentive to the crime of rape by the Negroes of the South and other sections of the country." [44]

Wright thus called for the adoption of an enforceable set of uniform federal narcotics laws so as to solve the problems associated with unregulated drug use. He found the various state pharmacy laws defective, "in that habit forming drugs may be bought without the prescription of a physician." [45] By insisting that narcotic drugs be available only by prescription, Wright championed a cause that was fundamental to early twentieth-century narcotics reform, but he also repeated an important demand of the medical professionalizers, who advocated stronger professional control of the access to all drugs. [46] Wright, who was himself a physician, accordingly suggested that a suitably empowered medical profession could solve the problems of addiction. Such professional empowerment was also the AMA's goal, and we thus begin to understand how its objectives harmonized with the aims of those who sought stricter regulation of narcotics. Wright's desire to combat the threat of addiction by strengthening the medical profession may seem contradictory, considering that he and many others felt that "the careless prescribing of physicians" was a major cause of addiction. [47] But he explained that unscrupulous pharmacists evaded state laws, as did "dishonorable physicians, dentists, or veterinarians, who regard their license to practice as a license to prescribe large quantities of these drugs for illicit use." [48] Wright echoed the professional discourse by suggesting that the control of narcotics be placed more firmly into the hands of "honorable" physicians while removing it from those whose prescription practices marked them as dishonorable, as inadequate to the challenges of modern medicine.

Calls for legislation that required a physician's prescription for narcotics enhanced the authority of professional medicine in three ways. First, such regulations amplified and endorsed the medical profession's claims of competence by handing it the task of solving what various writers had so strongly portrayed as a menacing condition that typified its age of appearance. Second, calls for federal legislation also offered a means for the profession to tighten its ranks, policing itself by weeding out the "dishonorable physicians" who failed to comply with federal standards of narcotic prescription. Wright's call for extensive record keeping on the part of government-registered wholesalers, doctors, and pharmacists might aid such a process. Such records would, in theory, forge a paper chain from production to consumption, thus enabling the investigation and enforcement of new, medicolegally authorized (and thus "honorable") federal prescription practices. Finally, tightening the prescription laws would increase the public's dependence on professional medicine. Wright complained that "many state laws are defective in that they do not make illegal possession of habit-forming drugs evidence for conviction."[49] By suggesting that simple, unauthorized possession might serve as sufficient proof of criminal wrongdoing, Wright offered a means to discipline the public, ensuring that the medical profession would hold the only legitimate right of access to the medications that many people wanted and needed.

Wright's testimony thus described both a condition—addiction—and a cure—professional control—that were thoroughly embedded in the modern cultural context which they both exemplified and helped to produce. By placing control of what was so often portrayed as a threatening product of modern technology more firmly into the hands of professional physicians, backed by the power of the federal government, Wright and other drug control advocates helped to boost the status and expand the power of professional medicine. By demanding legislation to this end, they asked for legal endorsement of that expanded power.

THE MENACE OF ADDICTION: HEARINGS BEFORE THE HOUSE COMMITTEE ON WAYS AND MEANS

Based largely on Wright's insights, the State Department produced the 1910 Foster Bill, which was the first federal attempt to regulate interstate trade in narcotics. Vermont representative David Foster, chairman of the House Committee on Foreign Affairs, introduced the bill to Congress on April 30, 1910.[50] It was proposed as a tax bill—which explains why the hearings were held before the Ways and Means Committee—and it would require all dealers in narcotics to register and pay a fee to the government for the maintenance of that

registration. It also required extensive record keeping on every narcotic transaction. Wright appeared before Ways and Means on May 31, 1910, to support
the bill and to reemphasize what he had written in the report that I discussed
above. The committee also heard the testimony of other concerned parties, including cure doctors, medical experts, and members of the (broadly defined)
pharmaceutical industry on two dates, December 14, 1910, and January 11,
1911.

Dr. Christopher Koch, vice president of the State Pharmaceutical Examining Board of Pennsylvania and chairman of the Legislative Committee of the
Philadelphia Association of Retail Druggists, appeared on December 14 to support the Foster Bill. He immediately informed the committee that he had recently presided over a "crusade, particularly in the city of Philadelphia, to wipe
out the illegal sale of cocaine and morphine" and that he was "entirely in accord
with Dr. Hamilton Wright." He declared that "the result of my investigation
has proved absolutely the facts which he brings forth in his report."[51] He then
proceeded to discuss many of Wright's concerns, while adding his own particularly colorful spin.

He began with a general discussion of the drug problem and then immediately associated drug taking with the criminal population. He claimed that "45
to 48 per cent of all criminals are dopes. That is almost 50 per cent." But especially important was that he paired his condemnation of the criminal drug users
with an apology for the more respectable user. He asserted his belief that "the
professional people who use these drugs use them when they are run down and
have a lot of work to do."[52] Echoing much of what we have read regarding middle-class drug use, Koch divided the addict population into respectable and disreputable categories—into groups of patients and of criminals. This distinction
followed the double meaning of addiction and served to excuse bourgeois drug
use by blaming it on modern social and economic conditions. It simultaneously
preserved the notion of moral responsibility and its attendant guilt for those
who found themselves in a less privileged position within that modern technological and economic world. The former group was protected by their
status as patients, whereas the latter was left vulnerable to charges of criminal
culpability.

Koch made clear to which others he referred when he moved from more abstract notions of crime and innocence to explicit racial imagery and fears of
miscegenation. He told the committee that "in the Chinatown in the city of
Philadelphia there are enormous quantities of opium consumed, and it is quite
common, gentlemen, for these Chinese or 'Chinks,' as they are called to have as

a concubine a white woman. There is one particular house where I would say there are 20 white women living with Chinamen as their common-law wives. A great many of the girls are girls of family, and the history of some is very pathetic." [53] In this passage, Koch entered much of what we have seen in the operation of the discourse of addiction into the congressional record. In a description of the way that drug use menaced middle-class identity ("girls of family") at its most vulnerable, feminine point, he mobilized images of a corrupt yet seductive racial otherness—a seduction that culminated in miscegenation and its implied racial degradation.

Koch soon turned his attention to cocaine. In a familiar pattern, he asserted the drug's modernity at the same time that he explained its peculiarly American popularity. Stating that "it was discovered about 20 years ago and the abuse of it started almost as early as its discovery," Koch argued that "it is essentially an American vice . . . they do not have it in foreign countries." [54] In what was also an unequivocal description of the threat of degradation, Koch found little legitimate use for the drug, claiming that "it has been estimated that 90 per cent or 135,000 ounces of cocaine goes to make 'fiends' out of human beings." [55]

But, as was the case in his discussion of opium, Koch reserved a special place in his testimony for racial others. He found that "a great many of the crimes that are committed in Pennsylvania . . . are directly traced to cocaine" and stated that "the colored population in Philadelphia is full of it, or was." He claimed that "the colored people seem to have a weakness for it." Among the problems that it produced was a tendency to get above one's social position. He felt that "persons under the influence of it believe they are millionaires" and, worse, that "they have no regard for right or wrong." Koch also repeated the logic of the lynch mob when he told the congressmen that "they would just as leave rape a woman as anything else and a great many of the southern rape cases have been traced to cocaine." He further contended that this problem was not only to be found in Philadelphia but that "the colored race in the South . . . is very much perverted by cocaine." [56]

He delivered what was perhaps his most colorful testimony when he described a police raid in Philadelphia. In a flurry of racialized and gendered illustrations of cocaine's menace to society, Koch explained that "we served a warrant on a little bit of a Negro wench who weighed less than 100 pounds. The detective read the warrant and she said: 'All right, I will go along with you.' She was lying in bed, with her clothes on, and she got out of bed, as he thought, and in getting she pulled this knife from under the pillow. She was just about to stab him in his groin, and if it had not been that there were two of them she would have stuck it in him. She was 'junked up' with 'coke.' There was a tussle. She bit one detective on the thumb and the other one she bit on the arm, right through his clothes."[57] Cocaine thus emancipated the physically powerful, slashing, biting, castrating beast that was otherwise caged within this "little bit of a Negro wench." Koch claimed that she lay in wait for the officer and, seizing her chance, went straight for his groin with her knife, attempting a literal emasculation of a man who, as a city detective, embodied municipal authority. In his testimony Koch drew upon racist fantasies of a latent African American racial viciousness, characterized by deception and sexual violence. He simultaneously reinforced those fears by spinning lurid tales of the modern pharmacological liberation of those same violent passions.

Koch also made clear to the congressmen that the threat held by cocaine was "not confined to the colored race entirely." He argued that "lots of white people use it, too. I am sorry to say that lots of professional people use it—people who ought to know better. . . . I mean lawyers, physicians—physicians principally—and some pharmacists and trained nurses."[58] As I pointed out above, Koch had already excused these people from the moral responsibility for their actions, contending that they took the drug in order to meet the challenges of their professional responsibilities. It was, however, nonetheless crucial to emphasize the narcotic habit as a threat to white, bourgeois Americans in order to spur congressional action.

Koch believed that antinarcotic legislation could have a significant effect in controlling the problems that he described. He shifted to a compassionate tone, pointing out that "the poor unfortunate 'dope fiend' is more sinned against than sinning. Had the law provided sufficient safeguards around the sale and distribution of these drugs, he would never have acquired such a habit." He believed that Congress should "make every man that handles these drugs responsible for his actions so that we have a record of the transaction from time of manufacture till it reaches the consumer."[59] Finding this record-keeping feature of the Foster Bill to be particularly useful, Koch noted that "this is a secret and a vile habit, and that the only way to eradicate it is to eliminate the secrecy. There is no better way of eliminating the secrecy than by turning on the limelight."[60] Koch believed that the Foster Bill would do just that.

Also appearing before the committee in support of the bill was Charles B. Towns, representing the Charles B. Towns Hospital at 119 West Eighty-first Street, New York City.[61] Much of his testimony only recapitulated the views he held that were discussed in the last chapter; but here its significance lies in the way that it entered what was both an esoteric professional debate and a sensational popular discourse into the legislative machinery of the United States Congress. In an amusing exchange, Congressman Boutell asked Towns if his institution was "one of the Keeley hospitals," thus confusing him with gold-cure doctor Leslie E. Keeley. Towns bristled, answering, "No, sir. This is Towns.' I have no secret methods or anything like that at all." [62] Towns thus sought to distance himself and his remedy from Keeley, but ironically it was Dr. Keeley, not the entrepreneur Towns, who held a medical degree. As we saw in chapter 2, however, Keeley was held in contempt by much of the medical mainstream, which based part of its claim to scientific legitimacy on the rejection of specific nostrums such as Keeley's gold cure, which was derived from a secret formula and advertised directly to the public. As Samuel Hopkins Adams wrote in his AMA-endorsed "Great American Fraud" series of 1905, "Any physician who advertises a positive cure for any disease, who issues nostrum testimonials, who sells his services to a secret remedy, or who diagnoses and treats by mail patients he has never seen, is a quack." [63] Keeley was guilty on all counts. Towns, on the other hand, allied himself with the advancing professional mainstream, mostly through the influence of his patron, Dr. Alexander Lambert, who published the formula for Towns's cure in the professional press. [64] Congressman Boutell's confusion, to Towns's evident displeasure, demonstrated the resilience of Keeley's influence, even though the doctor had been dead for ten years. Towns was determined not to be associated with Keeley, despite the latter's status as a physician, in an attempt to legitimate the his own cure by associating it with the growing power of professional medicine, but perhaps more significant, he established that legitimacy through an alliance with one segment of the medical profession against what was, by 1910, an older constituency whose star was fading.

This exchange lasted for only a few seconds, but in that instant the speakers struck a note that registered well beyond its brief duration. In it, we can distinguish once again how the discourse of addiction might help to draw distinctions within the medical ranks. Keeley was a licensed physician who held a degree from a legitimate, mid-nineteenth-century medical college, but changing notions of educational legitimacy and the control of licensing were controversial topics at the turn of the twentieth century. Like many others, Keeley believed strongly in the professional control of narcotic medication and addiction treatment, but he fell afoul of the mainstream in his insistence on the secrecy of his cure, in his advertising practices, and in the ornate, sentimental language of his writing. He thus represented a form of medical practice that the more "scientific" professionalizers of the AMA had struggled against for years. In 1910, these latter were well on their way to achieving dominance, and Towns was thus keen to distance himself from the infamous quack and his antiquated methods. Congressman Boutell's question, however, suggests that the lay public was not yet as willing to banish Keeley to the medical scrap heap as were those with whom Towns sought to curry favor.

These themes will reemerge in this book. As for Towns, having cleared up any confusion about his identity, he continued his testimony. His first goal as a witness was to describe what he saw as the remarkable potency of the narcotics themselves. Towns testified that a person given "an eighth of a grain of morphine twice a day over a period of three weeks . . . could not go without that drug." Elaborating, he claimed that "it would make no difference what his character was, how strong he was, or who he was; he would be in the grasp of that drug." [65] Such embellishment served to reinforce notions of the drug as a menace and helped to remind the congressmen, amid the pervasive racial imagery, that the threat of addiction extended across race, class, and gender boundaries. Towns was adamant about the power of the drug, claiming that "any drug that contains the slightest bit of opium in any form, . . . if that drug is taken over a given time, it makes no difference what the dose is, the man will become absolutely addicted to it." [66] As the proprietor of an addiction-cure hospital, Towns may have had his own interests in mind when he argued that "once a patient becomes addicted to the use of opium or morphine, or any of these alkaloids, it is absolutely impossible for that man to rid himself of that habit. No amount of will power on earth can relieve him of that habit." [67] His self-serving argument both emphasized the threat of addiction and also valorized his cure. Towns's *legal* remedy for what both the press and the expert witnesses described to the congressmen as a growing drug problem was to legislate the professional control of narcotics—in other words, to put them exclusively in the hands of the medical profession. He followed the prevailing political direction of the hearings, contending that "doctors should be made absolutely and wholly responsible for the habit-forming drugs." [68] By this he meant that narcotics should never be dispensed without the prescription of a licensed medical professional.

Towns left the stand after making clear the different categories of addicts for the committee. He reiterated the addiction concept's double meaning when he explained that the source of addiction "depends largely on the classes." He defined those addicts who lived "in the tenderloin of New York as an element that, through dissipation, has become addicted to the use of the drug." He placed this group beside the "thousands who have acquired the habit through the first ad-

ministration by a physician."[69] Once again we see that Towns's legal solution—
that is, medical prescription—would define the latter class as patients while
placing the former outside the law. He thus divided the addict population into
groups of criminals and patients. His patron, Dr. Alexander Lambert, followed
Towns, taking the stand briefly and confirming Towns's division of the addict
population.[70]

The largest group heard before the committee were the drug-manufactur-
ing and -retailing interests, which appeared on January 11, 1911. Like medical
practice, pharmacy was in the midst of a professionalization struggle during
the early twentieth century. The first attempts at professional pharmaceutical
organization had begun in the 1820s, but pharmacy, which was typified by the
sometimes competing interests of pharmacists and pharmacy owners, was even
less organized than was medical practice. As such, the history of pharmacy offers evidence of "a profession that has not been as effectively organized and uni-
fied as analogous professions such as dentistry, law, and medicine," according to
the historian Glenn Sonnedecker, who shows, however, that pharmacy was not
disorganized for the lack of trying.[71] The American Pharmaceutical Association (APhA) was founded in 1852 and, especially after the 1880s, tried to model
itself after the AMA. It spawned several "daughter" organizations, including
the National Association of Retail Druggists (1883), which represented the
business interests of the pharmaceutical profession. Professional pharmacy has
a long and complex history with its own issues and divisions, but its champions
in the APhA shared the AMA's desire to offer membership only to those who
were scientifically trained and to lose the taint of "quackery" by refusing to co-
operate with the nostrum sellers—something that posed a financial threat to
many pharmacists, whose livelihoods often came from marketing dubious ton-
ics and miracle cures. As its constitution made clear, however, the APhA also
sought to "restrict the dispensing and sale of medicines to regularly educated
druggists and apothecaries."[72] Though physicians and pharmacists often accused one another of professional turf violations, they faced related challenges
and held similar goals in terms of professionalization itself. It should therefore not be surprising that, like the physicians, the language of modern professionalization colored the pharmacists' testimony before the Ways and Means
Committee.

Committee chairman Payne explained that the committee was interested in
regulating the sale of narcotics in "the least burdensome manner to make the
law effective," which was why the representatives of the drug trades were asked
to comment.[73] The witnesses generally opposed the bill because they found its

extensive record-keeping requirements far too cumbersome for the average tradesman to heed. But even though the witnesses opposed the Foster Bill's means, we should be clear that its end—the regulation of narcotic use—went almost entirely unopposed. An interesting exception to this trend was Dr. William Muir, representing the New York Pharmaceutical Society. He testified that "we admit there is wrong comes from good things. We admit there are a good many people killed by automobiles; but there is a good deal of pleasure gotten from them; and this idea of stamping this out and killing it is wrong, because you can not stamp it out with any such means as this." He thus compared the dangers of other modern technological products to those held by narcotic drugs and concluded that their benefits outweighed their costs. Muir reminded the committee to "look at the remedial effect of opium to relieve pain; look at the good side. It is wonderful what it has done for pain, to relieve it. Every doctor has it in his saddlebags or his hand bag. Every one of them carries [it] in his pocket with a hypodermic."[74] Muir's testimony was in line with the many medical figures who commented on the positive aspects of narcotic medication, but his stronger statement and consequent ambivalence about the bill's goals stood out against the general tone of the hearings..

More typical of the industry response was that of Albert Plaut, representing Lehn and Fink of New York City, who supported the bill's goals and agreed with the division of users into two different classes when he stated that "half [of all drug habits] in my opinion, are caused by the careless prescribing of regular physicians, who prescribe, in this country particularly, morphine for every ache and pain." But he quickly added that "of course a very large number of drug fiends acquire the habit from association, from propinquity to other users."[75]

William J. Schieffelin, president of the National Wholesale Druggists' Association, appeared in order to declare his organization's support of the principle of the bill and further followed the tendency to divide addicts into two different classes, stating that "the drug trade wants to handle these things with clean hands, and only sell them for legitimate medicinal purposes, and have nothing to do with supplying the victims of the habit."[76] Likewise, Mr. William S. Richardson, who represented the National Association of Retail Druggists, appeared to state his group's desire to "confine [the use of narcotics] to strictly medicinal purposes."[77] Both these men differentiated between what they saw as the legitimate practice of medicine and the simple maintenance of addicts, engaging a debate that would grow in prominence over the course of the decade. They also implied that a more effectively professionalized drug trade could help to meet the challenges of addiction.

Finally, Mr. Donald McKesson appeared, representing wholesale druggists McKesson & Robbins of New York City. He discussed the significance of confining the drug to professional practice more directly than any other witness when he informed the congressmen that "in all European countries retail and wholesale druggists are professional men, the same as lawyers and doctors. They are men of high standing, and are recognized under the law, and their social standing is high, and the drug business is a business that requires just as high an education as any other profession, and is the poorest paid for the requirements of it; and I think this would be an opportunity for the retailer to appear in his proper light, and for that reason, as well as for the reason of elimination of habit-forming drugs, I think this is a very good measure, provided it is put into a practical form."[78] McKesson sensed that confining the access to narcotics to what all of the witnesses defined as legitimate medical channels held huge benefits for the status of professional medical practitioners, in this case, wholesale druggists and professional pharmacists. The legal recognition of their professional expertise to control such a dangerous technological product offered McKesson and others who shared his opinion an official stamp of approval as well as an enforceable legal claim to control both the potentially profitable narcotic product and the socially problematic addicted population. That most of the medical profession would soon reject this often difficult clientele is beside the point. McKesson sensed that professional prestige and authority might derive from federal narcotic legislation, which he clearly understood as the federal endorsement of a particular professional community's claims to special expertise.

Near the close of the proceedings, Hamilton Wright returned to the stand and summed up the threat that his bill hoped to counter. He reminded the committee that "seventy-five per cent [of opium] is used in debauchery. The conditions in this country to-day are just as bad as were found in China when the great opium evil was discovered in 1799; and although a large amount of the use of the morphine is confined to the criminal classes and the lower orders of society, it is creeping into the higher circles of society. The cocaine habit is greatly increasing in the South. . . . I have most reliable evidence that the crime of rape has largely been caused by the use of cocaine among the Negroes in the South in the last 10 or 15 years."[79] Wright drove home the linkage of racial difference, crime, and addiction, insisting that the problem was carried both within and without U.S. borders. He further made clear the State Department's demand that professional experts be given the power to control the menace in order to protect the middle and upper classes.

The Foster Bill was soon approved in committee but lingered on the floor of the 1911 lame-duck Congress because of the opposition of the drug trades. When the final session of the Sixty-first Congress ended, the Foster Bill was left on the table, effectively killed by the pharmaceutical companies. Until the powerful drug lobby could be placated, no federal antinarcotic action would be taken.

THE NATIONAL DRUG TRADE CONFERENCE OF 1913 AND THE HARRISON NARCOTIC ACT

Though Congress never passed the Foster Bill, the State Department and Hamilton Wright, because of their commitment to the International Opium Commission, kept up pressure to pass some sort of antinarcotic legislation. Soon after the Foster Bill's defeat, they and a joint committee of the State and Treasury Departments produced a new bill that they hoped would finally pass into law, even though it was clearly descended from the Foster Bill. New York representative Francis Burton Harrison, who was a member of the Ways and Means Committee that heard the testimony on the Foster Bill and recommended its approval, agreed to introduce the new bill and to guide it through the House.

To avoid a repeat of what happened to the earlier bill, drug-control advocates sought to secure the support of the drug trades, the medical profession, and the Internal Revenue Bureau, which would be responsible for the act's enforcement. At the same time, the drug trades, under the leadership of the American Pharmaceutical Association and with the aid of the American Medical Association, sensed that government action was imminent. Their representatives therefore met in Washington, D.C., on January 15, 1913, to make their own suggestions about the shape of antinarcotic legislation. Government officials, mainly Wright and Harrison, and representatives of the pharmaceutical and medical professions thus worked together to formulate legislation that was acceptable to all.

The National Drug Trade Conference (NDTC) was composed of representatives from the APhA, the National Wholesale Druggists' Association, the National Association of Manufacturers of Medicinal Products, the American Association of Pharmaceutical Chemists, the National Association of Retail Druggists, and also the AMA.[80] The conference proceedings provide a broad sample of the opinion of the leading professional medical organizations regarding narcotics legislation just prior to its enactment. Central to that opinion was their stated support of the *principle* of narcotics regulation. As we saw above in their testimony regarding the Foster Bill, the representatives of the drug trades voiced most of the same opinions on the drug threat that we have seen in development throughout the fifty years between 1870 and 1920. Their objections to the legislation lay rather in what they described as the bill's impractical and cumbersome clerical details and the way that the day-to-day operation of their businesses might bog down if the legislation were implemented.[81] James Beal, a pharmacist and lawyer and the editor of the *Journal of the American Pharmaceutical Association* (*JAPhA*), was one of the leading figures in the APhA and also at the conference. In the February 1913 edition of the journal, Beal summed up much of the professional opinion, writing that "all portions of the drug trade . . . are agreed that some Federal legislation is necessary to aid in controlling the traffic in habit-forming drugs, and the objections they have offered to the several Harrison Bills were addressed to details rather than to their substance, i.e., to the methods proposed for carrying the substantive provisions of the law into effect."[82] The participation of the various organizations at the NDTC helped to ensure that the Harrison Act's methods would both reflect and contribute to the growing power and authority of professional medicine in the early twentieth century.

Because the NDTC met only a short time after the failure of the Foster Bill, it is not surprising that most of the same themes emerged in its sessions. Of particular note, however, was the suggestion that more-effective professional organization might help to meet the challenge of regulating a modern, interconnected society. This theme arose at the conference's opening, when a letter was read into the record calling for the national registration of pharmacists to ensure the mutual recognition of the several state pharmacy boards' licensing procedures. Though the conference did not act upon the letter, which was outside its more strictly defined mission of formulating acceptable narcotics legislation, the letter's presence in the record is important. It helps to show that the connection between nationwide professional organization and federal narcotics legislation was a common one in the minds of some members of the drug trades.[83]

This connection was augmented by writers in the various professional journals who likewise demanded uniformity in medical practice and drug legislation. The AMA's M. I. Wilbert, a prominent member of the NDTC, wrote in March 1913 that "to even the cursory students of our American poison and narcotic laws it must be evident that we are . . . suffering from a lack of coordination or uniformity in the requirements of the several states" and that this condition made it "extremely difficult if not altogether impossible to enforce the laws of one state without imposing unnecessary hardships on, or placing a premium on, the ignoring of the existence of the law by the citizens of adjoining states." [84] In June 1913, pharmacist P. M. Lichthardt offered his readers an example of the way that both quackery and the narcotics trade thrived in an interconnected society, writing that "often a physician has reported to me that a patient of his is receiving treatment for a narcotic habit from a so-called doctor in some other state, and upon examining the remedial agent sent we find it to be essentially a solution of morphine or other habit-forming drug." [85] Resorting to railroad imagery, which by 1913 was a venerable image of modern interconnectedness, he wrote of "a little logging train that came into the State of California once a week with this 'dope.' " Lichthardt used these anecdotes to make clear that he was "heartily in favor of some law that would make it a crime to ship narcotics into a State in that way." [86]

The representatives of the drug trades believed that the federal government's role in helping to control what they characterized as a threatening interconnectedness ought to be one of effective information gathering. They believed that successful control required, most importantly, the collection of accurate information about the laws, practices, and obligations of the practitioners who lived in other states. James P. Finnerman wrote in 1913 that the professional organizations themselves were well-equipped to produce this kind of information. He claimed that the first assault on legal inconsistencies "must be made in our national drug organization, and why? Because the most of us have only a limited knowledge of just what is being done in our sister states, and have not the facilities of knowing exactly what the laws are on a given subject in other states. National organizations like the APhA have the facilities for getting this information." Finnerman hoped that the knowledge produced by and within national professional organizations like the APhA might aid in achieving his ultimate goal: "that boards of pharmacy should have full and complete supervision of the handling and sale of drugs." [87] The production of knowledge about drug distribution and use could thus augment the economic and social power of organized pharmacy, a process that would further develop as the public grew more dependent upon a profession whose demand for the exclusive control of drug distribution was based, at least partly, on its claims to competence in confronting the problems of an interconnected society.

Finnerman believed that his goal, the "complete supervision of the handling and sale of drugs," merited legal recognition and support. He finished his article by making two simple points. The first was that "boards of pharmacy should supervise sales of drugs in all stores, and all states should as far as possible have similar pharmacy laws," and the second, that "registered pharmacists only should be allowed to carry on the business." He therefore concluded that "the American Pharmaceutical Association should lend its purse and its influence towards uniform pharmacy laws in the various states."[88] Finnerman hoped to ground professional control of drug distribution in a uniform policy of pharmacist registration, supported by a framework of consistent, interstate pharmaceutical legislation. His article shows how the information-gathering resources of a professional organization might be used to augment and to implement demands for legally backed, professional control of the lucrative drug trade. Information produced in this manner might also be used to register the pharmacists themselves, providing a standard for policing the profession and eliminating those who violated its rules.

This broader, contextual linkage between information production and effective professionalization helps us to make sense of the NDTC's advocacy of the Harrison Act as an information-gathering tool, put in the service of the several states in order to trace and to control the interstate drug traffic. As we have seen, various members of the drug trades believed that the specialized knowledge produced by uniform pharmacy laws such as the Harrison Act might also be employed to regulate the profession. More effective pharmaceutical professionalization might, in turn, support attempts to subdue the modern threat of narcotic addiction. The NDTC thus added its voice to an intellectual context that believed in the authority of professional medicine—both pharmaceutical and practical—hoping to enhance it through a federally mandated, centrally administered gathering/production of specialized medical knowledge.

But here the conference entered dangerous territory. It most certainly did not wish to diminish its painstakingly established professional authority by allowing federal bureaucrats to meddle in its area of expertise—that is, in the prescription, handling and distribution of drugs—but the NDTC representatives sensed that federal narcotic legislation could open precisely that door. At the conclusion of the conference the NDTC resolved "that it is the sense of this Conference that the bill is not intended, and ought not to be intended, to regulate sales to consumers but only to trace narcotic drugs in commerce to the hands of the last distributor, and that the regulation of the sale of such drugs to the consumer in intrastate commerce should be left entirely to state, territorial and other local laws."[89] In other words, the NDTC did not support narcotics legislation as a federal prohibition act targeted at drug sellers and users. Still less did it endorse a police act. While the delegates agreed with popular representations of the addict and addiction, they believed that professional control, enhanced by the expanded production and gathering of specialist knowledge, would be the best response to the threat of narcotic addiction. They hoped that the Harrison Act would enhance their power and prestige through the establishment of a federally implemented, professionally administered information-gathering and registration system. They thus supported narcotics legislation as a way of combating the drug threat through the enhancement of their own professional power.

Drug Laws, Professionalism, and the Ambiguity of the Harrison Act

The support of the Wilson administration, which took office in March 1913, helped to move the Harrison Act through Congress.[90] On June 10, 1913, the NDTC approved a draft of the bill, and on June 26 the Harrison Act passed the House with little debate. Though the bill was held up in the Senate and in conference committees for several months, it finally passed and was signed into law by President Wilson on December 17, 1914.[91] In its final form, the law required the registration of narcotics dealers, who were obliged to keep records of all narcotic transactions, and ordered that they pay a slight tax of one dollar per year for their license. The law further stated that no one would receive narcotic drugs without the prescription of a registered medical doctor. It also declared that any nonregistered person who possessed the drugs without a prescription was presumed to be in violation of the law.

The bill's enforcement, however, remained unclear. While the drug trades believed that the act was primarily to be used for information gathering, Wright and others who envisioned the act as a condemnation of narcotic use itself hoped that it would be interpreted as a prohibition measure.[92] An editorial in the *Journal of the American Medical Association (JAMA)* explained that "following the enactment of any law of importance and especially of any law on a new subject, there is always a period of uncertainty and indefiniteness as to just what the law really means and how its provisions will be applied." The article went on, however, to reiterate the medical profession's general belief that "the law is not intended to, and does not, prevent the sale or distribution of habit-forming drugs for legitimate purposes. Neither does it undertake to limit the judgment of a physician as to the needs of his patient."[93] But what were legitimate purposes? Resolution of the extent of the regulatory and police powers implied by the Harrison Act would require several Supreme Court decisions, something that I take up in the next chapter. In the meantime, we need to be clear about two effects of narcotics legislation.

The first is that it served to enhance the already-growing power of professional medicine, which was evident in the act's legislative endorsement of medical expertise and also in the expansion of its scope. An editorial that appeared in the *Journal of the American Medical Association* of April 10, 1915, reported that "without doubt the law has forced numerous habitués, who otherwise might have been satisfied to continue as such, to apply to physicians and institutions for treatment." The article further claimed that "the increased admissions to these hospitals do not represent an increase in drug addictions; they are simply an objective manifestation of the operation of the Harrison law." Thus the editorial made clear that the act had produced more patients. It fashioned new subjects of institutional scrutiny and directly expanded the scope of professional power into areas formerly resistant to it. "There is no doubt that the large majority of these unfortunates will be freed of their habit," the *JAMA* article stated, with the suggestion that this submission to the legally mandated authority of professional medicine was actually an assertion of individual freedom.[94] Ironically, this freedom would be a consequence of surrendering oneself to the authoritative advice of the professional physician.

The second effect of antinarcotic legislation was to provide the forces of professional medicine with a tool to tighten their own ranks. In his role as editor of the *Journal of the American Pharmaceutical Association*, James Beal realized the Harrison Act's implications for policing the profession. In June 1913, when passage of the act was imminent, he expanded on a theme introduced by the editor of another journal, who wrote that "if the drug trade is to raise its standard, it must first discard the lower element of pharmacists. If right shall survive— wrong must perish. Do your part to eliminate undesirable druggists who are undermining the foundation wall of the profession."[95] Beal believed that druggists who evaded the letter or the spirit of antinarcotic legislation were certainly to be classed among the "lower element" of pharmacists whom the profession had to discard in order to maximize its authority. He felt that the acts of these pharmaceutical renegades discredited the entire profession and that "out of these facts grows the responsibility of a class for its members, and the obligation of members to their class, and just in proportion as these reciprocal relations are held in esteem or disregarded, so the class flourishes or retrogrades."[96] After this paean to professional solidarity, which laid the groundwork of his argument, Beal moved to the main point. Contending that the professional pharmacist best upheld his obligation to his class by observing and policing the ranks, he urged that "when a pharmacist has been detected in some violation of the law or in some gross offense against ethics[,] we cannot afford to wrap ourselves in the cloak of our own self-righteousness and leave the matter to the public. We should be the first to invoke the law and to see to his punishment, and unless we do this, we have no right to complain if we are regarded as *particeps crimis.*"[97] In 1916 an editorial in the *Boston Medical and Surgical Journal* suggested that physicians were following a path similar to the one that Beal had charted for pharmacists: "The profession has become accustomed to the slight annoyance caused by the necessary registration, with its attendant small fee, and has cooperated heartily in checking a great evil—the abuse of narcotics." Moreover, the *Journal* reported that "druggists are very generally obeying the law," and it echoed Beal's 1913 call for professional self-policing, claiming that "the federal authorities need, and should have, any assistance the right minded members of the profession can give in bringing to justice those who are thus stultifying themselves and their calling."[98] These statements clearly indicate how narcotics legislation served the process of professionalization, not only helping to legitimize the authority of professional medicine by recognizing and legislating its competence in such troubling and important social matters as narcotic addiction but also providing a tool by which the professional organizations could rank their potential members, rewarding "right-mindedness" while banishing the forces of "stultification."

Thinking about these effects in tandem provides an answer to one of the more perplexing questions about the Harrison Act and the discourse of addiction more broadly: If physicians were so widely blamed for spreading addiction, why were they given responsibility for bringing it under control? The texts discussed in this chapter suggest that accusations of medical culpability for the dissemination of addiction were far from a liability. For many writers, such accusations actually *served* their demands for increased professionalization by adding emphasis to their claims. Sensational indictments of medical incompetence helped to vivify the long-standing allopathic demand that all physicians meet the requirements of standardized education and licensing, overseen by the scientific regulars of the AMA. Put simply, the accusation of malfeasance on the part of *some* physicians, enabled the claim that proper professionals would prescribe responsibly. It thus proved the need for more rigorous, authoritative professionalization, forcing the conclusion that such a process could also help reduce the threat of addiction. The solution to the threat of narcotic addiction, therefore, was not simply to hand it over to a profession that stood accused of spreading the condition. The solution to the drug problem was medical professionalization *itself.* The degree to which strict, uniform narcotics regulation might empower professionalized medicine was the degree to which it might help to solve the drug problem.

Medical professionalization was thus a convincing solution because it answered two dissimilar queries that were asked by two different groups of people. The first was "how do we control the threat of narcotic addiction?" The second was "how do we improve medical care by setting it on a scientific basis?" The catalyst that dissolved each question into the other was located partly in the sometimes congruent aims and intentions of those who asked the questions, enabling the assembly of a coalition of antinarcotic reformers, diplomats, and medical professionals in support of the Harrison Act. But it was also, more subtly and significantly, located in the broader cultural context. Seen from that perspective, we can understand the linked questions of addiction and medical professionalization as typically turn-of-the-century engagements with the precarious status of independence and autonomy—individual and professional—in a modern, interconnected society. We have seen throughout this volume that narcotic addition figured a crisis that typified its historical moment of emergence because it epitomized the way that formerly independent people might become enslaved by new technologies. As Thomas Haskell has argued, modern professionalism offered a way to reconstruct causal narratives, reestablishing a sense of autonomy and independence in a complex, interconnected world. The liberty of the modern subject might thus be reestablished through the guidance of professionals, empowered by their private knowledges, exclusive organizations, and, if need be, federal legislation. Medical professionalization, put to work against the threat of addiction, resonated very strongly within this context, and understanding that cultural resonance helps us to understand the Harrison Narcotic Act.

The incredible irony of this response, however, seems to have evaded its champions. The independence and autonomy of the addicted patient might be restored, but only at the cost of surrendering oneself to the firm guidance of professional medicine. Likewise, the authority of medical professionals would be enhanced, but only to the degree that federal officials might confirm the legitimacy of their prescription practices. In contextual terms, then, the solution offered by the Harrison Act solved nothing. It simply replaced one type of dependence—narcotic addiction—with another—dependence on a medical profession that was itself dependent on the authority of the federal government. As such, we might think of the Harrison Act as an important contribution to what the historian T. J. Jackson Lears has described as an emergent twentieth-century therapeutic culture, typified by its ever-increasing reliance on powerful institutions and practices in the frantic attempt to establish a firm basis of identity.[99]

A final effect of the Harrison Act is the way that it inscribed the cultural crisis of modernity upon the bodies of the habitual drug users themselves. As we have seen, both lay and professional commentators spent a great deal of time assessing the relative innocence and guilt of those who had become addicted to the use of narcotic drugs. Several of the texts that we have engaged in this chapter were adamant in their descriptions of the different classes of drug user, and the Harrison Act, which paired medical treatment with penal sanction, confirmed this division of the addict population. This complex operation, which followed a logical pattern that I have identified throughout this book as the addiction concept's double meaning, is the subject of the final chapter.

CHAPTER 5

The Saved and the Damned

The Medicolegal Solution to the
Double Meaning of Addiction

Drug addicts may be divided into two general classes. The first class is composed of people who have become addicted to the use of drugs through illness, associated probably with an underlying neurotic temperament. The second class, which is overwhelmingly in the majority, is at the present time giving the municipal authorities the greatest concern. These people are largely from the underworld or channels leading directly to it. They have become addicted to the use of narcotic drugs largely through association with habitués and they find in the drug a panacea for the physical and mental ills that are the result of the lives they are leading.

—T. F. JOYCE, *New York Medical Journal*, August 14, 1920

I N THE INTRODUCTION I argued that a paradox lies embedded in the definition of the word "addict": that the word holds both a *juridical* meaning—an archaic legal usage that stood for the assignment by the court of a duty or status—and a *volitional* one, which is the more common usage that means simply to devote oneself to a preferred practice or object. Various turn-of-the-century experts struggled with this paradox in their attempts to define what was, in their estimation, the growing threat of an obsessive desire, held by some people, for narcotic drugs.

This struggle to define narcotic addiction took place in the sentimental language of cure doctors and journalists as well as in the specialized vocabularies of medical science and law. In chapter 2 we saw that a diverse group of experts defined, organized, and presented their perceptions of habitual narcotic use in ways that both reflected and contributed to the broader discursive production of turn-of-the-century modernity as cultural crisis. Much of this perceived crisis lay in an alleged and peculiarly modern threat to older notions of middle-class identity—an apprehension that bourgeois autonomy and independence might be dissolved into the interdependent, technological labyrinth that signified modernity. At the same time, we saw that some people, particularly those who were beneficiaries of modern America's rapidly expanding technological/ industrial economy, were provided with an excuse for their drug taking. They were widely characterized as victims of the stress and strain of the modern economy who turned to drugs to bolster themselves against its ever growing demands.

This juridical notion of addiction, the idea that narcotic addicts were assigned a particular status owing to their participation in the modern economy and were therefore addicted through no fault of their own, was not extended to all people. In chapter 3, I argued that the concept of addiction was often enunciated in terms that both reflected and reinforced contemporary stereotypes of racialized and gendered others. We saw that the relatively safe haven of victimhood was often denied to Chinese immigrants and to African Americans because they were allegedly free from the strains of modern economic and social competition. They therefore had nothing and no one but themselves to blame for what many observers described as disproportionately high rates of drug use. Writers used terms that marked these people as volitional addicts, drug users whose inner corruption made itself visible in the willful decision to take drugs. The identity that bore this burden, however, was not the same rational and independent subject whose status was, for the most part, reserved for middle- and upper-class white men. Writers often assigned the responsibility for addiction in such cases to an essential and racially specific inability to control one's desires. Because such inability to control desire typified the narcotic addict's plight, these racial others made convenient figures for the threat held by the unregulated use of narcotics for the white bourgeoisie.

Yet no one believed habitual narcotic use to be restricted to racial or ethnic minorities. In chapter 3, for instance, I discussed how white women were located in a somewhat ambiguous position within the discourse of addiction. Experts often described women as predisposed to the seduction of drugs because of an innate, biological vulnerability, but because middle-class women were not marginalized with the same exclusionary vehemence as were racial minorities, they threatened to infect the bourgeois home. Many writers argued that these women were victimized by their physicians and by the escalating demands of modern society, as were their husbands, sons, and brothers, but these pressures were multiplied by the demands of female reproductive biology. Middle-class women's drug use, therefore, did not offer evidence of depravity but rather of feminine delicacy—a vulnerability which harmonized with sentimental and somewhat nostalgic narratives of male-dominated households and which required masculine protection. Sorting out the subtle differences between the various types of users and the treatment appropriate to each required a fine rhetorical balance if the addiction concept was to maintain any sort of cultural coherence. The challenge that confronted addiction experts was to formulate a historically appropriate concept that could account for both types of addicts, the juridical and the volitional. Their formulation helped to determine the proper social response to what they characterized as the nation's growing drug menace, as it simultaneously inscribed the cultural crisis of modernity upon the bodies of those it identified and named as addicts.

In chapter 4 I took a first look at that response by examining how medical and legal experts first posited and then, in the 1914 Harrison Narcotic Act, legislated professional medical authority as a remedy for the drug problem. The Harrison Act relied on a logic of legislated professional authority—in this case *medical* authority—as a remedy for what it described as the unequivocally modern problem of narcotic addiction. But the Harrison Act did more than this. It also affirmed the paradox at the heart of the addiction concept by dividing the drug-using population into groups of criminals and patients. To understand this operation, however, we first need to consider the extent of the act's police powers. A series of Supreme Court decisions, issued between 1915 and 1919, clarified these powers. Over this four-year period, the Court reinterpreted the primary aim of the Harrison Act, moving away from the act's definition as an information—and revenue-gathering measure to an assertion of its role as a law with broad police powers aimed at the prohibition of narcotic use.[1]

On December 7, 1915, before the new law had been in effect for one year, the Supreme Court heard *U.S. v. Jin Fuey Moy*. Here the Court ruled that the Harrison Act was intended primarily as a measure for revenue—and information-gathering and not as a prohibition act with regulatory power over suppliers and consumers of the drugs. The defendant, a doctor, was accused of prescribing a small quantity of morphine to an addict solely for the purpose of maintaining his addiction. The Justice Department argued that the addict's unauthorized possession of these drugs, prescribed only to maintain an addiction and thus "in bad faith," was grounds for conviction.[2]

The Court ruled 7–2 in favor of the defendant. Justice Oliver Wendell Holmes delivered the majority opinion, writing that "only words from which there are no escape could warrant the conclusion that Congress meant to strain its powers almost if not quite to the breaking point in order to make the probably very large proportion of citizens who have some preparation of opium in their possession criminal or at least prima facie criminal and subject to the serious punishment made possible by § 9." While noting that "it may be assumed that the statute has a moral end as well as revenue in view," Holmes explained that the Court was "of opinion that the district court, in treating those ends as to be reached only through a revenue measure, and within the limits of a revenue measure, was right."[3] The Court thus ruled that the act was constitutional insofar as it was a registration and tax act and that for Congress to go further was to exceed its powers. Simple possession of narcotics by addicts who had received the drugs through properly registered and taxed channels was not, in Holmes's majority interpretation, a violation of the new law.[4] The Court's ruling implicitly denied the constitutionality of using federal police powers in direct attempts to reduce or prohibit the use of narcotics.

In less than five years, however, the Court reversed itself in two cases decided on March 3, 1919. In the first, *U.S. v. C. T. Doremus*, the justices affirmed the constitutionality of the government's regulation of Dr. Doremus's practice, finding that a doctor could not prescribe large quantities of narcotic drugs to a known addict, or "a person popularly known as a 'dope fiend,' "[5] merely for the purpose of maintaining an addiction. Justice William R. Day wrote for the majority, arguing that "the [Harrison] act may not be declared unconstitutional because its effect may be to accomplish another purpose as well as the raising of revenue."[6] The "other purpose" to which Day referred was the reduction of narcotic use, and he voiced the Court's new opinion that the pursuit of such a goal—beyond mere revenue collection—was indeed constitutional. This ruling meant that federal enforcement of the Harrison Act did imply broad police powers, including the regulation of private medical practice, in order to stem the narcotic habit. Day wrote that the act's provisions "tend to diminish the opportunity of unauthorized persons to obtain the drugs and sell them clandestinely without paying the tax imposed by the Federal law."[7] This case thus affirmed that Congress was within its constitutional powers to pursue that goal and supplied it with a judicial stamp of approval.

In the second case decided that day, the Court determined what was to be considered legitimate, or authorized, possession of narcotics. It ruled in *Webb et al. v. U.S.* that Webb, a physician working in tandem with a druggist to produce a large number of morphine prescriptions at a rate of fifty cents each, was in violation of the act. Justice Day once again delivered the Court's opinion, writing that "to call such an order for the use of morphine a physician's prescription would be so plain a perversion of meaning that no discussion of the subject is required."[8] Day stated that the simple maintenance of addiction was not going to be considered a prescription in good faith and that people who had received narcotics for this purpose, even from a properly licensed physician, were therefore not authorized to have them. Henceforth, the doctor *and* the patient in such cases would be considered in violation of the law.

This change in opinion is striking, and there are many reasons why the Court so quickly and clearly reversed its interpretation of the Harrison Act. A general and growing intolerance of outsiders, particularly resulting from the recently concluded First World War, played an important role, as did fears that Russia's Bolshevik movement might spread to the United States. Changes within the demographic makeup of the addict population itself further helped to accentuate the unsavory aspects of narcotic use and shift broad sections of public opinion against its practitioners.[9] Several historians have noted the importance of these factors, but an excessive focus on the refusal to countenance narcotic use explains the public's attitude to only one portion of the addict population, that is, to those criminal addicts who refused to accede to the authority of professional medicine in all things pharmaceutical.

What I would like to suggest, however, is that the 1919 interpretation of the Harrison Act as a prohibition measure with broad police powers did more that just say "no" to narcotic addiction. It confirmed the paradox essential to the addiction concept itself. The separation of the addict population into groups of criminals and patients followed the logical contours of the double meaning of addiction that I have examined throughout this book. This logic inhabited the discourse of addiction beginning at least as early as the 1870s. The debate over and passage of the Harrison Act in 1914, along with its reinterpretation between 1915 and 1920, thus mark the culmination of a logic long in construction. The expansion of the act's police powers both reflected and helped to produce a clear demographic division within the drug-using populace. The

Harrison Act's distinction between patients and criminals affirmed the paradoxical double meaning of addiction as it simultaneously inscribed the cultural crisis of modernity upon the bodies of those it named as addicts. As such, the medicolegal solution to the problem of narcotic addiction begins to look very much like an attempt to remedy a much larger and more vexing condition—that is, it begins to resemble an attempt to alleviate the cultural crisis of modernity itself.

In this final chapter, therefore, I explore this medicolegal logic of inscription more directly. Engaging a series of texts published between 1914 and 1920 will show how the paradox inherent in the concept of addiction found a provisional settlement by 1920. Why provisional? Because through the twenties, newly popular psychological models of addiction would come to replace the more properly physiological definitions that were dominant around the turn of the twentieth century. Yet, by 1920, a settlement of the status of addiction and of the addict was clear in the Supreme Court's *Doremus* and *Webb* decisions. After examining the provisional resolution of this double logic, I will consider two reports: The 1919 report of the U.S. Treasury Department and the 1920 report by the AMA's Special Committee on Addiction make clear the legal and the medical halves of the solution to the double meaning of addiction.

HOPE AND HOPELESSNESS IN CHARLES B. TOWNS'S
Habits That Handicap

As I explained in chapter 3, William Rosser Cobbe's *Dr. Judas* of 1895 offered a particularly strong division of the addict population into two groups based on their preference of smoking opium as opposed to the refined concoctions employed by the medical mainstream. In 1916, Charles B. Towns wrote *Habits That Handicap*, which shared many of the concerns expressed in *Dr. Judas*. Writing twenty-one years later, Towns agreed with Cobbe about the popular emphasis on those phases of the drug problem "which make themselves manifest in the underworld or among the Chinese. I am," he continued, "reasonably certain that until very recently the world had heard nothing of the blameless men and women who had become drug-users as the result of illness." [10] Towns, though generally less racially biased in his writings than many of the writers I have discussed, nonetheless persisted in grouping the "underworld" with the Chinese in this description of the differing faces of addiction. Like Cobbe, he lamented the public's ignorance of what both writers saw as the distinct differences between groups of addicts, contrasting the underworld addict with "the blameless men and women who had become drug-users as the result of illness." Towns hoped to make both the public and especially the cure doctor more aware of the definitive difference that he believed existed between these groups. Crucially, Towns differentiated between groups of addicts in his discussion of the possibility of an addiction cure, advising the cure doctor to "classify his subjects of investigation, recognizing the hopeful ones and admitting the hopeless to be hopeless." [11] He felt that this division would be the key to a successful treatment. Towns's differentiation of the hopeful and the hopeless was reminiscent of Cobbe's distinction between the smoker and the morphine user.

Towns invoked what I have described as the double meaning of addiction when he divided the addict population into groups. Though he began with three rather than two groups, his distribution nonetheless followed the broader division of addicts according to volitional and juridical status that lies embedded within the concept of addiction. Towns explained that "the first and largest [group] is created by the doctor, the second is created by the druggist and the manufacturer of proprietary and patent medicines, and the third, and smallest, is due to the tendency of certain persons toward dissipation." Towns's first two groups thus conformed to Cobbe's group of medical addicts who became drug users through no fault of their own. They were, in effect, assigned their status by broader social factors, including professional irresponsibility or even malfeasance. Like Cobbe, Towns found this group to be blameless. Effectively collapsing these first two groups into one, he wrote that their "major importance" lay in their greater number but also in "the pitiful fact that such victims are always innocent." [12]

These innocent victims were Towns's favorite subjects for cure. He explained that his "preferred risk" lay "among the victims of the drug habit . . . who have acquired it through the administration of a narcotic by physicians in time of pain or illness." He felt that such cases, "if treated before too great a deterioration has taken place, may be considered almost certain of relief." [13] These "innocent" addicts were thus the hopeful and proper subjects for the ministrations of professional medicine. He believed that they responded well to medical authority and its offer of a cure. This should not be surprising, considering that many of them had become addicted in the first place when they acquiesced to the claims of professional medicine. Put another way, they became addicts, at least in part, because they accepted their doctor's authority to diagnose and treat their illnesses.

Innocent, juridical addicts were, however, not to be confused with the volitional addicts who became addicted on their own and were much more difficult
to work with. Towns wrote that "where the drug habit is the direct or indirect
result of alcoholic dissipation or sexual excesses, or is a social vice, . . . the lack
of moral standards and the loss of pride are serious handicaps."[14] In other
words, those who acquired their addiction from channels outside of the medical,
and whose moral standards and sense of pride differed from those of the practitioner, were not likely to respond well to medical efforts to cure them. Towns
elaborated on the membership of this group, explaining that those who had become addicts "through a tendency toward dissipation are almost invariably
denizens of the under-world." More ominous, he asserted his belief that "if it
were not for the fact that the contagion of their vice may spread, they might
well be permitted by society to drug themselves to death as speedily as possible."[15] As part of this underworld, addicts participated in a network that operated beneath the surface of the institutionally and legally sanctioned American
mainstream, implicitly denying the authority of the power that constituted that
mainstream. To acquire or to continue one's drug habit from a nonmedical
source was to be, by definition, part of an underworld. Moreover, Towns feared
that the "contagion" born in and borne by these addicts threatened the broader
society, which might otherwise permit these people to "drug themselves to
death."[16]

Towns believed that these patients were not likely to be cured. He thus
echoed Cobbe's 1895 suggestion that for this group, addiction was not a temporary and remediable condition but a symptom of an alarming, irredeemable corruption of character. Towns sought to correct those among his colleagues who
might believe that "after a patient has once been through the process of treatment for a drug or drink habit he will be entirely made over." Instead, he hoped
that they would realize that "the elimination of drugs or drink from a degener-
ate will not eliminate degeneracy. Nothing, in fact, will eliminate it except stopping the breeding of degenerates."[17]

Addiction, then, was merely a symptom of a much more disturbing heredi-
tary condition in these addicts. The ultimate and perhaps utopian resolution of
the problem would thus be eugenic, but in the meantime there remained the
problem of a proper response to the existence of these underworld types in the
present. Towns suggested measures even stronger than Cobbe's for their treatment: "Those among this class who have become public charges and refuse to
work should be forced to do so by state or municipal authority. Society or their

own families should not bear the burden of their useless existence. They should be segregated in some place where they will be physically comfortable, where they may be made industrious and useful, and where a separation of the sexes will prevent the increase of their worthless kind." Towns advocated the construction of work camps to deal with the problem of the volitional addict. These would be places where "they should be permanently kept." He argued that "through this course alone society will be spared the periodical havoc they will be sure to work during their intervals of freedom." [18] Most important, he paired this confinement with professional treatment and guidance for those who, by their acceptance of the doctor's authority, proved themselves to be both worthy and blameless.

Towns thought that such harsh measures were justified in order to contain what he saw as the threat of widespread degradation brought by these addicts to the rest of society. Unlike Cobbe, however, Towns argued for a much stronger identification between the two groups of addicts. He believed that "whether a man has acquired the habit knowingly or unknowingly, its action is always the same . . . the drug at once begins to loosen his sense of moral obligation, until in the end it brings about absolute irresponsibility." [19] Towns thus argued that the blameless addict, the addict who became so at the hands of his or her doctor, was at risk of becoming every bit as depraved as the "dissipated" addicts who willed their own subjection. The threat of addiction to those of the better class was thus one of decline—a reduction to a level equivalent to that of the degraded, volitional addict of the underworld.

Towns continued his point by providing a set of examples that might have frightened the most securely bourgeois reader with the possibility of his or her own unwitting decline. Declaring that "the drug habit is no respecter of persons," Towns described "exemplary mothers and wives who became indifferent to their families; clergymen of known sincerity and fervor who became shoplifters and forgers; shrewd, successful business men who became paupers, because the habit left them at the mercy of sharpers after mental deterioration had set in." [20] From exemplary motherhood to careless indifference, from respectable clergyman to skulking shoplifter, and from successful businessman to duped pauper, Towns made sure that his audience understood the threat of decline that he believed narcotics held for even the most comfortable among them.

Because he thought the threat was so potent and so widespread, Towns advocated harsh legal measures, paired with the authority of professional medicine, to arrest its progress. He believed that a partnership between legal and medical disciplinary systems might help to control the distribution and use of narcotics. While he admitted that medicolegal prohibition might not entirely cut the illicit drug supply, he felt that "the passage of restrictive legislation and the enforcement of such laws will tend to prevent the descent of many into the criminal class."[21] Towns testified to his hope for a medicolegal partnership in the control of drug use. "With the government as the first distributor and a physician as the last, drug-taking merely as a habit would cease to be."[22] Thus, for Towns, a medicolegal apparatus was the solution to the drug problem. He suggested professional medical care and especially guidance for the innocents who acknowledged scientific medicine's therapeutic authority, paired with permanent incarceration for those recalcitrants of the underworld who exercised their own volition by rejecting that authority.

THE DOUBLE MEANING OF ADDICTION IN THE PROFESSIONAL MEDICAL JOURNALS

As I have noted, neither Cobbe nor Towns was a physician. Nonetheless, the ideas that they so strongly set forth were very much in evidence in the professional journals of mainstream medicine. In chapter 4 I introduced Perry Lichtenstein's 1914 research on the addict population of City Prison, Manhattan. Lichtenstein also compared addict demographics, explaining in the *New York Medical Journal* that "the greater number are of the gangster type and consequently are mental and moral degenerates." But he was surprised to find out how many addicts there were of the "better class." Among these, he numbered "physicians, nurses and actresses" but also found "some of the very richest of our people" within the group. These were people who "frequently have elaborate 'lay outs' in their homes, richly furnished, and stocked with the handsomest jeweled opium pipes."[23] At first glance, the contradiction between Lichtenstein's discovery of an underworld majority, paired with a small but distinctly "better class" of addict, and Towns's allegation that "respectable" users made up the majority of the addict population is somewhat perplexing. Yet contrasting findings like these tend to highlight the different population samples from which Lichtenstein and Towns drew their results.[24] Their differing findings suggest a great deal about the way that the discourse of addiction both reflected and produced a particular notion of class difference among habitual narcotic users.

Lichtenstein wrote that "many of [the better class of addicts] naturally never attract our attention because of the absence of marked physical changes, due to good surroundings, good meals, etc."[25] Put another way, access to the good surroundings and good meals guaranteed by a good paycheck rendered middle-class addicts, quite literally, invisible to a prison researcher such as Lichtenstein. Presumably, we could also add medical care to this list of goods, which would explain the visibility of respectable addicts as a majority to such cure promoters as Towns but would also highlight the class specificity of the so-called respectable addicts.[26] We have seen that experts considered addicts who came to drug use through medical channels to be respectable, to be pitied rather than censured. Those who became addicted through nonmedical channels, however, were fit subjects for penal institutions and thus surfaced more often in Lichtenstein's prison studies.

In 1916, Solomon Rubin wrote at length on this subject for the *Boston Medical and Surgery Journal.* After reminding his readers that his several strategies for the cure and maintenance of patients applied only to those who had become drug users through medical channels, a group that he called "social users," he declared that "the criminal and delinquent type, of which there are approximately twenty percent, are subjects for the penologist and criminologist. This class of users is the most hopeless and most dangerous element to deal with. They are intractable, cunning, designing, and wholly devoid of moral responsibility. It is their ambition to enlist new victims in the army of drug users."[27] Likewise, Walter Bloedorn followed and amplified Rubin's logic in 1917, writing in the *U.S. Naval Medical Bulletin* that "under these circumstances a drug addict becomes a focus of infection, as it were, and through contact with susceptible individuals serves to spread the evil."[28] It was precisely this notion of the addict as a focus of infection, as an underworld agent in the dissemination of an evil habit, that justified the suggestion by Rubin and many others of a twinned medicolegal approach to what they saw as a growing drug problem. Doctors performed a police function in this system, identifying criminal subjects for incarceration, while police officers played a medical role, rooting out and neutralizing contagious sources of infection.

Rubin was quick, however, to qualify his position. He cautioned the legal authorities against overzealous pursuit of their duties. He wrote to "commend" the authorities for their efforts to round up the "criminal class of users" but hoped that they would not make general what he described as their "crusade." His greatest fear was that legal enforcement might be extended to "the redeemable social user." For the rehabilitation of these "unfortunate victims," he recommended "the employment of medico-social measures instead of penal measures."[29] The respectable, "unfortunate victim" was thus the proper subject for the medical profession to exercise what Rubin called its "medico-social" role.

The criminal class of user, on the other hand, was left to be rounded up by the authorities and committed to a regime of "penal measures."

A particularly illustrative discussion of the two classes of drug users and their respective memberships appeared in the *American Journal of Clinical Medicine* in 1918. After dividing the addict population into two general groups, George D. Swaine wrote that "in class one, we can include all of the physical, mental, and moral defectives, the tramps, hoboes, idlers, loafers, irresponsibles, criminals, and denizens of the underworld." These were the people who had begun and maintained their drug use outside the channels of professional medical authority. Though the class element in this statement is obvious, we should also note that Swaine included within this group idle, rich women who "began taking the drug for the intoxication it produces and have kept it up until they have become slaves to its devilish power." He explained that "these are the drug fiends," a group that did "not want to be cured."[30]

He contrasted these "drug fiends" with a second group, finding that "in class two, we have many types of good citizens, who have become addicted to the use of the drug innocently and who are, in every sense of the word, 'victims.' " In language that showed the influence of Charles Towns, whose book had been published only two years before, Swaine wrote that "morphine is no respecter of persons, and the victims are doctors, lawyers, ministers, artists, actors, judges, congressmen, senators, priests, authors, women, girls, all of whom realize their conditions and want to be cured." For these people, he argued that "morphine-addiction is not a vice, but, an incubus, and, when they are cured they stay cured."[31] Most important, "fiendishness" was to be determined by one's desire to be cured, that is, by a drug user's willingness to accept the ministration of professional medicine.

These are just a few examples, drawn from many, which show that by 1918 it was possible to distinguish a growing consensus regarding the existence of two clearly defined groups of addicts within the pages of the nation's professional medical journals. Popular authorities such as Towns and Cobbe, along with professionals such as those just discussed, were coming into broad agreement as to the double meaning of addiction—something that I have argued is implicit within the concept itself. In 1920 the *Journal of the American Medical Association* crowned this effort with its own special report from the AMA's Committee on the Narcotic Drug Situation in the United States. That report concludes this book, but I first will consider how the same notion of addiction was present in another landmark report, that of the U.S. Treasury Department's Special Narcotic Committee, delivered in June 1919.

THE DOUBLE MEANING OF ADDICTION AND THE
U.S. TREASURY DEPARTMENT

On March 25, 1918, Secretary of the Treasury William McAdoo appointed a special committee to look into the country's narcotic problem. The committee's findings offer a picture of the federal government's position on drug control in 1918 and 1919, according to David Musto, who further explains that the committee was appointed to challenge and rectify Court decisions that had impeded the government's battle against addiction maintenance.[32] Composed of influential members of the U.S. Public Health Service and chaired by the future Speaker of the House, Representative Henry T. Rainey of Illinois, the committee issued a report that offers the legal half of what I have termed the medicolegal solution to the problem of addiction.

In its final report, the committee described its purpose as an investigation of "the traffic in opium, its preparations and habit-forming alkaloids and coca leaves." It chose these substances to investigate because "these are the drugs which are definitely covered by the Harrison Act and are most pernicious from the standpoint of habit formation."[33] The Treasury Department's assessment was intended to investigate the use of "pernicious" substances over which federal authorities might hope to have some influence, and the investigation took place during the same months that the Supreme Court was busily reinterpreting the Harrison Act.

The committee began its work by preparing and distributing questionnaires to the 125,000 physicians and 48,000 pharmacists who were registered as part of the Harrison Act's regulations. It also surveyed nonprofit organizations that provided addiction treatment; the chiefs of police of every American city with a population greater than five thousand; county, federal, and state penal institutions; and the superintendents of state, county, and municipal almshouses, state hospitals, insane asylums, and county municipal hospitals.[34] Though the highest rate of reply (an average of about 35%) came from the medical professions, the committee received a very limited response to its survey.[35] This did not, however, stop the committee from interpolating from the replies it received and from making very powerful recommendations for a course of action. In fact, it sometimes used this lack of access to data as way to dismiss responses that did not confirm its basic belief that "the consumption of narcotic drugs in this country has steadily increased from the date of their introduction."[36]

In regard to the prisons that responded to the survey, the committee found that the reports of a low rate of prisoner addiction "would apparently indicate that only a small percentage of persons incarcerated in penal institutions are addicted to drugs." Yet the committee demonstrated its firm belief in the prevalence of addiction when it explained away this result, claiming that "this is an assumption which is partly [negated] by the fact that only a very small percentage of such institutions kept any records relative to drug addiction." [37] In other words, the committee was convinced that had these institutions kept any records, the numbers would have confirmed its suppositions.

The committee had similar difficulties with local administrators, whose responses showed "that a great majority of these officials kept no records and therefore had no information upon the subject." But, again, the committee concluded that "this condition is believed to be due principally to a lack of knowledge of the seriousness of the situation." [38] The committee did not, for instance, entertain the possibility that these people failed to take the situation seriously because they had not experienced a serious problem. I note this not to make an empirical claim for or against the reality of a drug threat but only to suggest that committee members seemed to have made up their minds independently of what the data indicated. Further, the committee hoped to remedy this public ignorance and complacency by recommending "that educational campaigns be instituted in all parts of the United States for the purpose of informing the people of this country, including the medical profession, of the seriousness of drug addiction and its extent in the United States, and thereby secure their aid and cooperation in its suppression." [39] If the American public and even the medical profession were unaware of what the committee was determined to interpret as a growing threat, the Treasury Department was going to make quite sure that they heard about it soon. In any case, and despite the lack of response to its surveys, the committee estimated that "the total of addicts in this country probably exceeds 1,000,000 at the present time," [40] a number that was quoted more than any other statistic in the report, according to Musto. In fact, this number, which was broadcast to Congress in August 1918 as part of a preliminary report, helped convince Chairman Rainey's congressional colleagues of the need to strengthen the Harrison Act by amending it. [41] As I pointed out in the introduction to this book, the most reliable estimates that we have today suggest that the figure of 1 million addicts was more than double the actual number of habitual users.

In addition to its estimate of the number of addicts, the committee had a great deal to say about the composition of the addict population, arguing that "addiction to the use of these habit-forming drugs is not restricted to any particular race, nationality, or class of people." [42] Such a contention broadened the threat of addiction, applying it to everyone and making clear that no one was immune to the effects of drug use. Such claims were necessary to sustain fears of a narcotic threat to the white middle class because depictions of addiction had relied so heavily upon sensational scenes of allegedly ethnic and racially based moral squalor. An insistence on the contagiousness of drug addiction ensured that the middle and upper classes felt that addiction was their problem as well—that they could indeed be reduced to the level of what many writers had depicted as their ethnic and racial inferiors if they allowed themselves to be snared in the web of narcotic addiction. The committee completed this line of thought by turning to a physiological argument that both confirmed the possibility of addiction's spread and argued for the necessity of professional assistance in its removal. It found that "anyone repeatedly taking a narcotic drug over a period of 30 days, in the case of a very susceptible individual for 10 days, is in grave danger of becoming an addict, and when addiction has been established, it is impossible for the individual to discontinue use of the drug without outside assistance." [43] Human frailty thus made professional intervention necessary as protection against the powerful threats of modern medical technology.

But even though, as this passage makes clear, human physiology served as an equalizer, guaranteeing the spread of addiction to all classes, the committee was quick to differentiate between addicts according to the source of their addiction and the type of drug to which they were addicted. It noted that "the habit of using opiates or cocaine is acquired through association with addicts, through the physician, and through self-medication with these drugs, or patent or proprietary preparations containing the same." But if the possibility of addiction was shared by all, the condition itself was not always the same, and it mattered by which of these methods one became addicted. The Treasury Department's committee therefore divided the addict population into two broad classes, "namely, the class composed principally of addicts of the underworld and the class which is made up almost entirely of addicts in good social standing." [44]

As to whom the committee called "the addict of good social standing" and whom I have identified as the juridical addict—those who were relieved of the responsibility for their condition—the committee explained that some "become addicted to the use of these drugs through self medication, while a few first indulge as a social diversion." But the committee's key finding was that its evidence "points to the physician as the agent through whom the habit is acquired in the majority of cases." The committee thereby asserted the relative innocence of the bourgeois addict. Following a familiar pattern, the Treasury committee compared this group of addicts with those of the "underworld" whom we have seen repeatedly classified as volitional addicts—those who were responsible for creating their own condition. It found that "the addict of the underworld, in a large majority of cases, acquires the habit of using these drugs through his or her associates. This is probably due to the fact that addicts of this class make use of heroin and cocaine most frequently, these drugs being employed as a snuff. . . . In addition, these drugs are made use of by 'white slavers' in securing and holding their prey, and by prostitutes in entertaining their callers."[45] The Treasury Department's report thus gave government backing to the division of the addict population into two classes. The report was intended to aid those who wished to strengthen the Harrison Act and also to bolster the Justice Department in its cases against Webb and Doremus before the Supreme Court. We have already witnessed the Justice Department's success at the bar. This report made clear the legal opinion of the federal government in regard to the status of narcotic addiction.

THE DOUBLE MEANING OF ADDICTION AND THE AMA

The American Medical Association added its opinion to that of the Treasury Department when it offered its solution to the paradoxical meaning of addiction. In April 1920 the association held its seventy-first annual meeting in New Orleans, where the assembled physicians received the report of the Committee on the Narcotic Drug Situation in the United States. This report presented the AMA's version of the history of narcotics in the United States and also offered a set of suggestions that professional medicine might follow to "stamp out" drug addiction, a condition that, adopting a phrase used by the New York City Board of Health, the committee declared a "pestilence."[46] If the Treasury Department's report stood as representative of the federal government's attitude toward narcotic addiction at the close of the second decade of the twentieth century, then the AMA report served the same function for professional medicine, providing the medical half of the medicolegal solution to the double meaning of addiction.

The doctors stated their general argument at the beginning of the report, which effectively sums up much of the literature that has been the basis of this book. After noting the novelty of the public's growing concern about habitual drug use and blaming addiction's newfound notoriety on the Harrison Act and its reinterpretation by the Supreme Court, the committee made its first important point: "Drug addiction in the sense in which we ordinarily use the word at the present time is a modern problem." The committee explained its contention by placing addiction within the broader context of the mid—to late nineteenth-century technological and scientific change that typified the emergence of what it quite self-consciously described as modernity. This move recapitulated the modern technological ambivalence displayed by many of the experts that I have discussed. By noting that it had "few facts to indicate that drug addiction came to notice as a menace among Western peoples until after the discovery of the opium alkaloids, particularly morphin, and after the perfecting of the hypodermic syringe," the committee described the condition as a distinctly modern menace, as a product of recent historical change.[47] Addiction was a hazard produced by modern medical technology. It was unleashed by the isolation of the chemicals themselves and then amplified through their injection by mechanical syringe.

Likewise, the committee described the addicts themselves as products of modern technology. Its members distinguished between drug users past and present in a manner reminiscent of the several writers that I considered in chapter 2: "The facts stated indicate that we are not dealing with the opium smokers or eaters of another age and civilization but with a problem which in one phase dates back to the middle of the nineteenth century with the introduction into use of the hypodermic needle."[48] Again, the syringe served as an example of a modern, mechanical instrument that produced and enhanced a condition of technological dependence, but the use of "addiction" as a distinct term signified something that was historically specific and quite different from older manifestations of habitual drug use. The doctors made it clear that "drug addict" was not a synonym for "opium eater" and that the difference lay in an intensification of effect over time rooted in the development of medical technology. In other words, the drug addict was both a product and a marker of the history of medicine.

The committee further established the modernity of addiction by locating it within what we have seen described as the increasingly interdependent modern economy. The doctors ascribed narcotic addiction's widespread dissemination to "reasons connected in part with commerce and the spread of civilization." Modern interconnectedness—figured as the "close association" experienced within growing cities—threatened an even greater incidence of addiction in the future.[49] Modern commerce and urbanization, but also the expanded possibility and ease of communication, thus amplified the menace of narcotic addiction. This intensification, combined with the technological development of the drugs themselves, created the distinctly modern menace of addiction.

The committee's choice of causes had a direct influence on its choice of cures. It thus proposed a distinctively modern method for eradicating the "pestilence" of drug addiction. Declaring that members of "the medical profession should take the lead to which their position entitles them, and should not be compelled to follow in the wake of the great work already begun of stamping out drug addiction," the physicians proposed a solution that required the twinned and complementary forces of medical and legal authority in its implementation. Fearing an increase in the incidence of addiction, the committee urged colleagues to "take advantage of the present interest and get control of the situation through law and the care of those already victims."[50] If, however, there was any doubt as to which drug users ought to be subject to "law" and which ones were fit for medical "care," the physicians had a solution. The formula lay in the immanent and paradoxical double meaning of the addiction concept itself.

The Two Classes of Drug Users

Suggesting that "the habitual users of narcotic drugs may be divided into two classes," the committee developed a sophisticated distinction between categories of drug users, grouping "in Class 1 . . . all those who suffer from a disease or ailment requiring the use of narcotic drugs." It explained that "patients in this class are legitimate medical cases," but this group was more narrowly defined than were previous groups of relatively innocent *juridical* addicts.[51] The committee restricted this class to the comparatively small group of patients who remained directly under a physician's care and whose treatment required the continued administration of narcotics. Other writers were concerned with the medical creation of a class of users who continued their drug use after the physician had finished with them. The AMA's "Class 1," however, was restricted to patients who were under close medical supervision. The committee even refused to call these people "addicts."

The doctors explained that after excluding the first group, "we have left for consideration those who are addicts—those who use narcotic drugs for the comfort they afford and continue their use solely by reason of an acquired habit." This second class of drug users, which was described by the committee as consisting of "those who are suffering from a functional disturbance with no physical basis expressed in a pathologic change," were thus the only group to which it applied the word "addict." Class 1, made up of people whose continuing illness required narcotic medication, was for the AMA quite clearly an object of professional medical supervision. Class 2, the much larger group, consisted of people who persevered in drug taking without the medical profession's direct management. This group therefore included both juridical and volitional addicts. The committee suggested four subgroups within Class 2-"correctional cases, mental defectives, social misfits and otherwise normal persons"[52]—and it is here, with the different approaches to addiction within these groups, that the AMA's medicolegal resolution of the double meaning of addiction became clear.

The AMA's Position on "Addicts"

Of the four subgroups in Class 2, the committee sought to confine the first three in one institution. It claimed that "under a proper system of classification, in the institution for the after-care of the addict, it will be necessary to segregate the correctional, the mental defective, and the social misfit groups."[53] The fourth group, "otherwise normal persons," was excluded from the institution, and I will return to it later. Here, I want to clarify the nature of this institution and the care and identity of its inmates.

The committee's suggestions for the treatment of the first two groups, the "defectives" and the "correctional cases," mirror Charles B. Towns's ominous suggestion of lifelong internment in work camps for those cases he termed "hopeless." The AMA's committee argued that "the correctional cases should be committed to institutions with no age limit—from the cradle to senility, if necessary." Further, it seemed to rule out the possibility of a permanent cure for this group, suggesting that "if they show marked improvement, they could be put on probation under the care of a technically trained person acting as probation officer."[54]

The doctors further echoed Towns in their suggestion of a treatment for the "defectives," arguing that "institutional care must be provided where they can be comfortable and often self-supporting, but where they shall not be permitted to reproduce their kind."[55] For both these groups, then, the committee suggested permanent confinement or, at the least, a lifetime of close, professional supervision. Though the committee made no overtly racial or class-based judgments concerning the makeup of these groups, we have seen the prevalence of such thinking in the work of other addiction experts. It is not too much to suppose that, for much of the report's AMA readership, traces of these assessments may have adhered to the committee's suggestion of permanent incarceration for such hopelessly degraded characters.

The committee was less reticent to make class-based judgments for the "misfits," the third group to be institutionalized. Though it stated that "misfits are found in all social strata," [56] the committee reserved its greatest fears for those misfits of the "drifting industrial population" who it felt had become visible within the last generation. Put another way, the committee understood these characters as markers of historical change, as evidence of modernity. While noting that "the facilities may have to be increased," the committee affirmed that "we already have state provision for the care of correctional cases and mental defectives." But the doctors worried that "the problem of the misfit and of the drug user who appears normal except for the drug weakness has yet to be solved." [57] They warned that "the misfit can no longer be ignored. He is too numerous; he has learned the lesson of organization; and he has learned through association means of cheap satisfaction that deaden for a time his elemental cravings, even though they return him to society more of a menace and a care than before." [58] The "means of cheap satisfaction" that he had "learned through association" were, of course, narcotic, and this method of discovery situated him firmly within the volitional class of addict. Furthermore, this group sought only to "deaden" what the committee described as its "elemental cravings"— something that will be a key marker of the group's difference from the "otherwise normal" class of users, whose addictive desire held redeeming elements that could be professionally attuned to the greater good of society. The AMA committee's proposed treatment for the "misfits" was based on the promise that they believed the extension of their professional authority held for society. It also demonstrates the enormous power that might accrue from this proposed application of medical expertise to stubborn social problems. The committee's suggestion thus implied a professional agenda that went far beyond merely curing the sick.

The "Social Misfit"

The committee argued that the person they called the "social misfit" was, like all addicts, a product of modern intellectual and economic development. They believed that these misfits had "become much more of a problem with the spread of individualism and rationalism" because "an earlier world accepted unhappiness and disease with resignation as the hand of Providence." [59] The social misfit was thus a product of a modern intellectual environment that precluded the resigned acceptance of "unhappiness and disease" as a part of his or her fate.

These cultural developments were exacerbated by an economy that differed from older models whose "unremitting toil and consequent deadened nerves prevented such problems as arise with the change from a 'pain economy' to a 'pleasure economy,' so that it may be said that a society which has enough of a surplus for leisure will also have more misfits." Heightened nervous sensitivity—caused by a "remission of toil"—combined with an individualistic, rational culture, was thus to blame for the phenomenon of the social misfit, whose problem was, according to the doctors, "getting into the right place to enjoy the surplus and the leisure" generated by the new "pleasure economy." Social misfits were thus people who did not know their place in an economy based not on the grinding, endless production of necessities but rather on relatively leisured consumption of a surplus. They had too much time on their hands, or at least more than they could profitably manage, and they were most certainly a product of modern industrial change. This "drifting industrial population" had, according to the committee, "brought home to the commercial world what an expense on business is the social misfit, who is also an economic misfit; for the restlessness of inner life works its way out in drifting from job to job." And, what was perhaps most problematic for the committee, this drifting misfit had a penchant for "listening to any agitator who assures him that this dissatisfaction and restlessness are the fault of some one besides himself." [60]

For the modern worker, the committee concluded, "the minute subdivision of labor of the modern factory system" meant that "if he has 'nerves,' some day he will get a nightmare vision of himself as a piece of social waste, a victim of conditions far more far-reaching than his individual life. When he becomes organized and vocal, society awakens to the fact that he is an I.W.W., a Bolshevik, or what not." [61] In other words, the committee theorized that the experience of modern factory labor caused many workers, who were deprived of older fatalistic belief systems, to become restless and dissatisfied with their lot in life. Further, what the doctors saw as the workers' growing leisure provided them with the opportunity to reflect on their condition. The result was that a particularly sensitive individual who realized himself to be caught up in a complex, interdependent society—a "victim of conditions far more far-reaching than his individual life"—was likely show his dissatisfaction by organizing in order to threaten and change that society.

Yet the doctors argued that the misfit "is not wholly to blame" for his restless dissatisfaction. [62] They turned to modern psychology to define the "original nature of man as eternal restlessness, curiosity and constructiveness," contending that "we like to do things which we feel are useful and for which we are given credit" but that modern industrial society, typified for the worker by its "minute sub-division of labor," inhibited this means of arriving at a sense of self-worth and that "if such primary instincts are forever thwarted, the social misfit develops."[63]

The committee thus felt that the social misfit's problem lay in the frustration resulting from a perceived powerlessness in a modern, interdependent society typified by what the committee called a "pleasure economy." Such frustration could lead to organized revolt, but because the doctors' idea of a pleasure economy was one where consumption replaced production, we should not be surprised to find that the misfit's frustration might lead him to "drift" toward profoundly destructive consumption practices. In other words, the social frustration of the industrial population threatened also to make itself manifest through the habitual consumption of narcotics. The doctors brought together many of their apprehensions about the modern world when they argued that the misfit's inability to manipulate his environment might lead him to "seek forgetfulness in some form of self-gratification" which was all too readily available "in the unwholesome environment of the ordinary city street." Here, if "he comes in contact with those using narcotic drugs, they will find him responsive." [64] The committee thus invoked a combination of historically specific cultural, economic, and urban contexts in order to explain the social misfit's diffuse frustration, which was in turn condensed, made visible, and grounded by two closely associated social lightening rods: radical politics and the runaway consumption of narcotics.

Yet this description of the social causes of the misfit's drug dependence—of what must be interpreted as his partial innocence—is what spared him from a lifelong sentence to the work camp along with the so-called mental defectives and correctional cases. Crucially, however, the misfit needed to be closely guided by professional experts who were well acquainted with the challenges and problems he presented. The doctors suggested "vocational guidance" as a means to arrest the drift from which the social misfit suffered. They emphasized the professional's role as a guide through the confusing labyrinth of modernity when they explained that "this whole movement is based on the belief that happiness is a by-product of normal, useful activity, and that the child can be directed along the way, whether he be brilliant, mediocre or stupid. [The vocational guidance movement's] social philosophy teaches that the goal of society is to provide so flexible a social system that there shall be no misfits among the normal members of a population as a result of lack of guidance and training." The committee thus emphasized professional guidance and training as a way to channel and focus the human drives whose expression was first frustrated by modern conditions of labor and then appropriated by the destructive forces of radical politics or narcotic addiction. The professional's responsibility in such a system was to find and to reconcile the misfit to his proper place in society. This notion of professional guidance was to be continued beyond the recovery of the addicted misfit, perhaps throughout the addict's life, ensuring that he remained in his place. The committee argued that an effective "probation system" would be necessary "to counteract [restlessness] with the cured addicts." It felt that "many an otherwise hopeless misfit can be permanently saved by the supervision of a wise and experienced probation officer, acting with authority." [65] It is imperative to note the vast increase in the role of the professional expert in this suggestion. The committee hoped to solve much more than drug addiction, which it mobilized as a symptom of vast, seemingly intractable social problems spawned by a modern society that was marked by its expanding corporate, industrial economy. Professional guidance could provide a solution not only to the drug problem but also to the threat posed by radical labor politics. It would do so by identifying misfits and reconciling them to their proper place in the modern world.

Yet the committee's demand for expanded professional guidance enforced by state authority applied primarily to the misfit class and was paired with its recommendation for the permanent incarceration of "mental defectives" and "correctional cases" in work camps. The committee hoped that this would solve the problem of these three groups whose condition roughly corresponds to various shadings of the volitional meaning of addiction. But the problem of what to do with the last group still awaited resolution. The committee therefore turned its attention to the problem of the "otherwise normal" addict.

Addicts "Otherwise Normal"

The committee made the class position of this final group of addicts clear, especially in comparison with the misfits of the drifting industrial population, when it placed among them "the literary genius who has to finish his manuscript for the publisher; the social worker whose district must be covered at whatever cost to herself; the physician or nurse with an epidemic sweeping the city, and who must not stop—any of these may realize too late that he has become a slave to the drug." These people knew their place and were by no means part of the drifting industrial population. They sought not to change their place or to challenge the society that assigned it but rather to fulfill more completely its ever increasing demands. Though the social misfits were not "wholly to blame" for their condition, the otherwise normal addict was much less so. The committee explained the incidence of this type of addict, writing that "we may have such a person working under too great strain. Then the 'last straw' is laid on the burden, and in the altogether human search for relief . . . the drug is perhaps taken occasionally, and the habit finally formed."[66] This "altogether human search for relief" from the pressure of maintaining a position atop the economic and social pyramid was completely different from the misfit's attempt to deaden "elemental cravings" in the pursuit of "self-gratification," something the committee linked to the inability to accept one's unhappy lot in life, to the failure to know one's place. The otherwise normal addict, whom the committee depicted as a physician or a nurse, a literary genius or a social worker, was a victim of the demands of society on an individual whose only fault was trying too hard to serve that society. In a manner that we have seen repeatedly in the discourse of addiction, these otherwise normal addicts completely fulfilled the juridical sense of the word "addiction."

Because they quite clearly knew their place, vocational guidance was an inappropriate form of professional intervention for the otherwise normal addict. Foreshadowing what would become perhaps the dominant approach to the question of addiction in the 1920s and through much of the remaining century, the committee suggested instead "psychanalysis" as the most productive way to help these respectable addicts. It described the treatment as "a form of mental therapy" whose goal was "the reclamation of [the unconscious] part of the ego." Committee members believed that it offered "the greatest hope for the salvation of the otherwise normal person whose will is not strong enough to shake off the drug habit." The committee argued that this treatment, which required the analyst to discover "the 'sore spot' in the individual subconscious mind," was "a process of reeducation" whose "theory holds that there will be released an increased energy." The professional's role was to release and redirect those otherwise blocked or inappropriately directed channels of energy in order to resuscitate the weakened will. The committee suggested that "the reclamation of this 'normal' addict will depend on the power he will have, under guidance, to direct this libido into higher thought and emotional levels."[67] The "reclamation" of the addict thus stood on his or her ability to "irradiate and sublimate this libido which he is so wantonly wasting on the fetish of drug addiction," but such a success was possible only under the guidance of a professional expert.

Most important, the professional expert could turn the otherwise normal addict's overpowering but misdirected desire to his or her own and to society's good. The committee declared that the respectable addict's "strong desire is a measure of his energy. Let him be taught to direct that energy into wholesome channels which will give him as great pleasure and which will recreate his soul." By now, the assumptions that animated this statement should be obvious. We have seen throughout this book that various marginalized groups, especially the Chinese, African Americans, and the discontented "misfits" of the industrial class, displayed not their "wholesome" yet misdirected energy in their addiction to narcotics but rather their inner degradation or inability to reconcile themselves to their places in the modern world. What I have termed the double meaning of addiction, the paradoxical opposition between juridical and volitional senses of the word, helps us to understand this division between the respectable and the disrespectable, the hopeful and the hopeless, the innocent and the guilty. But perhaps of greater significance is that the double meaning also suggests a cure for the condition. The committee concluded that "such is the task of the men and women in charge of the institution for the educated men and women who are drug addicts: They are to be both trained and sympathetic, wholesome and strong-willed; friends and guides into a new life in which the base desire for self-gratification is, not suppressed, but directed into new channels which will make for the happiness of the individual and the race." [68] This clear juxtaposition of "suppression" with "direction" betrays the AMA's medicolegal solution to the problem of addiction. The AMA's report embodied a logic wherein professional authority served as a means of *directing* the desire of the "better class" of addicts into more productive channels while at the same time *suppressing* the desire for self-gratification held by addicts of social positions deemed inferior to this better class. As we have seen, the means of suppression ranged from permanent incarceration in work camps to the close supervision of vocational counselors, backed by what the committee described simply as "authority." This last embellishment was evidently unnecessary for the "wholesome and strong-willed friends" who were to gently coach and guide those of the better class into their new lives. Thus in its report, the committee solved the paradoxical double meaning of addiction by affirming it. The committee hoped to assign the juridical addicts—those of the "better class"—to the supervision of professional medicine while sentencing the volitional addicts to the jurisdiction of the penal authorities.

The combination of the Treasury Department and the AMA reports suggests that a provisional, medicolegal resolution of the double meaning of addiction was in place by 1920. Their juxtaposition indicates a consensus between the forces of professional medicine and federal police power in the definition and solution of what by then had been characterized for fifty years as a particularly challenging instance of modern technology's threat to the autonomy of the human subject. Their consensus is the culmination of a logical process that we have seen at work in the years between 1870 and 1920. What these studies both suggested was that the professional management of human desire could provide people who went along with this system and assumed the role of "patient" with something like a new, monitored autonomy, put in the service of a reinvigorated modern identity that could more adequately meet the challenges of the new century.

Their solution also provided a space for those recalcitrant subjects who could not or would not accede to the professional authority of organized medicine. As we have repeatedly seen, these people were often typed by their racial or class position and were left to the jurisdiction of the police. On January 1, 1920, the enforcement of antinarcotic laws was turned over to the newly created Narcotic Division of the Prohibition Unit of the Internal Revenue Bureau. Armed with the Supreme Court decisions in the Webb and Doremus cases and augmented by a strengthened Harrison Act, the federal government, in partnership with organized medicine, was well equipped to launch its enforcement of this newly minted medicolegal logic. They were authorized to begin the "war on drugs" whose clashes continue to reverberate across the landscape of the early twenty-first century.

Throughout this book, I have argued that a wide array of writers debated and ultimately affirmed the paradoxical double meaning that animates the addiction concept of habitual narcotic use within the broader context of what intellectual and cultural historians have called the cultural crisis of modernity. As such, addiction appeared as the epitome of that crisis, and the consequence of its affirmation was to divide the drug-using population into groups of criminals and patients while also helping to expand the roles of professional medicine and federal police authority. Many medical professionals would eventually chafe at the increasingly intrusive government regulation of their prescribing practices, but that is beside the point. The deed was done, and whether practitioners realized it or not, the Harrison Act was part of the early twentieth-century expansion of the cultural authority, prestige, and power of professional medicine, backed by the power of the state. The act implicitly recognized and helped to establish professional expertise as adequate to the task of solving what so many had described as a menace that was emblematic of the broader threats carried within late nineteenth- and early twentieth-century modernity. Likewise, the act offers an example of the continuing expansion of interventionist state power, backed by the imprimatur of scientific authority, into the regulation and the disciplining of bodies and their desires.

Moreover, we have seen that the insistent and perhaps inevitable resort to the immediate cultural context as a means of describing and explaining the drug habit bound together the concepts of modernity and addiction. As such, I have suggested that the addiction concept played a metonymic role in turn-of-the-twentieth-century American culture—that it offered a significant example of the way that one relatively minor element of the broader culture might come to stand for an entire syndrome of historical changes that contributed to the perception of the period as a moment of crisis. But figures of speech have power, and thus the addiction concept did more that simply reflect its cultural context. It also helped to *produce* it by adding to the sense of its modern historical moment as a time of crisis. As such, it was embedded in the culture of which it was part. The addiction concept stood as the embodiment of cultural crisis, and it would soon become a common way to describe the compulsive desire for many other substances and practices, while it also continued to mark the novelty of the ever changing present in terms of its newest addictive technologies. The concept performed those tasks for most of the twentieth century, and it continues to do so today.

But the texts we have confronted in this book push us still further, suggesting that we extend the metaphor by thinking of the medicolegal solution to the problem of addiction in terms of its status as a remedy, not merely for the problems of habitual drug use but also for the cultural crisis of modernity itself. Because the modern cultural crisis was rooted in a perceived inadequacy of older descriptions of middle-class identity, based on challenged notions of autonomy and independence, we might think of the Harrison Narcotic Act as one attempt to shore up that hemorrhaging conception of subjectivity. In an interdependent, complex world, relations of obligation and responsibility—perhaps the crucial concepts in the establishment of subjectivity—are difficult to ascertain. Professional experts offer specialized knowledge that can help to negotiate those confusing pathways, but as I hope we have seen, that knowledge comes at a price. Today we live in an immensely complex, interdependent world where deference to the authority of professional experts has become the norm. We are used to having our desires interpreted, assessed, and fed back to us by powerful social institutions. Diverse professions, ranging from psychology and medicine to advertising, law, and criminology, specialize in delimiting personal responsibility and obligation by praising some desires—and those who have them—

while censuring others. Those who resist the expertise of these institutions, choosing instead to indulge unsanctioned, unconventional, or "excessive" desires, risk consequences that run from social exclusion to incarceration. In this speculative sense, and in a way that goes well beyond the bounds of a book about turn-of-the-twentieth-century culture, the addiction concept suggests an important approach to the analysis of modern subjectivity. Further research may show that it is precisely at this crossing where we find the most significant and long-lasting intersection of the concepts of addiction and modernity.

Finally, I hope that it is clear that the addiction concept and the notion of modernity as cultural crisis, as I have discussed them in this book, were far from abstract, nor are they mere excuses for theoretical exercises in the close reading of historical texts. In the words of historian Caroline Jean Acker, "We now have in the United States a two-tier system of response to drug dependence: treatment for the middle and upper classes and incarceration for most others, including the poor, the uninsured, ethnic minorities and immigrants."[69] Though today's conditions are vastly changed from those of one hundred years ago, the contextualization of otherwise arcane debates about technology, medicine, and modern subjectivity may tell us much about contemporary attitudes toward drug use. In the end, the addiction concept served as a medicolegal formula that inscribed the cultural crisis of modernity on the bodies of those whom it identified and named as addicts. This century-old textual process therefore had, and continues to have, real consequences—not simply for those who were assigned the burden of the condition but for us all.

NOTES

Introduction

1. There is a vast literature on DeQuincey. To begin an exploration of its resonance in the discussion of narcotics, see Althea Hayter, *Opium and the Romantic Imagination* (Berkeley: University of California Press, 1968). For a more historical approach, see Virginia Berridge, *Opium and the People: Opiate Use and Drug Control Policy in Nineteenth and Early Twentieth Century England*, rev. ed. (London: Free Assoriciation Books, 1999).

2. The authoritative source on the history of the syringe remains Norman Howard-Jones, "A Critical Study of the Origins and Early Development of Hypodermic Medication," *Journal of the History of Medicine and Allied Sciences* 2, no. 2 (1947): 201–49.

3. On Civil War battlefield application and for the estimate of 4.59 per thousand, see David T. Courtwright, *Dark Paradise: A History of Opiate Addiction in America* (Cambridge: Harvard University Press, 2001), 54–55, 9, 3. I derived the figure of 10.9 per thousand based on a total U.S. population in 1910 of 91,641,195. See University of Virginia Geospatial and Statistical Data Center, *United States Historical Census Browser*, http://fisher.lib.virginia.edu/census/.

4. David F. Musto, M.D., *The American Disease: Origins of Narcotic Control*, 3rd ed. (New York: Oxford University Press, 1999). Joseph Spillane has made an important contribution to this debate, showing that public opinion had turned against recreational cocaine use long before the Harrison Narcotic Act stigmatized the practice as illegal. See Joseph F. Spillane, *Cocaine: From Medical Marvel to Modern Menace in the United States, 1884–1920* (Baltimore: Johns Hopkins University Press, 2000), 141–57. On the changing medical notions of addiction, from the perspective of both researchers and patients, see Carolyn J. Acker, *Creating the American Junkie: Addiction Research in the Classic Era of Narcotic Control* (Baltimore: Johns Hopkins University Press, 2002). On the history of treatment, see William L. White, *Slaying the Dragon: The History of Addiction Treatment and Recovery in America* (Bloomington, Ill.: Chestnut Health Systems, 1998). For a broad, comparative overview of the new historical research on drugs and alcohol emerging at the opening of the twenty-first century, see Caroline J. Acker and Sarah W. Tracy, eds., *Altering American Consciousness: Essays on the History of Alcohol and Drug Use in the United States, 1800–1997* (Amherst: University of Massachusetts Press, 2004).

5. Musto, *The American Disease*, 11.

6. Courtwright, *Dark Paradise,* 4

7. Although the cultural history of the drug problem is a relatively recent development, the history of the drug culture has an established presence on library shelves. See, for instance, H. Wayne Morgan, *Drugs in America: A Social History, 1800–1980* (Syracuse: Syracuse University Press, 1974); John C. Burnham, *Bad Habits: Drinking, Smoking, Taking Drugs, Gambling, Sexual Misbehavior, and Swearing in American History* (New York: New York University Press, 1993); and Jill Jonnes, *Hep-Cats, Narcs, and Pipe Dreams: A History of America's Romance with Illegal Drugs* (New York: Scribner, 1996). The influence of the newer, cultural approaches has been particularly evident in works that have focused on the gendered aspects of the discourse. See Nancy D. Campbell, *Using Women: Gender, Drug Policy, and Social Justice* (New York: Routledge, 2000); Mara L. Keire, "Dope Fiends and Degenerates: The Gendering of Addiction in the Early Twentieth Century," *Journal of Social History* 31 (Summer 1998): 809–22; and Stephen R. Kandall, *Substance and Shadow: Women and Addiction in the United States* (Cambridge: Harvard University Press, 1996). For literary and theoretical treatments, see Avital Ronell, *Crack Wars: Literature, Addiction, Mania* (Lincoln: University of Nebraska Press, 1992); David Lenson, *On Drugs* (Minneapolis: University of Minnesota Press, 1995); Sadie Plant, *Writing on Drugs* (New York: Faber and Faber, 2001); and, most helpfully, Jacques Derrida, "The Rhetoric of Drugs," *Differences* 5, no. 1 (1993): 1–25. On visual elements of the discourse of addiction, see Timothy A. Hickman, "Heroin Chic: The Visual Culture of Narcotic Addiction," *Third Text: Critical Perspectives on Contemporary Art and Culture* 16, no. 2 (June 2002): 119–36.

8. On embeddedness, see Louis A. Montrose, "Professing the Renaissance: The Poetics and Politics of Culture," in *The New Historicism,* ed. H. Aram Veeser (London: Routledge, 1986), 15–36.

9. On the necessity of critical approaches to "banal" cultural objects, see Lauren Berlant, *The Queen of America Goes to Washington City: Essays on Sex and Citizenship* (Durham: Duke University Press, 1997).

10. On inscription, see Franz Kafka, "In the Penal Colony," in *The Penal Colony: Stories and Short Pieces,* trans. Willa Muir and Edwin Muir (New York: Schocken Books, 1976), 191–227.

11. This theme has been persistent in the historiography of the Gilded Age and the Progressive Era since (at least) the 1950s, when Richard Hofstadter explained the Spanish-American War in terms of the "psychic crisis of the 1890s." See Richard Hofstadter, *The Paranoid Style in American Politics and Other Essays* (London: Jonathan Cape, 1964), 148. See also Robert H. Wiebe, *The Search for Order, 1877–1920* (New York: Hill and Wang, 1967); Henry F. May, *The End of American Innocence: A Study of the First Years of Our Own Time, 1912–1917* (New York: Alfred A. Knopf, 1959); Alan Trachtenberg, *The Incorporation of America: Culture and Society in the Gilded Age* (New York: Hill and Wang, 1982); Nancy Cott, *The Grounding of American Feminism* (New Haven: Yale University Press, 1987); James Livingston, *Pragmatism and the Political Economy of Cultural Revolution* (Chapel Hill: University of North Carolina Press, 1994); and Clive Bush, *Halfway to Revolution: Investigation and Crisis in the Work of Henry Adams, William James, and Gertrude Stein* (New Haven: Yale University Press, 1991). Theoretical takes on modernity abound, but a good start is Marshall Berman's *All That Is Solid Melts into Air: The Experience of Modernity* (New York: Penguin, 1988);

Matei Calinescu, *Five Faces of Modernity: Modernism, Avant-Garde, Decadence, Kitsch, Postmodernism* (Durham: Duke University Press, 1987); and Reinhart Kosselleck, *The Practice of Conceptual History: Timing History, Spacing Concepts*, trans. Todd Samuel Presner (Stanford: Stanford University Press, 2002). For more recent applications of and challenges to the crisis model that incorporate race, class, and gender difference, see Gail Bederman, *Manliness and Civilization: A Cultural History of Gender and Race in the United States, 1880–1917* (Chicago: University of Chicago Press, 1995); Grace Elizabeth Hale, *Making Whiteness: Southern Segregation, 1890–1940* (New York: Random House, 1999); and Robert G. Lee, *Orientals: Asian Americans in Popular Culture* (Philadelphia: Temple University Press, 1999). On the limitations of the crisis model, see especially Bederman, *Manliness and Civilization*, 11.

12. June Howard, *Form and History in American Literary Naturalism* (Chapel Hill: University of North Carolina Press, 1985), xi.

13. On the experience of modernity as a "paradoxical . . . unity of disunity," see Berman, *All That Is Solid*, 15. My sense of modernity, however, is closer to Jean-François Lyotard's description of *post*modernity as the latest instance of modernity. See Jean-François Lyotard, "Answer to the Question: What Is Postmodernism?" in *The Postmodern Condition: A Report on Knowledge*, trans. Geoff Bennington and Brian Massumi (Manchester: Manchester University Press, 1984), 71–82.

14. Calinescu, *Five Faces of Modernity*, 1–92.

15. Harry Gene Levine, "The Discovery of Addiction: Changing Conceptions of Habitual Drunkenness in America," *Journal of Studies on Alcohol* 39, no. 1 (1978): 143. Levine's notion of a paradigm shift is drawn from Thomas Kuhn, *The Structure of Scientific Revolutions*, 2nd ed., enlarged (Chicago: University of Chicago Press, 1970). Kuhn's work is also fundamental to my own.

16. Levine, "Discovery of Addiction," 144, 151.

17. Ibid., 148.

18. Ibid., 158.

19. Levine first quotes Reverend S. Danforth, who in 1709 wrote that "God sends many sore judgments on a people that addict themselves to intemperance in drinking" (147). He contrasts this with Benjamin Rush's 1814 contention that "the persons who have been addicted to [strong liquors] should abstain from them suddenly and entirely" (152). In the first example the word is used as a reflexive verb, in the second it is passive but still a verb. While it does illustrate a shift in the assertion of moral responsibility for habitual drunkenness, the term does not refer to a distinct physiological condition that these earlier writers would have recognized as "addiction."

20. This change in terminology is clear in an examination by Charles E. Terry and Mildred Pellens, *The Opium Problem* (1928; reprint, Montclair, N.J.: Patterson Smith, 1970). The older terms for habitual drug use continue to appear after the turn of the century, but their use diminishes as they are rapidly replaced by the words "addiction" and "addict."

21. *The Oxford English Dictionary*, compact ed. (1971), s.v. "addict." Emphasis added.

22. Most historians refer to this discrepancy as a conflict between the disease and vice concepts of habitual drug use. Rather than arguing over which notion is dominant at which time, I hope that my turn to something like the literal meaning of the word "addiction" itself demonstrates how both notions could operate simultaneously, in one

concept. Also important is that the division of the sick into guilty and innocent camps was not inaugurated at the turn of the century. The addiction concept helped to formalize this older medical approach to "social" diseases. For further exploration of this tendency, see Alan Brandt, *No Magic Bullet: A Social History of Venereal Disease in the United States since 1880,* expanded ed. (New York: Oxford University Press, 1987). Caroline J. Acker explores this process as it operated in medical attitudes regarding opiates and addiction in "Stigma or Legitimation: A Historical Examination of the Social Potentials of Addiction Disease Models," *Journal of Psychoactive Drugs* 25, no. 3 (1993): 193–205.

23. As we will see, such arguments can be found in many places. Among the most interesting and influential are George Miller Beard's *Stimulants and Narcotics; Medically, Philosophically, and Morally Considered* (New York: G. P. Putnam and Sons, 1871), 24; Leslie E. Keeley, M.D, *Opium: Its Use, Abuse and Cure; or, From Bondage to Freedom* (Chicago: Banner of Gold, 1897), 39–41; T. D. Crothers, *Morphinism and Narcomanias from Other Drugs: Their Etiology, Treatment and Medicolegal Relations* (Philadelphia: W. B. Saunders and Company, 1902), 33; and L. L. Stanley, "Morphinism," *Journal of the American Institute of Criminal Law and Criminology* 6 (1915–16): 586.

24. This interpretation of the Harrison Act required several years of legal haggling. Especially important were the Supreme Court's 1919 decisions in *Webb et al. v. U.S.* and *U.S. v. Doremus.* See Musto, *The American Disease,* 131–32.

Chapter One

1. This brief synopsis is drawn from Althea Hayter, *Opium and the Romantic Imagination* (Berkeley: University of California Press, 1968), chap. 1. A corresponding story is told by Virginia Berridge in *Opium and the People: Opiate Use and Drug Control Policy in Nineteenth and Early Twentieth Century England* (London: Free Associciation Books, 1999). For a study of opiate use and regulation in medieval France, see Walton O. Schalick III, "To Market, to Market: The Theory and Practice of Opiates in the Middle Ages," in *Opioids and Pain Relief: A Historical Perspective,* ed. Marcia L. Meldrum (Seattle: IASP Press, 2003). For a wide survey of medical writing about opium use before 1928, see Charles Terry and Mildred Pellens, *The Opium Problem* (1928; reprint, Montclair, N.J.: Patterson Smith, 1970).

2. John Jones, *The Mysteries of Opium Revealed* (London: Richard Smith, 1701), 32.

3. Berridge, *Opium and the People,* 53.

4. In 1989, for instance, William S. Burroughs felt compelled to question DeQuincey's legacy. He told the historian David Courtwright that "the opium dream as a stimulus to creativity is definitely a myth. . . . DeQuincey knew that if, say, he built up a very heavy habit, when he got down to a much lighter habit, he'd have this renewal, and then he felt like writing." See David Courtwright, Herman Joseph, and Don Des Jarlais., *Addicts Who Survived: An Oral History of Narcotic Use in America, 1923–1965* (Knoxville: The University of Tennessee Press, 1989), 246.

5. DeQuincey's book, though autobiographical and narrated in the first person, was published anonymously. He never names or refers directly to himself as narrator anywhere in the text. I therefore refer to the person, Thomas DeQuincey, by his real name and to the character in his book when I discuss "the opium-eater."

6. Samuel Morewood, *An Essay on the Inventions and Customs of Both Ancients and Moderns in the Use of Inebriating Liquors* (London: Longman, Hurst et al., 1824), 106.

7. Morewood further commends DeQuincey's writing as offering a description of "the struggles he underwent to break the charm which kept him spell-bound for such a length of time," which he described as "highly interesting and curious" (ibid., 106–7).

8. Edward W. Said, *Orientalism* (New York: Vintage Books, 1979), 1, 3.

9. Thomas DeQuincey, *Confessions of an English Opium-eater and Other Writings*, ed. Grevel Lindop (Oxford: Oxford University Press, 1985), 56.

10. Ibid., 57.

11. Ibid., 5. The Latin passage is from Terrence and is translated by Grevel Lindop as "he deems nothing alien to him."

12. Ibid., 72.

13. Ibid., 78.

14. William Blair, "An Opium-Eater in America," *Knickerbocker*, July 1842, available from the Schaffer Library of Drug Policy (online database), http://www.druglibrary.org/schaffer/heroin/history/blair.htm, 3.

15. C. B. Macpherson, *The Political Theory of Possessive Individualism: Hobbes to Locke* (Oxford: Oxford University Press, 1961), 3.

16. Gordon S. Wood, *The Radicalism of the American Revolution* (New York: Vintage Books, 1991), 104.

17. William J. Rohrbaugh, *The Alcoholic Republic: An American Tradition* (New York: Oxford University Press, 1979), 176.

18. Ibid., 87.

19. Mark Edward Lender and James Kirby Martin, *Drinking in America: A History*, revised and expanded ed. (New York: Free Press, 1987), 205–6.

20. Rohrbaugh, *Alcoholic Republic*, 89, 90.

21. Lender and Martin, *Drinking in America*, 74–77.

22. Abraham Lincoln, "Temperance Address," *Sangamo Journal*, March 25, 1842, available from the Schaffer Library of Drug Policy, (online database) http://www.druglibrary.org/schaffer/History/ancient/TempAddr.htm, 6.

23. Ibid.

24. Ibid.

25. This biography of Ludlow is drawn from James Grant Wilson and John Fiske, eds., *Appleton's Cyclopaedia of American Biography* (New York: Appleton and Company, 1888). Available from the Lyceaum (online database), http://www.lycaeum.org/~sputnik/Ludlow/Texts/appleton.html, 1. Ludlow is something of a cult figure whose life and writing are often celebrated by various drug countercultures. These groups can be credited with preserving the memory of this otherwise obscure figure. The Fitz Hugh Ludlow Memorial Library existed in San Francisco during the 1970s and early 1980s. The most extensive biography of Ludlow, "A Brief Biography of Fitz Hugh Ludlow," has been put together by Dave Gross and is available at http://www.lycaeum.org/~sputnik/Ludlow/THE/Biography/biography.html.

26. Fitz Hugh Ludlow, *The Hasheesh Eater: Being Passages from the Life of a Pythagorean* (New York: Harper and Brothers, 1857; Upper Saddle River, N.J.: Gregg Press, 1970), ix.

27. Ibid., ix–x.

28. "Literary Notices," *Harper's New Monthly Magazine*, November 1857, 834–35, quoted in Gross, "A Brief Biography of Fitz Hugh Ludlow," 10.

29. D. W. Cheever, "Narcotics," *North American Review* 95, no. 197 (1862): 405.

30. Louis J. Bragman, M.D., "A Minor DeQuincey," *Medical Journal and Record* 121 (January–June 1925), available from the Lycaeum, http://www.lycaeum.org/~sputnik/Ludlow/Texts/bragman.html.

31. See Gross, "A Brief Biography of Fitz Hugh Ludlow," 23.

32. Ludlow, *Hasheesh Eater*, vi.

33. Ibid., v.

34. Ibid., vii.

35. Gross, "A Brief Biography of Fitz Hugh Ludlow," 1, 4.

36. Fitz Hugh Ludlow, "If Massa put Guns into our Han's," *Atlantic Monthly* 15, no. 90, 1865, available from the Lycaeum, http://www.lycaeum.Org/~sputnik/Ludlow/Texts/massa.html, 1.

37. Ibid. Note also the persistent racialism, if not outright racism, that pervades this pro-abolitionist piece.

38. Ibid.

39. Ibid., 4, 7.

40. Ibid., 6.

41. "The Household Angel" began on May 30, 1868, and concluded on August 22, 1868.

42. Gross, "A Brief Biography of Fitz Hugh Ludlow," 35. See also the selection of the Ludlow family's correspondence that Dave Gross has made available online at the Lycaeum (online database), http://www.lycaeum.org/~sputnik/Ludlow/Texts/letters.html.

43. Gross, "A Brief Biography of Fitz Hugh Ludlow," 35.

44. Horace Day, *The Opium Habit, with Suggestions as to the Remedy* (New York: Harper and Brothers, 1868), 5.

45. Ibid., 7.

46. Fitz Hugh Ludlow, "What Shall They Do to be Saved?" *Harper's Magazine*, August 1867, 10–11 available from the Schaffer Library of Drug Policy (online database), http://www.druglibrary.org/schaffer/history/saved1867.htm.

47. Ibid., 4.

48. Ibid., 5.

49. Ibid., 4.

50. It is important to remember, however, that opium was something far different from alcohol. On page 5 of "What Shall They Do?" Ludlow explained that "the grasp with which liquor holds a man when it turns on him, even after he has abused it for a lifetime, compared with the ascendancy possessed by opium over the unfortunate habituated to it for but a single year, is as the clutch of an angry woman to the embrace of Victor Hugo's Pieuvre."

51. Ibid.

52. Ibid., 12.

53. Ibid., 14.

54. Ibid.

55. Ibid., 16.

56. Ibid.

Chapter Two

1. T. J. Jackson Lears, *No Place of Grace: Anti-Modernism and the Transformation of American Culture, 1880–1920* (New York: Pantheon Books, 1981), 12–13. Lears argues that fin de siècle, elite cultural critique had lost its formerly solid grounding in communitarian social institutions, especially the Protestant Church. Turn-of-the-century cultural elites therefore resorted to various ideologies of the individual in what Lears argues were their multiple resistances to modernity. Lears concludes that this "therapeutic" approach to individual selfhood was (and is) precisely the logic of the modernity supposedly under attack and therefore served only to strengthen an emergent world of corporate capitalism and its consumer ethos.

2. See Alfred D. Chandler Jr., *The Visible Hand: The Managerial Revolution in American Business* (Cambridge: Harvard University Press, Belknap Press, 1977), 1–14.

3. Lears, *No Place of Grace*, 32.

4. Mark Wahlgren Summers, *The Gilded Age, or, The Hazard of New Functions* (Upper Saddle River, N.J.: Prentice Hall, 1997), 78.

5. Alan Trachtenberg, *The Incorporation of America: Culture and Society in the Gilded Age* (New York: Hill and Wang, 1982), 122–23.

6. Thomas Haskell, *The Emergence of Professional Social Science: The American Social Science Association and the Nineteenth-Century Crisis of Authority* (Urbana: University of Illinois Press, 1977), 1.

7. Ibid., 39–40.

8. For a useful set of distinctions between studies of alcohol and drug habits, the most pertinent of which rests on the relative marginality of narcotic use in the nineteenth century and later, see Mariana Valverde, *Diseases of the Will: Alcohol and the Dilemmas of Freedom* (Cambridge, England: Cambridge University Press, 1998), 9. From my perspective, the study of narcotic addiction contributes to our understanding of a tenacious social problem but also reveals a microlevel performance of a modern cultural crisis. Other maladies of dependence might be explored to complementary ends. See, for instance, Leslie Camhi, "Stealing Femininity: Department Store Kleptomania as Sexual Disorder," *Differences* 5 (Spring 1993): 26–50. On alcohol use in America, see Mark Edward Lender and James Kirby Martin, *Drinking in America: A History,* revised and expanded ed. (New York: Free Press, 1987). For antebellum practices, see William J. Rohrbaugh, *The Alcoholic Republic: An American Tradition* (New York: Oxford University Press, 1979). For twentieth-century practices, with special attention to gender, see Lori Rotskoff, *Love on the Rocks: Men, Women, and Alcohol in Post–World War II America* (Chapel Hill: University of North Carolina Press, 2002). For a broader, comparative view, see Susanna Barrows and Robin Room, eds., *Drinking Behavior and Belief in Modern History* (Berkeley: University of California Press, 1991). Literary approaches are on display in David S. Reynolds and Debra J. Rosenthal, eds., *The Serpent in the Cup: Temperance in American Literature* (Amherst: University of Massachusetts Press, 1997).

9. David T. Courtwright, *Dark Paradise: A History of Opiate Addiction in America* (Cambridge: Harvard University Press, 2001), 45, 85; David F. Musto, M.D., *The American Disease: Origins of Narcotic Control,* 3rd ed. (New York: Oxford University Press, 1999), 69; Joseph F. Spillane, *Cocaine: From Medical Marvel to Modern Menace in the United States, 1884–1920* (Baltimore: Johns Hopkins University Press, 2000), 8–9;

T. D. Crothers, M.D., quoting a Dr. Luria, in *Morphinism and Narcomanias from Other Drugs: Their Etiology, Treatment and Medicolegal Relations* (Philadelphia: W. B. Saunders, 1902), 22. Experts praised cocaine in a similar manner; see Spillane, *Cocaine*, 7–24.

10. George Miller Beard, M.D., *Stimulants and Narcotics; Medically, Philosophically, and Morally Considered* (New York: G. P. Putnam and Sons, 1871), 24. Beard had begun to use the term "neurasthenia" in his published work two years previously. See George Miller Beard, M.D., "Neurasthenia, or nervous exhaustion" in the *Boston Medical and Surgical Journal* 80 (1869): 217–221.

11. Ibid., 84. He refers here to the isolation of morphine in 1817 and cocaine in 1844, the invention of the hypodermic syringe in 1843, and the considerable growth in both the medical and recreational uses of these substances, especially during and after the Civil War.

12. Ibid., 24.

13. Harry Hubble Kane, *The Hypodermic Injection of Morphia: Its History, Advantages and Dangers* (New York: Chas. L. Bermingham and Co., 1880), 13, 19. The authoritative source on the history of the syringe remains Norman Howard-Jones, "A Critical Study of the Origins and Early Development of Hypodermic Medication," *Journal of the History of Medicine and Allied Sciences* 2, no. 2 (1947): 201–49.

14. Crothers, *Morphinism*, 33.

15. Joel D. Howell defines "technology" as being comprised of three layers. It can be a physical artifact or a machine, an activity (a treatment or practice), or a specific knowledge. See Howell, *Technology in the Hospital: Transforming Patient Care in the Early Twentieth Century* (Baltimore: Johns Hopkins University Press, 1995), 8. The use of the refined products of opium and coca had elements of all three of these aspects of technology. Their use can—and should—be seen as a part of the modernizing medical technology of the late nineteenth and early twentieth centuries.

16. Roberts Bartholow, M.D., *Manual of Hypodermic Medication* (Philadelphia: J. B. Lippincott, 1873), 26–27.

17. Ibid., 28.

18. Ibid., 81.

19. Roberts Bartholow, M.D., *The Treatment of Diseases by the Hypodermic Method: A Manual of Hypodermic Medication* (Philadelphia: J. B. Lippincott, 1879), 6.

20. Ibid., 90–91.

21. Ibid., 91.

22. Roberts Bartholow, M.D., *A Manual of Hypodermatic Medication: The Treatment of Diseases by the Hypodermatic Method* (Philadelphia: J. B. Lippincott, 1882), 5.

23. Roberts Bartholow, M.D., *A Manual of Hypodermatic Medication: The Treatment of Diseases by the Hypodermatic or Subcutaneous Method* (Philadelphia: J. B. Lippincott, 1891), 261.

24. I have explored this fundamental discrepancy—a principle of internal difference—as the definitive element of the discourse of addiction in several places. See, for instance, "Heroin Chic: The Visual Culture of Narcotic Addiction," *Third Text: Critical Perspectives on Contemporary Art and Culture* 16, no. 2 (2002): 119–136 or "Drugs and Race in American Culture: Orientalism in the Turn-of-the-Century Discourse of Narcotic Addiction," *American Studies* 41, no. 1 (2000): 71–91.

25. Bartholow, *Manual of Hypodermatic Medication* (1891), 261.

26. Ibid.

27. Ibid., 262.

28. Ibid.

29. George Miller Beard, *Certain Symptoms of Nervous Exhaustion,* reprint from the *Virginia Medical Monthly,* June 1878, 1. Pamphlet available at the Library of the College of Physicians of Philadelphia.

30. George Miller Beard, "Causes of the Recent Increase of Inebriety in America," *Quarterly Journal of Inebriety* 1, no. 1 (1876): 30.

31. Ibid., 34.

32. Beard, *Certain Symptoms,* 1.

33. George Miller Beard, M.D., *American Nervousness: Its Causes and Consequences* (1881; reprint, New York: Arno Press and the New York Times, 1972), 138.

34. Ibid., 8, viii, 30–31.

35. W. F. Waugh, "Opium Inebriety," *Quarterly Journal of Inebriety* 16 (October 1894): 310. On the way fears of overcivilization affected the construction of race and gender difference, see Gail Bederman, *Manliness and Civilization: A Cultural History of Gender and Race in the United States, 1880–1917* (Chicago: University of Chicago Press, 1995).

36. Beard, *Certain Symptoms,* 10.

37. Beard, "Causes of the Recent Increase," 34.

38. Beard, *Certain Symptoms,* 10.

39. H. H. Kane, *Drugs That Enslave: The Opium, Morphine, Chloral and Hashisch Habits* (Philadelphia: Presley Blakiston, 1881), 17.

40. Henry G. Cole, *Confessions of an American Opium Eater: From Bondage to Freedom* (Boston: James H. Earle, 1895), 7, 8. This section of Cole's book has also been excerpted in H. Wayne Morgan's *Yesterday's Addicts: American Society and Drug Abuse, 1865–1920* (Norman: University of Oklahoma Press, 1974).

41. L. L. Stanley, "Morphinism," *Journal of the American Institute of Criminal Law and Criminology* 6 (1915–16): 586. Quoted in Charles E. Terry and Mildred Pellens, *The Opium Problem* (1928; reprint, Montclair, N.J.: Patterson Smith, 1970), 113.

42. For a detailed analysis of the Foster Bill's struggles in Congress, see Musto, *The American Disease,* 40–48.

43. See ibid., 54–68.

44. The influence of Wright's report, which was designated Senate Doc. 377, Sixty-first Congress, Second Session, was made clear by Martin I. Wilbert, a pharmacist in the Public Health Service and a member of the American Medical Associations's (AMA's) Council on Pharmacy and Chemistry, who wrote that "the conditions outlined in these several messages, with other evidence that has accumulated, will, no doubt, tend to bring about the enactment of radical if not drastic laws for controlling the traffic in narcotic or habit-forming drugs of all kinds." See *Journal of the American Pharmaceutical Association* 2, no. 3 (1913): 309.

45. Hamilton Wright, M. D., "Report on the International Opium Commission and on the Opium Problem as seen within the United States and its Possessions" contained in *Opium Problem: Message from the President of the United States,* U.S. Senate Doc. 377, 61st Cong., 2nd sess., February 21, 1910, 37.

46. Ibid., 47.

47. The association's debt to and differences with the temperance movement are outlined in Joseph Parrish, M.D., "The Temperance Cause and Its Departures," *Quarterly Journal of Inebriety* 5, no. 1 (1883): 1–7.

48. Theodore L. Mason, M.D., "Inebriety, a Disease," *Quarterly Journal of Inebriety* 2, no. 1 (1877): 1.

49. J. B. Mattison, M.D., "The Treatment of Opium Addiction," *Quarterly Journal of Inebriety* 7, no.1 (1885): 1. The distinction is an important one and is covered in greater detail by Harry Gene Levine in "The Discovery of Addiction: Changing Conceptions of Habitual Drunkenness in America," *Journal of Studies on Alcohol* 39, no. 1 (1978). Also helpful is Valverde, *Diseases of the Will.*

50. Alonzo Calkins, M.D., *Opium and the Opium Appetite* (Philadelphia: Lippincott, 1871), 19; Horace Day, *The Opium Habit, with Suggestions as to the Remedy* (New York: Harper and Brothers, 1868).

51. Calkins, *Opium and the Opium Appetite*, 20.

52. Joseph Parrish, M.D., "Opium Poisoning," *Proceedings of the Fifth Meeting of the American Association for the Cure of Inebriates, Held in New York City on 29 September 1874* (New York: The Association, 1874), 2.

53. Also clear is the continuity of a rhetoric that I have elsewhere argued was derived, on the one hand, from the abolitionists (users were "enslaved") and, on the other, from temperance (the abandonment of "self").

54. This chronology of Crothers's life is drawn from an editorial by Louis M. Gaynor, M.D., in the *Quarterly Journal of Inebriety* 24, no. 1 (1902): 97–98.

55. Crothers, *Morphinism*, 33.

56. Ibid., 5.

57. Though many of Crothers's patients were women, I use the masculine pronoun in reference to the restoration of subjectivity because, in the discourse of addiction as elsewhere, the rational, autonomous subject was often constructed as "masculine" against an irrational, dependent, and "feminine" other. See Joan W. Scott, *Gender and the Politics of History* (New York: Columbia University Press, 2000). On the classical republican tradition's exclusion of women, precisely because of their alleged status as dependents, see Gorcon S. Wood, *The Radicalism of the American Revolution* (New York: Vintage Books, 1991), 104.

58. T. D. Crothers, M.D., "Legal Opinions of Inebriety," *Quarterly Journal of Inebriety* 5, no. 2 (1883): 90.

59. Ibid., 92.

60. T. D. Crothers, M.D., "Historical Notes concerning the Legal Responsibility of Inebriates," *Quarterly Journal of Inebriety* 5, no. 2 (1883): 157.

61. Ibid., 158.

62. Ibid.

63. This project was helped along by others who published their work in the *QJI*. See, for instance, E. C. Clevenger, M.D., "Medico-Legal Relations of Morphine and Other Addictions," *QJI* 20, no. 2 (1898): 265–72. See also Geo. R. Villeneueve, M.D., "Case of Morphinism Associated with Theft," *QJI* 22, no. 1 (1900): 84–90.

64. Crothers, *Morphinism*, 231–32.

65. Ibid., 232.

66. Ibid., 233, 232, 242.

67. J. L. Bowman, M.D, "Psychical Aspects of the Morphine Addict," *Journal of Inebriety* 30 (Spring 1908): 40, 41. On page 42 Bowman acknowledges Crothers's influence on his thought. In the same edition of the *Journal of Inebriety*, an Indiana doctor wrote that "the man who acquires a drug habit is a different man from what he was before," whereas other sorts of habit left the habitué unchanged. See Charles W. Carter, "What Is the Morphine Disease?" ibid., 28.

68. Henry Freeman Walker, M.D., "Some Remarks on the Morphine Habit," *Quarterly Journal of Inebriety* 18, no. 3 (July, 1896): 235, 236.

69. Asa P. Meylert, *Notes on the Opium Habit* (New York: G. P. Putnam's Sons, 1885), 11.

70. Ibid., 12, 46.

71. T. D. Crothers, M.D. "To What Extent Are Morphine Addicts Responsible for Their Crimes?" *Medical Standard* 34, no. 3 (1916): 103.

72. Alexander Lambert, "Alcohol, Morphinism, Cocaine," in *Modern Medicine: Its Theory and Practice*, ed. William Osler (Philadelphia: Lea and Febiger, 1914), 438–39.

73. I discuss the relationship between narcotics and professional medicine at greater length in chapter 4. Musto, in *The American Disease*, and especially Caroline J. Acker in *Creating the American Junkie: Addiction Research in the Classic Era of Narcotic Control* (Baltimore: Johns Hopkins University Press, 2002) also look at this theme, though mostly from the perspectives of the individuals involved. The best general treatment on the professionalization of American medicine is Paul Starr's *The Social Transformation of American Medicine: The Rise of a Sovereign Profession and the Making of a Vast Industry* (New York: Basic Books, 1982).

74. George A. Barclay, "The Keeley League," *Journal of the Illinois State Historical Society* 54 (1964): 341–65.

75. William L. White, *Slaying the Dragon: The History of Addiction Treatment and Recovery in America* (Bloomington, Ill.: Chestnut Health Systems, 1998), 50–52.

76. Morgan, *Yesterday's Addicts*, 75.

77. Beard, "Causes of the Recent Increase," 44.

78. T. D. Crothers, M.D., "The Gold Cures," *Quarterly Journal of Inebriety* 17, no. 3 (1895): 284.

79. Leslie E. Keeley, M.D., *Opium: Its Use, Abuse and Cure; or, From Bondage to Freedom* (Chicago: Banner of Gold, 1897), 37.

80. Ibid., 23.

81. Ibid., 15.

82. Ibid., 20.

83. Ibid., 36.

84. Ibid., 79.

85. On the cultural meaning of the gold standard, see Walter Benn Michaels, *The Gold Standard and the Logic of Naturalism: American Literature at the Turn of the Century* (Berkeley: University of California Press, 1987).

86. David A. Wells, *Robinson Crusoe's Money; or the Remarkable Financial Fortunes and Misfortunes of a Remote Island Community*, with illustrations by Thomas Nast (1876; reprint, New York: Peter Smith, 1931), 57. Wells's text is rapidly becoming canonical, thanks largely to Michaels's use of it in *The Gold Standard*. See also Michael O'Malley's excellent "Specie and Species: Race and the Money Question in Nineteenth-Century America," *American Historical Review* 99, no. 2 (1994): 369–95.

87. Wells, *Robinson Crusoe's Money*, 63.
88. Ibid., 40.
89. Ibid., 63.
90. Keeley, *Opium*, 83.
91. Ibid., 85, 82, 75.

Chapter Three

1. Leslie E. Keeley, M.D., *Opium: Its Use, Abuse and Cure; or, From Bondage to Freedom* (Chicago: Banner of Gold, 1897), 8.
2. Ibid., 8.
3. Andrew Carnegie, *Triumphant Democracy: or, 50 Years' March of the Republic* (London: Sampson Low, 1886), 1. An interesting discussion of the American "cult of the new" can be found in William Leach, *Land of Desire: Merchants, Power, and the Rise of a New American Culture* (New York: Vintage, 1994), 4–5.
4. Keeley, *Opium*, 8.
5. Ibid., 8.
6. Ibid., 104.
7. Ibid., 105.
8. Ibid.
9. Ibid., 104–5.
10. Ibid., 24.
11. Robert G. Lee, *Orientals: Asian Americans in Popular Culture* (Philadelphia: Temple University Press, 1999), 22, 28. My goal in this section is to show several examples of the way that Orientalism, especially as manifested in anti-Chinese racism, inhabited the addiction concept of habitual narcotic use at the turn of the century. Those more interested in the other side of the equation—the role played by allegations of opium use in anti-Chinese rhetoric—could begin with Stuart Creighton Miller's *The Unwelcome Immigrant: The American Image of the Chinese, 1785–1882* (Berkeley: University of California Press, 1969). The work of Ronald Takaki, especially *Iron Cages: Race and Culture in Nineteenth-Century America* (New York: Alfred A. Knopf, 1979), is also quite helpful, as is Shih-shan Henry Tsai's *The Chinese Experience in America* (Bloomington: Indiana University Press, 1986). Among the more recent works, see Charles J. McClain, *In Search of Equality: The Chinese Struggle against Discrimination in Nineteenth-Century America* (Berkeley: University of California Press, 1994), James S. Moy's *Marginal Sights: Staging the Chinese in America* (Iowa City: University of Iowa Press, 1993), and Sucheng Chan's *Asian Americans: An Interpretive History* (Boston: Twayne Publishers, 1991). Finally, Chan has edited two volumes that provide a very strong overview of Chinese American studies: *Entry Denied: Exclusion and the Chinese Community in America, 1882–1943* (Philadelphia: Temple University Press, 1991) is particularly helpful for the legal history of Chinese exclusion, and *Claiming America: Constructing Chinese American Identities during the Exclusion Era* (Philadelphia: Temple University Press, 1998), edited with K. Scott Wong, offers a broader, cultural perspective of the same period.
12. Peter Clark Macfarlane, "The 'White Hope' of Drug Victims: An Everyday American Fighter," *Collier's*, November 29, 1913, 17.

13. David F. Musto, M.D., *The American Disease: Origins of Narcotic Control*, 3rd ed. (New York: Oxford University Press, 1999), 79. In light of Musto's claim, the attention I have given to Leslie Keeley may seem unwarranted, but this is not the case. Historian H. Wayne Morgan claimed that Keeley's name was "almost a household word." These writers seem to contradict each other, but I believe that their different emphases account for their disagreement on the relative importance of the two cure doctors. Musto's concern is with the passage of the Harrison Act and the government wrangling that attended its birth. As such, he gives much greater weight to the institutional power and influence wielded by Towns through his mentor, Alexander Lambert. Morgan, on the other hand, offers a cultural history of drug use, and therefore Keeley's status as a popular figure holds great attraction for him. I attempt to cross these boundaries and explore the confluence of the popular and the institutional.

14. MacFarlane, "The 'White Hope' of Drug Victims," 16.

15. Ibid., 16.

16. This biography of Towns is drawn from Musto, *The American Disease*, 79–82.

17. Macfarlane, "The 'White Hope' of Drug Victims," 16.

18. Ibid., 29, 16.

19. Ibid., 29.

20. William Rosser Cobbe, *Doctor Judas: A Portrayal of the Opium Habit* (Chicago: S. C. Griggs and Company, 1895), 124.

21. Ibid., 125.

22. Ibid., 127.

23. Ibid., 132.

24. Ibid., 125.

25. Ibid., 126.

26. Ibid., 131.

27. Ibid., 125.

28. Ibid., 131.

29. Ibid., 129.

30. See George Miller Beard, *Stimulants and Narcotics; Medically, Philosophically and Morally Considered* (New York: G. P. Putnam and Sons, 1871), 46–47.

31. Cobbe, *Doctor Judas*, 125–26, 128.

32. Ibid., 133.

33. As we saw above, in a contradiction that seems to have eluded its author, Cobbe argued that the opium smoker, a type of addict who "entered into [addiction] with deliberation" (ibid., 132) and who was morally responsible for his condition because of the "independent action" (125) that brought it about, only affirmed a preexisting state of slavery when he or she "freely" chose to smoke opium. The volitional user's offense would then seem to be that his one act of volition was to surrender his autonomy.

34. Ibid., 133.

35. Ibid., 126.

36. Ibid., 126–27.

37. David Brion Davis, *Slavery in the Age of Revolution, 1770–1823* (Ithaca, N.Y.: Cornell University Press, 1975), 263.

38. Tillman served in the Senate from 1898 to 1909 following a stint as governor, which began in 1890. He was also quite active on the Chautauqua circuit after 1901. Tillman

is quoted in Francis Butler Simkins, "Ben Tillman's View of the Negro," *Journal of Southern History* 3, no. 2 (1937): 164.

39. Ibid., 167, 166.

40. Thomas Nelson Page, "The Lynching of Negroes—Its Cause and Its Prevention," *North American Review* 178 (1904): 33–48.. Available from Kathryn Kish Sklar, Thomas Dublin, Melissa Doak, and Erin Shaughnessy, eds., *Women and Social Movements in the United States, 1600–2000* (online database) at http://womhist.bing hampton.edu/aswpl/doc5.htm, 5–6, 12.

41. Winfield H. Collins, A.M., Ph.D., *The Truth about Lynching and the Negro in the South* (New York: Neale Publishing Co., 1918), 58.

42. Tillman, quoted in Simkins, "Ben Tillman's View of the Negro," 164.

43. Ibid., 172.

44. Joel Williamson, *The Crucible of Race: Black-White Relations in the American South since Emancipation* (New York: Oxford University Press, 1984), 118.

45. Page, "The Lynching of Negroes," 13, 5–6.

46. Collins, *The Truth about Lynching*, 95.

47. Recent researchers have shown that the frequent assertion of disproportionate cocaine use in the African American population was a dubious proposition at best. David Musto points to a survey conducted over the five years between 1909 and 1914 at Georgia's Midgeville State Asylum wherein only two African Americans—from the 2,100 admitted—were found to be suffering from a cocaine problem. Interestingly, the director of the institution suggested that poverty might prevent African Americans from developing the habit to the same degree as whites. In other words, he reserved the possibility that blacks might be inordinately predisposed to using cocaine through his implication that he would have seen more black addicts had they been able to afford it. See Musto, *The American Disease*, 8. Joseph F. Spillane argues that the glaring racism in so much of the period's writing is enough to make us doubt its claims, but he further reminds us that the historical record is ambiguous about the actual level of cocaine use in the African American population. He also explains that both employers and work practices in many of the fields open to black laborers, particularly in physically demanding occupations such as dockwork, encouraged cocaine use. See Spillane, *Cocaine: From Medical Marvel to Modern Menace in the United States, 1884–1920* (Baltimore: Johns Hopkins University Press, 2000), 95. If the contemporary observations were not outright lies but rather exaggerations of a not entirely inaccurate perception, then sociologist John Helmer has placed the blame upon the working conditions of many black Southerners. Pointing out that cocaine was widely marketed in patent cures for bronchial diseases like asthma, he reasons that those most susceptible to these diseases were the ones most likely to be exposed to cocaine. The living and working conditions—especially in the dusty cotton and textile industries—of the lower classes promoted such diseases, which could help to explain a prevalence of cocaine use. See John Helmer, *Drugs and Minority Oppression* (New York: Seabury Press, 1975), 49.

48. "This Drug-Endangered Nation," *Literary Digest*, March 14, 1914, 687.

49. Spillane, *Cocaine*, 7–8.

50. Dr. W. Scheppegrell, M.D., "The Abuse and Dangers of Cocain [*sic*]," *Medical News* 73, no. 14 (October 1, 1898): 419.

51. Ibid., 419–20.

52. T. D. Crothers, M.D., *Morphinism and Narcomanias from Other Drugs: Their Etiology, Treatment and Medicolegal Relations* (Philadelphia. W. D. Saunders, 1902), 273; Towns is quoted in Samuel Merwin, "Fighting the Deadly Habits: The Story of Charles B. Towns," *American Magazine*, October 1912, 710.

53. Scheppegrell argued that the results of cocaine use were "not only as dangerous as those of the morphin habit but are claimed by some to be even more rapid" ("Dangers of Cocain," 420).

54. Ibid., 421.

55. *Atlanta Constitution*, December 27, 1914, 1.

56. Edward Huntington Williams, "The Drug Habit Menace in the South," *Medical Record* 85 (1914): 247.

57. Edward Huntington Williams, "Negro Cocaine 'Fiends' Are a New Southern Menace," *New York Times*, February 8, 1914, 12.

58. J. W. Watson, "Cocaine Sniffers," *New York Tribune*, June 21, 1903, 15.

59. Harvey W. Wiley and Anne Lewis Pierce, "The Cocaine Crime," *Good Housekeeping* 58, no.3 (March, 1914), 393–94.

60. A good example of the tradition can be found in Frederick Douglass, *My Bondage and My Freedom* (1855; New York: Dover Publications, 1969), when he refers to a fellow slave as "Sandy the root man" (284) and describes him as a "genuine African" with "magical powers" (238).

61. Scheppegrell, "Dangers of Cocain," 421.

62. T. J. Happel, M.D., "Morphinism from the Standpoint of the General Practitioner," *Journal of the American Medical Association* 35, no. 7 (1918): 409.

63. Ibid., 408.

64. *Traffic in Narcotic Drugs—Report of Special Committee of Investigation appointed March 25, 1918, by the Secretary of the Treasury, June 1919*, quoted in Charles E. Terry and Mildred Pellens, *The Opium Problem* (1928; reprint, Montclair, New Jersey: Patterson Smith, 1970), 472.

65. Alonzo Calkins, M.D., *Opium and the Opium Appetite* (Philadelphia: Lippincott, 1871), quoted in ibid., 469.

66. American Pharmaceutical Association (AmPhA), *Proceedings of the Fifty-First Annual Meeting* (Baltimore: AmPhA, 1903), 468.

67. Ibid.

68. AmPhA, *Proceedings of the Fiftieth Annual Meeting* (Baltimore: AmPhA, 1902), 570.

69. AmPhA, *Proceedings* (1903), 476.

70. L. L. Stanley, "Morphinism and Crime," *Journal of the American Institute of Criminal Law and Criminology* 8 (1917–18), quoted in Terry and Pellens, *The Opium Problem*, 114.

71. Calkins, *Opium and the Opium Appetite*, quoted in Terry and Pellens, *The Opium Problem*, 469.

72. Keeley, *Opium*, 36.

73. See Barbara Welter, "The Cult of True Womanhood: 1820–1860," part 1, *American Quarterly* 24, no. 2 (1966): 151–74.

74. George Miller Beard, M.D., *American Nervousness: Its Causes and Consequences* (1881; reprint, New York: Arno Press and the New York Times, 1972), 26, 185.

75. Ibid., 96.

76. Ibid., 137.
77. Ibid., 73.
78. Keeley, *Opium*, 41.
79. Ibid., 29.
80. Asa P. Meylert, M.D., *Notes on the Opium Habit*, 3rd ed. (New York: G. P. Putnam's Sons, 1885), 24.
81. Beard, *American Nervousness*, 76–77.
82. See especially Carroll Smith-Rosenberg, "The Abortion Movement and the AMA, 1850–1880," in her *Disorderly Conduct: Visions of Gender in Victorian America* (New York: Oxford University Press, 1985), 217–44.
83. Crothers, *Morphinism and Narcomanias*, 87.
84. Ibid., 204. Crothers made this conclusion based on the work of a Dr. Macnaughton Jones, whose findings in Britain, Crothers believed, were confirmed by "the experience in this country."
85. O. Marshall, "The Opium Habit in Michigan," *Annual Report of the Michigan State Board of Health* 6 (1878): 61–73, quoted in Terry and Pellens, *The Opium Problem*, 96.
86. Lucius P. Brown, "Enforcement of the Tennessee Anti-Narcotic Law," *American Journal of Public Health* 5, no. 4 (1915): 323–33, quoted in Terry and Pellens, *The Opium Problem*, 476.
87. This is not to say that doctors never blamed themselves for spreading narcotic addiction, for they did. I explore their logic at length in the next chapter.
88. AmPhA, *Proceedings* (1903), 472.
89. Keeley, *Opium*, 13.
90. Ibid., 99.
91. Ibid., 107. In this passage, Keeley quoted Fitz Hugh Ludlow, "the American opium eater."
92. AmPhA, *Proceedings* (1902), 572.
93. C. B. Pearson, "Is Morphine 'Happy Dust' to the Addict?" *Medical Council* (Dec. 1918, Jan. 1919), quoted in Terry and Pellens, *The Opium Problem*, 153 (emphasis added).
94. Archibald Church and Frederick Peterson, *Nervous and Mental Diseases*, 8th ed. (1914), quoted in Terry and Pellens, *The Opium Problem*, 455.
95. W. M. Krauss, "An Analysis of the Action of Morphine upon the Vegetative Nervous System of Man," *Journal of Nervous and Mental Diseases* 48, no. 1 (1918), quoted in Terry and Pellens, *The Opium Problem*, 461.
96. J. V. Shoemaker, *Materia Medica and Therapeutics* (1908), quoted in Terry and Pellens, *The Opium Problem*, 193.

Chapter Four

1. Samuel Hopkins Adams, *The Great American Fraud* (n.p.: Collier and Son, 1905 and 1906).
2. Paul Starr, *The Social Transformation of American Medicine: The Rise of a Sovereign Profession and the Making of a Vast Industry* (New York: Basic Books, 1982), 131.
3. Thomas Haskell, *The Emergence of Professional Social Science: The American Social Science Association and the Nineteenth-Century Crisis of Authority* (Urbana: University of

Illinois Press, 1977), 27. Those wishing to read more fully about the history of profes-sionalization might begin with the excellent anthology of essays edited by Haskell ti-tled *The Authority of Expertsː Studies in History and Theory* (Bloomington: Indiana University Press, 1984). Also helpful is Alexandra Oleson and John Voss, eds., *The Or-ganization of Knowledge in Modern America, 1860–1920* (Baltimore: Johns Hopkins Uni-versity Press, 1979). More recent work can be found in Dorothy Ross, ed., *Modernist Impulses in the Human Sciences, 1870–1930* (Baltimore: Johns Hopkins University Press, 1994). Those specifically interested in medical professionalization might begin with Starr's *Social Transformation of American Medicine.* Judith Walzer Leavitt and Ronald L. Numbers, *Sickness and Health in America: Readings in the History of Medicine and Public Health* (Madison: University of Wisconsin Press, 1978), is also quite helpful, as is Joel D. Howell's *Technology in the Hospital: Transforming Patient Care in the Early Twentieth Century* (Baltimore: Johns Hopkins University Press, 1995). In addition to its sugges-tive and useful insights, Martin S. Pernick's *A Calculus of Suffering: Pain, Professional-ism, and Anesthesia in Nineteenth-Century America* (New York: Columbia University Press, 1985) offers a thorough bibliography of both primary and secondary sources in the study of the history of medical professionalization.

4. Haskell, *Emergence of Professional Social Science,* 18.

5. See Starr, *Social Transformation of American Medicine,* chap. 3.

6. James G. Burrow, *AMA: Voice of American Medicine* (Baltimore: Johns Hopkins Press, 1963), 49–50. Still more significant, according to Burrow, was the growth in the num-ber of AMA fellows. This number, which referred to those who paid full fees and sub-scribed to the *Journal of the American Medical Association,* rose by 500% during these years. While the number of subscribers to the journal rose from 4,633 in 1900 to 30,032 in 1920, its influence was probably much greater because, according to Burrow, it was available to about 80% of the profession.

7. Starr, *Social Transformation of American Medicine,* 142, 18.

8. Ibid., 18–19.

9. J. A. Witherspoon, M.D., "A Protest against Some of the Evils in the Profession of Medicine," Oration on Medicine before the Fifty-First Annual Meeting of the Ameri-can Medical Association, Atlantic City, N.J., June 5–8, 1900, *Journal of the American Medical Association* 34, no. 25 (1900): 1591. David F. Musto, M.D., cites this passage to demonstrate the growing medical consciousness of the narcotic habit in *The Ameri-can Disease: Origins of Narcotic Control,* 3rd ed. (New York: Oxford University Press, 1999), 303.

10. Witherspoon, "Protest," 1591.

11. Ibid., 1591–92.

12. S. F. McFarland, "Opium Inebriety and the Hypodermic Syringe," *Transactions of the New York State Medical Society* (1877), 289–93, quoted in Charles E. Terry and Mildred Pellens, *The Opium Problem* (1928; reprint, Montclair, N.J.: Patterson Smith, 1970), 96.

13. C. W. Earle, "The Opium Habit," *Chicago Medical Review* 2 (1880): 442–93, quoted in Terry and Pellens, *The Opium Problem,* 98.

14. C. C. Whorley, "Psychopathologic Phases Observable in Individuals Using Narcotic Drugs in Excess," *Pennsylvania Medical Journal* 17 (June 1913), quoted in Terry and Pellens, *The Opium Problem,* 108–9.

15. F. X. Dercum, "Relative Frequency of Drug Addiction among Middle and Upper Classes; Treatment and Final Results," *Pennsylvania Medical Journal* (February 1917), quoted in Terry and Pellens, *The Opium Problem,* 117.

16. Archibald Church and Frederick Peterson, *Nervous and Mental Diseases,* 8th ed. (1914), quoted in Terry and Pellens, *The Opium Problem,* 113.

17. Witherspoon, "Protest," 1592.

18. David Courtwright has argued that national anti-addiction legislation became possible only when the perception of a change in the addict population—from white, middle-class women to a demimonde fringe—became widespread. It is clear, however, that even though medical researchers often noted demographic changes, the argument that the majority of the blame be placed upon the physician who had inflicted the condition upon an innocent patient remained a vital part of the discourse. While Courtwright makes a compelling argument regarding the criminalization of narcotic use, I hope to point out how the noncriminal addict was likewise placed under the authority of a powerful social institution. See Courtwright, *Dark Paradise: Opiate Addiction in America* (Cambridge: Harvard University Press, 2001), 1–8.

19. P. M. Lichtenstein, "Narcotic Addiction," *New York Medical Journal* (November 1914), quoted in Terry and Pellens, *The Opium Problem,* 112. He went on to explain the presence of these twenty among the others, invoking a gender distinction that was very important to the definition of addiction. He mobilized notions of an inherent women's weakness, based on reproductive biology, when he explained that "most of these victims were women who had been suffering from tubal disease," thus designating one group of addicts who, because of the vulnerability signified and imparted by their gender, were somewhat less to blame for their addiction while still maintaining the existence of another group whose active agency in their drug use rendered them proper objects of penal attention.

20. Ibid.

21. Alexander Lambert, "The Treatment of Narcotic Addiction," *Journal of the American Medical Association* 60 (June 1913), quoted in Terry and Pellens, *The Opium Problem,* 110.

22. For further reading on the foreign policy aspects of the drug trade, see William B. McAllister, *Drug Diplomacy in the Twentieth Century* (London: Routledge, 1999).

23. The power of the pharmaceutical industry was based primarily in its advertising money. Any political figure who supported legislation unpopular with the drug trades could well return to his home district for reelection only to find the local press supporting the opposition.

24. Hamilton Wright, M.D.," Report on the International Opium Commission and on the Opium Problem as seen within the United States and its Possessions," contained in *Opium Problem: Message from the President of the United States,* U.S. Senate Doc. 377, 61st Cong., 2nd sess., February 21, 1910, 63.

25. Ibid., 44.

26. Ibid., 64.

27. In one of the many contradictions that characterize the discourse of addiction, as we will see, Wright will argue that, especially in terms of cocaine use, the drug use was fundamentally *American.*

28. Wright, "Opium Problem," 65.

29. Ibid., 46, 48.

30. Ibid., 54.

31. Ibid., 44.

32. Ibid., 45. This contradicts what he had claimed only two pages earlier, where he argued that "if we allow for 35 percent of smokers among our Chinese population—which is almost wholly adult male—we are well within the mark" (43).

33. Ibid., 45.

34. Ibid., 40.

35. Ibid., 41, 45.

36. See Musto, *The American Disease*, 44.

37. Wright, "Opium Problem," 34.

38. Ibid., 48.

39. Ibid., 40.

40. Ibid., 51.

41. Ibid., 49.

42. Ibid., 51, 48.

43. Ibid., 49.

44. Ibid., 50.

45. Ibid., 59.

46. On the AMA's campaign for the control of pharmaceutical advertising and access, see Starr, *Social Transformation of American Medicine*, 127–34.

47. Wright, "Opium Problem," 47.

48. Ibid., 59.

49. Ibid.

50. See Musto, *The American Disease*, 40–44.

51. *Importation and Use of Opium: Hearings before the Committee on Ways and Means of the House of Representatives on H.R. 25240, H.R. 25241, H.R. 25242, and H.R. 28971*, 61st Cong., 3rd sess., December 14, 1910, and January 11, 1911, 10.

52. Ibid., 13.

53. Ibid., 11.

54. Ibid., 20.

55. Ibid., 11.

56. Ibid., 12.

57. Ibid., 16.

58. Ibid., 12.

59. Ibid., 26.

60. Ibid., 21.

61. Ibid., 139.

62. Ibid., 143.

63. Adams, *The Great American Fraud*, quoted in Starr, *Social Transformation of American Medicine*, 131.

64. Alexander Lambert, "The Obliteration of the Craving for Narcotics," *Journal of the American Medical Association* 53, no. 13 (1909): 985–89.

65. *Importation and Use of Opium*, 140.

66. Ibid., 142. Towns's dire warnings did not stop with the drug itself; he also attacked the use of the syringe, a piece of modern medical machinery whose use we have already

seen as an issue in the period's professional medical journals. He concluded that "I have gone into this matter in every phase of it, and I would amend this bill so that a hypodermic syringe could not be had except upon the prescription of a physician" (143).

67. Ibid., 140.

68. Ibid., 142.

69. Ibid., 143.

70. Ibid., 145.

71. Glenn Sonnedecker, *Kremers and Urdang's History of Pharmacy*, 4th ed. (Philadelphia: J. B. Lippincott, 1976), 211.

72. *Constitution and By-Laws of the American Pharmaceutical Association* (Washington, D.C., [1961]), 2, quoted in Sonnedecker, *Kremers and Urdang's History of Pharmacy*, 202.

73. *Importation and Use of Opium*, 126.

74. Ibid., 125.

75. Ibid., 134, 136.

76. Ibid., 6, 120.

77. Ibid., 31. Richardson relayed his association's resolution, adopted at their national convention held in Pittsburgh on September 12–14, 1910, "that the association use all its efforts to have passed an interstate narcotic law, the terms of which will prohibit all illegitimate traffic in narcotic and habit-forming drugs and confine their sale and uses to proper channels and for strictly medicinal purposes" (31).

78. Ibid., 132.

79. Ibid., 22–23.

80. C. M. Woodruff, "Proceedings Relating to the Organization of the National Drug Trade Conference," *Journal of the American Pharmaceutical Association* 2, no. 2 (1913): 235.

81. Their objections are listed in ibid., 236.

82. Ibid., 239. The NDTC made this position its official policy when it resolved "that the National Drug Conference hereby expresses its approval of uniform state and federal drug legislation in line with the action of associations in other lines and hereby instructs its executive committee to endeavor to bring about such uniform drug legislation in state and nation" (ibid., 239). Among the "associations in other lines" to which the resolution referred was the AMA, which, at its Ninth Annual Conference on Medical Legislation, held in Chicago on February 25, 1913, resolved "that the Council on Health and Public Instruction and the members of the Annual Conference on Medical Legislation of the American Medical Association hereby express their approval of all legislative efforts which may be necessary to restrict the employment of habit forming drugs to proper and legitimate uses." See Martin I. Wilbert, "The Need for Restricting the Interstate Traffic in Habit Forming Drugs," *JAPhA* 2, no. 4 (1913): 518.

83. Woodruff, "Proceedings," 239–40.

84. Martin I. Wilbert, "The Need for Uniformity in Laws Regulating the Sale and Use of Poisons and Narcotics," *JAPhA* 2, no. 3 (1913): 311.

85. P. M. Lichthardt, "Business and the Opium Traffic," *JAPhA* 2, no. 6 (1913): 689.

86. Ibid., 691.

87. James P. Finnerman, "Past, Present and Future Pharmacy Laws," *JAPhA* 2, no. 3 (1913): 312.

88. Ibid., 313.

89. Minutes of the second meeting of the National Drug Trade Conference, Washington, D.C., April 10–11, 1913 (second session), in *JAPhA* 2, no. 5 (May, 1913): 631–32.

90. In August 1913, after the Harrison Act had passed the House, Wilson wrote to the Senate that "I earnestly urge that this measure, to the adoption of which this Government is now pledged, be enacted as soon as possible during the present session of the Congress." See "Letter of Transmittal," *Second International Opium Conference: Message from the President of the United States,* S. Doc. 157, 63rd Cong., 1st sess., August 9, 1913, 3.

91. Musto, *The American Disease,* 59–63.

92. Wright had been removed from his position by Secretary of State Bryan in 1914. For the details of his firing and also of the various institutional interpretations of the Harrison Act, see Musto, *The American Disease,* 61–62.

93. Editorial, "The Harrison Anti Narcotic Law," *Journal of the American Medical Association* 64, no. 11 (1915): 912.

94. Editorial, "Effects of the Harrison Law," *JAMA* 64, no. 15 (1915): 1250.

95. Beal, quoting the editor of *New Idea,* in "Class Obligation and Responsibility," *JAPhA* 2, no. 6 (1913): 670.

96. Ibid.

97. Ibid., 674.

98. *Boston Medical and Surgical Journal* 174, no. 12 (1916): 434.

99. T. J. Jackson Lears, *No Place of Grace: Anti-Modernism and the Transformation of American Culture, 1880–1920* (New York: Pantheon Books, 1981).

Chapter Five

1. See David F. Musto, M.D., *The American Disease: Origins of Narcotic Control,* 3rd ed. (New York: Oxford University Press, 1999), 128–32, for a more comprehensive description of the details and the constitutional issues explored in these cases.

2. The federal government's assault on drug maintenance approaches to narcotic addiction becomes particularly important in the period that directly follows that under study in this book. See ibid., 121–51.

3. Justice Oliver Wendell Holmes, *U.S. v. Jin Fuey Moy,* decided June 5, 1916, *Supreme Court Reporter* (1915), 1064, 1065.

4. Perhaps we should not be surprised that Holmes, a member of a famous medical family, should voice the same interpretation of the law that had been heard from professional medicine.

5. Justice Horace Day, *U.S. v. C. T. Doremus,* decided January 19, 1919, *Supreme Court Reporter* (1919), 495.

6. Ibid., 496.

7. Ibid., 497.

8. *Webb et al. v. U.S.,* decided January 19, 1919, *Supreme Court Reporter* (1919), 499.

9. David Musto argues quite convincingly that this refusal to tolerate drug addicts or addiction came at a time of growing national intolerance. He compares the refusal to tolerate narcotic use to both the Palmer raids and to preparations for alcohol prohibition. See Musto, *The American Disease,* 132–34. David Courtwright argues that changing demographics within the addict community, toward a preponderance of underworld

users, led to a growing intolerance of narcotic use. See Courtwright, *Dark Paradise: Opiate Addiction in America* (Cambridge: Harvard University Press, 2001), 3.

10. Charles B. Towns, *Habits That Handicap: The Menace of Opium, Alcohol, and Tobacco, and the Remedy* (New York: Century Co., 1916), xi.

11. Ibid., 210.

12. Ibid., 61.

13. Ibid., 210.

14. Ibid.

15. Ibid., 56.

16. Interestingly, Towns invoked the populist rhetoric of the superiority of productive labor to a parasitic elite when he added the wealthy to the membership of the group of "difficult" addicts. He argued that "the idle rich to whom money has no value cannot usually be classed among hopeful subjects for treatment." But his main concerns were reserved for "those for whom others take financial responsibility, paying the cost of their treatment. If such cases do not already belong in the human scrap-heap, this mistaken kindness is very likely to place them there." This attack on both the richest and poorest members of the addict population identifies Towns's writing as a distinctively middle-class critique. Ibid., 211.

17. Ibid., 208–9.

18. Ibid., 211–12.

19. Ibid., 7.

20. Ibid.

21. Ibid., 244.

22. Ibid., 26.

23. P. M. Lichtenstein, "Narcotic Addiction," *New York Medical Journal* (November 1914), quoted in Charles E. Terry and Mildred Pellens, *The Opium Problem* (1928; reprint, Montclair, N.J.: Patterson Smith, 1970), 492.

24. I make a similar claim regarding a comparison between Lichtenstein's work and that of Towns's partner, Alexander Lambert, in chapter 4. This sort of direct contradiction as to demographics is something that we encounter again and again in the discourse of addiction. Foster Kennedy, in "The Effects of Narcotic Addiction," *New York Medical Journal* 100 (1914), quoted in Terry and Pellens, *The Opium Problem*, 147, wrote that "morphinism is a disease, in the majority of cases, initiated, sustained and left uncured by members of the medical profession." On the other hand, Walter Bloedorn, in "Studies of Drug Addicts," *U.S. Naval Medical Bulletin* 11, no. 3 (1917), quoted in Terry and Pellens, *The Opium Problem*, 117, wrote that "the number of individuals who begin the use of drugs through illness, insomnia, or persistent pain, while constituting a large aggregate, is believed to form a relatively small percentage of the total. The great majority take their first step through being unfortunate enough to meet and associate with addicts." This lack of demographic certainty, however, did not stop medical authorities from suggesting far-reaching solutions based on these inconclusive reports.

25. Lichtenstein, "Narcotic Addiction," 492.

26. Although Towns was not a physician, his partner, Dr. Alexander Lambert, provided him with this medical authority.

27. Solomon Rubin, "Drug Addiction and Modern Methods for Control," *Boston Medical and Surgery Journal* (1916), quoted in Terry and Pellens, *The Opium Problem*, 878.

28. W. A. Bloedorn, "Studies of Drug Addicts," *U.S. Naval Medical Bulletin* 11, no. 3. (1917), quoted in Terry and Pellens, *The Opium Problem*, 111.

29. Rubin, "Drug Addiction," 070.

30. G. D. Swaine, "Regarding the Luminal Treatment of Morphine Addiction," *American Journal of Clinical Medicine* (1918), quoted in Terry and Pellens, *The Opium Problem*, 496.

31. Ibid.

32. Musto, *The American Disease*, 135.

33. U.S. Treasury Department, Special Narcotic Committee, *Traffic in Narcotic Drugs*, report of a special committee of investigation appointed March 25, 1918, by the Secretary of the Treasury (Washington, D.C.: GPO, 1919), 5.

34. Musto, *The American Disease*, 137, 351, n. 44.

35. Musto points out that the rate of return for the questionnaires varied from a low of 3.9% from penal institutions to 32% from chiefs of police (ibid., 351n.44).

36. U.S. Treasury Department, *Traffic in Narcotic Drugs*, 8.

37. Ibid., 15–16. The committee based its belief in the increase of narcotic use in growing import figures. It found that "cocaine was first introduced into this country about 30 years ago, and at the present time the annual consumption of coca leaves, from which cocaine is obtained, amounts to 1,048,250 pounds." But the committee's questionable use of deductive logic is evident in its conclusion that the existence of cocaine substitutes "shows that there is undoubtedly a large quantity of cocaine used for illegitimate purposes, namely, for the satisfaction of addiction." See ibid., 8.

38. Ibid., 27.

39. Ibid., 28.

40. Ibid., 20.

41. Musto, *The American Disease*, 138.

42. U.S. Treasury Department, *Traffic in Narcotic Drugs*, 28.

43. Ibid., 22–23.

44. Ibid., 23.

45. Ibid.

46. Committee on the Narcotic Drug Situation in the United States, "Report," proceedings of the New Orleans Session, minutes of the Seventy-first Annual Session of the American Medical Association, New Orleans, April 26–30, 1920, *JAMA* 74, no. 19 (1920): 1324.

47. Ibid.

48. Ibid., 1325.

49. Ibid., 1324

50. Ibid.,

51. Ibid., 1326.

52. Ibid.

53. Ibid., 1327.

54. Ibid., 1326.

55. Ibid.

56. Ibid.

57. Ibid., 1327.

58. Ibid., 1326.

59. Ibid.

60. Ibid.

61. Ibid., 1327.

62. Ibid.

63. Ibid., 1326.

64. Ibid., 1327.

65. Ibid.

66. Ibid.

67. Ibid., 1328.

68. Ibid.

69. Carolyn Jean Acker, *Creating the American Junkie: Addiction Research in the Classic Era of Narcotic Control* (Baltimore: Johns Hopkins University Press, 2002), 9.

INDEX

Timothy A. Hickman was born in Santa Monica, California, and grew up in California, Colorado, and Oregon. He received his Ph.D. from the University of California at Irvine and, after spending one year as a Fulbright lecturer in the American Studies Department at Georg-August Universität, in Göttingen, Germany, he accepted a permanent appointment to teach in the History Department of Lancaster University in northwest England. He continues to live and teach in Lancaster, at the edge of the Lake District National Park, with his wife Nicola, their son Henry, and Dewey the dog.